DOMINIC RAAB has worked as an international lawyer in the City, at the human rights organisation *Liberty* and for six years as a legal adviser at the Foreign and Commonwealth Office. Since 2006, he has served as chief of staff to respective Shadow Home Secretaries, taking time out in 2008 to act as chief of staff on David Davis's by-election campaign, fought on the single issue of the government's relentless erosion of British liberty.

DOMINIC RAAB

The Assault on Liberty

WHAT WENT WRONG WITH RIGHTS

FOURTH ESTATE • *London*

First published in Great Britain in 2009 by
Fourth Estate
An imprint of HarperCollinsPublishers
77–85 Fulham Palace Road
London W6 8JB
www.4thestate.co.uk

1

A catalogue record for this book is
available from the British Library

ISBN- 978-0-00-729339-1

Set in Minion

Printed in Great Britain by Clays Ltd, St Ives plc

Mixed Sources
Product group from well-managed
forests and other controlled sources
www.fsc.org Cert no. SW-COC-1806
© 1996 Forest Stewardship Council

FSC

FSC is a non-profit international organisation established to promote the
responsible management of the world's forests. Products carrying the FSC
label are independently certified to assure consumers that they come
from forests that are managed to meet the social, economic and
ecological needs of present and future generations.

Find out more about HarperCollins and the environment at
www.harpercollins.co.uk/green

For Erika

CONTENTS

ACKNOWLEDGEMENTS

I am very grateful for all of the support and comments I have received in the course of writing this book. Any shortcomings in the text remain my own. The aim is to give an overview of two main, recent, developments in the field of human rights law as they impact on people's ordinary lives. There are many other micro-trends and themes that have not been addressed in detail. At the risk of oversimplifying the relative positions in England, Scotland, Wales and Northern Ireland, I have not explored their particular historical evolution, relying instead on the common historical legacy of liberty in which all parts of the United Kingdom share. Nor have I explored differences in interpretation of the Human Rights Act under the devolved arrangements, since the Human Rights Act applies throughout the United Kingdom.

Too many people provided insights, ideas and comments that contributed to this book to name them all, but I should particularly mention a few. My sincere thanks to David Davis, Dominic Grieve and Peter Oborne, with whom the first ideas were originally discussed. I am indebted to Andrew Gordon at David Higham and Robin Harvie at Fourth Estate for their invaluable support and guidance from start to finish. I am also grateful to Laura Davies and Gary McKenzie-Smith for their general comments on the draft text. Gareth Crossman at Liberty and Dr Benjamin Goold at the Oxford University Centre for Criminology provided expert insights on surveillance. I benefited enormously from a diverse range of legal perspectives on Parts II and III, and would like to express my particular gratitude to Anthony Speaight QC at 4 Pump Court and

Andrew Warnock at 1 Chancery Lane. Above all, my thanks to Erika, who endured the *'Assault'* with patience, wit and wisdom throughout.

FOREWORD

Liberty matters. That statement may seem self-evident, but the freedom under the law that we have historically enjoyed in Britain is more fundamental to the entire nature of our society than many realize.

Freedom is a pervasive virtue, and it has a material impact on many aspects of our national history. Freedom of speech has encouraged freedom of thought, and that is the bedrock of our extraordinary creativity over the centuries – whether it is in literature, or science, or political philosophy for that matter. In conjunction with the freedom of action available to British citizens, buttressed by property rights, it engendered the industrial revolution and made us one of the richest and most powerful nations in the world.

As a rich and powerful nation, our political ideas – foremost amongst them freedom under the law – have been disproportionately disseminated around the world. Those countries that embraced those ideas – from America to Australia to India – are amongst the most successful and civilized nations both today and in the future.

So it is a particular tragedy that we in Britain are slowly abandoning the very characteristics that have made us and others so successful and civilized. It is also ironic that we are doing so often in response to a threat from people that have no respect for those values – who despise tolerance, liberty, and diversity.

The last decade has witnessed an accelerating erosion of liberty on many fronts, all carefully documented in this timely book. The attack on the fundamental liberties, such as habeas corpus, is at the front of the public mind because of the pitched parliamentary battles on ninety days and more recently forty-two days detention without charge.

But these assaults are only the most visible part of the attack. Equally pernicious are the massive intrusions on our privacy with the growth of the huge government databases and the identity card register, the pernicious growth of a surveillance state with cameras seemingly on every corner, the creation of a 'suspect society' with the recording of the DNA of a vast number of innocent people, all in conjunction with the undermining of the institutional structures that have historically protected us from excessive state power, most notably jury trials.

Each and every one of these actions has a sensible idea at the core, but one which has been massively overused to the point where it ceases to be a challenge to the guilty and becomes a threat to the innocent.

Why does this happen? What has happened in government to create this soft tyranny in Britain?

Is it that our New Labour masters have decided to covertly put in place the pieces of a dictator state? Hardly, although one or two of their Home Secretaries may have had unhealthy instincts in that direction. Most British politicians are broadly altruistic, and would be horrified to be seen to be the instruments of such action.

No, the problem is more systemic than that, and as a result this is a book that should be read as a cautionary warning by would-be ministers of any political colour, and by those who want to keep an eye on them, be they elector or commentator.

The first of the culprits is the concept of the 'continuous campaign'. This idea, imported from Bill Clinton's America, is that political parties should not stop campaigning once they are elected, but should carry on as though they are still in mid election whilst they are in government. Although this sounds mundane, it is at odds with the real behaviour of most British governments down the decades. Most of them just thought about the campaign in the last year before an election, and up until then just ran the country in the interests of the electorate.

The danger of the continuous campaign is that it encourages ministers to use the apparatus of the state to promote the cause of one party or even one minister. The first effect of this is to make everything much more short term. Favourable headlines take the place of favourable outcomes as primary objectives to be achieved. This trend is reinforced by the twenty-four-hour media's hunger for news.

Add this to a set of policy problems that are relatively intractable, such as Islamist terrorism, or persistent rising crime, and the tendency is to go for more and more tough and dramatic sounding headlines – and therefore for ever more draconian policies. This tendency is reinforced when politicians sell a simplistic analysis of the problem to a worried public. It is reinforced even more when the politicians overdramatize the risks.

So we end up with vast numbers of security cameras that are largely useless for crime prevention or detection, and for which there are precious few privacy protections – but the minister got his '10,000 new cameras' headline. We end up with huge databases that carry vast amounts of acutely personal information on us all, and which put our privacy and even security at risk – but the minister gets his 'High tech Health Service' headline.

Of course history catches up. Now the papers are full of stories of lost personal details, and we see everything from bank account details to soldiers' lives put at risk. We see stories of so-called security cameras used to spy on young women, or on a more mundane level used to maximize council revenues rather than minimize personal risks.

We can be sure that there will be much more to come. The government has begun to make a habit of trying to short circuit legal process, by curbing jury trials, cutting back the powers of magistrates courts, and replacing some court appearances with summary justice in the form of fines and cautions. The effect will make the figures for clear up of crime look good, but it will achieve the interesting double of under-punishing the guilty whilst risking destroying an innocent person's life with a miscarriage of justice. This, and some of the other effects of the erosion of our freedoms and protection under the law, will take years to surface in the public mind. But surface it will, and when it does the British people will not be impressed.

The other assault on our freedoms comes from a complex nexus of actions whose aim, paradoxically, is to improve our rights. The growth of a rights culture, with an inflation of what fundamental rights really are, in conjunction with well-intentioned but flawed approaches like some of the decisions of the Strasbourg Court and some of the British courts under the Human Rights Act, has led to a peculiar dilution of British freedoms and a signal failure to defend some of those freedoms when they came under serious threat.

The irony here is that the vested interests that defend these flawed institutions are often those that fight a sterling battle in defence of our freedoms in other contexts. The argument is therefore harder to make, but no less important for all that.

Dominic Raab has been at the middle of the battle to defend our freedoms from these many different threats, and also brings an understanding of the international dimension to the table. He is uniquely placed to analyse the problems and propose thoughtful solutions in this book. His first-class forensic analysis is likely to provoke some strong responses, but the cause of freedom is never defended without some discomfort.

Rt Hon. David Davis MP, *November 2008*

INTRODUCTION

A visitor to Britain arriving on International Human Rights Day might be bemused to read the following newspaper headline: 'The liberties stripped from the weak today could be lost to us all tomorrow'. He will be positively perplexed if he compares it to another just a few weeks earlier: 'Human rights is merely a sweetener for rapists, murderers and violent criminals'.

This is not an isolated example of the conflicting views on 'human rights' in Britain today.

On the one hand, we now regularly hear that the government is seizing the ancient birthright of Britons, tearing up freedoms nurtured since the thirteenth century and ushering in a dark new chapter in British history. Over the last twelve years, the police have clamped down on freedom of speech, restricted public demonstrations and stifled peaceful protests – using an array of new powers bestowed by a blizzard of legislation, hastily enacted by Parliament on the flimsy pretext of national security. Wave upon wave of anti-terrorism measures have been introduced by an increasingly authoritarian government, including proposals to extend police detention without charge that even the former head of MI5 describes as draconian. Wide new surveillance powers allow half a million private conversations between British citizens to be bugged each year by snooping spooks, including hundreds of local authorities.

Meanwhile, our traditional pillars of justice are also crumbling under the immense strain of law enforcement short cuts taken in the name of fighting crime. Basic safeguards put in place to protect the innocent have been wrenched from our justice system by politicians desperate for tabloid headlines: the presumption of innocence reversed, the burden of proof watered down, our courts sidelined and the right to trial by jury subject to sustained, and ongoing, assault.

The creeping powers of the state at every level – from the intelligence agencies through to quangos and councils – are creating a surveillance society, with neighbourhood spies even checking our rubbish and following innocent children home from school to confirm that they qualify for the local catchment area. The Home Office's imminent national identity register will store masses of sensitive personal details, for each and every British citizen, on a vulnerable central government database. Careless and unaccountable civil servants will then liberally share our private information around the disparate, sprawling and utterly unreliable arms of government – as likely to lose or abuse as protect our personal data.

To cap it all, Britain, the cradle of liberal democracy, now has the unsavoury honour of topping a dubious array of international league tables – including boasting the largest DNA database and the most CCTV cameras in the world.

On the other hand, our visitor may draw little sense of public order or security, as might be expected from a government with such a heavy-handed reputation. On a daily basis, we read about the steady stream of human rights rulings undermining law enforcement, criminal justice and national security. Common sense turned on its head – warped by the European Court of Human Rights in Strasbourg, and magnified by Labour's feckless Human Rights Act – allows human rights to be wielded to protect and compensate serious criminals rather than their victims. Police now invoke the human rights of fugitive killers, to protect their privacy rather than alert the law-abiding public. The Prison Service compensates drug-addicted prisoners for the hardship of going clean, and gives jailed criminals access to fertility treatment. Airline hijackers successfully claim their 'rights' to fend off deportation, illegal immigrants sue the immigration service for holding them in detention and bogus asylum seekers claim access to state benefits. Children show off their novel rights like new toys, challenging authority at every level – including police officers in the street, teachers in the classroom and even their parents at home.

Add in, for good measure, the reams of new government regulation that have spawned a health and safety culture – preventing the police from rescuing a child drowning in a pond, but prosecuting them for mistakes made during the heat of a counter-terrorism operation – and the prevailing sense of confusion is complete.

The conventional explanation is that these are two mutually hostile positions, set amidst a polarized debate that pits a liberal elite against a populist press. But what if, far from antagonistic, there is a kernel of truth, and some measure of substance, to support both sides in this debate?

The British idea of liberty, developed over eight hundred years, is now caught between conflicting tides, cast adrift from its natural moorings. It has been both corroded and conflated. It has been corroded by the government's direct assault on our fundamental freedoms, including freedom of speech, the presumption of innocence and freedom from arbitrary police detention. British liberty was hard won over centuries – millions died in the struggle, revolts and wars that secured and then defended those freedoms. Yet, since 1997, in a vain effort to prove itself tough on crime and counter-terrorism, historically weak flanks for the Labour Party, the government has hyperactively produced more Home Office legislation than all the other governments in our history combined, accumulating a vast arsenal of new legal powers and creating more than three thousand additional criminal offences. As the power of the state has grown, so has the scope for its abuse, whether by police officers operating under ever-increasing pressure, invisible civil servants concealed within grey bureaucracies or over-zealous council officials relishing their windfall of extended authority over local residents. These incremental extensions in the reach and authority of government, and the mounting abuse of power by its agents and officials, have led to a tectonic shift in the relationship between the state and the citizen. As our liberal democracy becomes less liberal, the government is inflicting lasting damage on the very bedrock of what it means to be British – undermining the fundamental freedoms we enjoy as citizens, our sense of fair play as a society and the checks and balances that restrain the state's ability to interfere in our daily lives.

At the same time, and in parallel, the British tradition of liberty has been conflated as swathes of other comparatively minor grievances, claims and interests have been shoe-horned into the ever-elastic language of inalienable, unimpeachable and judicially enforceable rights. In place of our most basic – fundamental – freedoms, steadily eroded and undermined since 1997, we have witnessed the expansion of a range of novel, often trivial, rights.

Over the last thirty years successive governments have tried to grapple with, or plain ignored, the inflation of human rights by the European Court of Human Rights in Strasbourg. But since 1997 the government has fuelled the proliferation of rights by passing its flagship Human Rights Act, importing lock stock and barrel into British law the European Convention of Human Rights and all of its accompanying case law. The Act forms part of a broader government strategy that seeks to anchor Britain to Europe and introduce a socialist conception of human rights, fundamentally at odds with the British legacy of liberty going back hundreds of years.

The result has been to upgrade endless ordinary claims – including to social services, NHS treatment, welfare payments and even police protection – to the status of fundamental human rights.

Civil servants, the courts, police, prison officers and numerous other officials have struggled to keep up, distracted by the growing number of rights they are forced to service along with the wider public interest, and baffled by the legal confusion it has created. There is a real and rising risk that this exponential expansion of new, individual rights will drown out a balanced assessment of public service priorities, displace broader social interests, fuel a growing compensation culture and undermine this country's traditional ethos of civic duty and social responsibility.

The dramatic expansion of rights in the UK is not the result of public debate, nor has it been endorsed by our democratically elected representatives. On the contrary, it has emerged by stealth, pioneered by judges in Strasbourg – and more recently the UK – at the expense of any meaningful British democratic control. Whatever the differing views on human rights – and those on the left and the right may reasonably disagree – the massive proliferation of rights through the courts is difficult to square with basic ideas about how a democracy should function.

If these twin developments have frayed the threads of our liberal democracy, they are not yet beyond repair. As a general election beckons, with all three political parties proposing constitutional reform – including proposals for a modern British Bill of Rights – this book aims to inform that debate, by drawing on our history, constitution and a consideration of the practical impact of human rights on our daily lives. To do that it is necessary to ask – in the mother of parliamentary democracies, which enshrined the first fundamental freedoms some eight hundred years ago – what went wrong with rights?

PART I

WHERE DID RIGHTS COME FROM?

1

Runnymede

'You mustn't sell, delay, deny,
A freeman's right or liberty.
It wakes the stubborn Englishry,
We saw 'em roused at Runnymede!'

RUDYARD KIPLING,
'What Say the Reeds at Runnymede?'

Where did our 'rights' come from? Winston Churchill described the Magna Carta of 1215 as 'the foundation of principles and systems of government of which neither King John nor his nobles dreamed'. At Runnymede, near the royal home of Windsor, the seeds of British liberty were sown. Centuries before the Enlightenment gave birth to the French Revolution and American Declaration of Independence, and with a fraction of the bloodshed, English nobles persuaded their monarch to cede rights and freedoms that charted a course towards liberal democracy.

Magna Carta was preceded by war between England and France, as King John strove to recover lands lost to the French king, Philip Augustus (Philip II). In pursuing his revenge, John placed an increasingly intolerable strain on what was left of the barons' goodwill and financial resources, already tested by his abuse of feudal prerogatives. John depended on financial and political support from the barons to implement his foreign policy and military strategy. In a deft reversal of his isolation – and excommunication – by the Pope, Innocent III, John turned the tables on both the French and the barons by accepting papal authority over England. Magna Carta was the embodiment of a disingenuous truce, which bought off the barons, kept the French at bay and capitulated to the spiritual authority of Rome. As such, it proved a temporary rather than lasting settlement, and one John had no intention of keeping. His refusal to adhere to its terms led swiftly to domestic rebellion, French attack and his own death.

In reality, Magna Carta's sixty-three clauses were more concerned with the immediate interests of the barons – feudal rights, tax and trade – than the rights of man. There was no mention of any broader representation beyond the ruling class, no enunciation of democratic principles and no lofty declaration of fundamental rights. Notwithstanding this triumph of pragmatism over principle, 1215 nevertheless marks the historical starting point for the modern debate on 'rights'. It may not have been consumed by, or the product of, some deeper political emancipation, yet three of its nascent principles – the rule of law, habeas corpus and trial by one's peers – still represent the earliest articulation of liberty capable of resonating with a modern audience.

Numerous articles throughout Magna Carta sought to subject John to some basic ground rules in the exercise of royal power. The text is littered with articles that restrict the arbitrary use of royal authority and restrain the levying of feudal dues. Article 17 requires courts to be held in fixed location and article 40 expounds that: 'To none will we sell, to none deny or delay, right or justice.' This codified the most basic idea of the rule of law – requiring the authority of state to be exercised in a clear, transparent and consistent way, not at the arbitrary whim of those with power. The pervasive value of 'legal certainty' is easily overlooked today, as we take it for granted that the law of the land will be applied impartially and consistently through independent courts. But it provides the foundation for all the other freedoms. Predictable rules are essential not just for individuals, but also companies and even government to plan their business and lives around. So, when the government introduced indefinite detention without trial for foreign terrorist suspects after 9/11, the legislation was heavily criticized by the House of Lords, Lord Nicholls stating that 'indefinite imprisonment without charge or trial is anathema in any country which observes the rule of law'.

Likewise, Article 39 of Magna Carta set out one of the earliest constitutional expressions of habeas corpus and trial by jury. The right of habeas corpus – translated literally as 'you may have the body' – is the individual's right to know and challenge the legal basis of his detention by the state. Today, the principle reflects a basic level of due process we expect from the police, in return for their power to interfere with our freedom. If stopped by a police officer, we expect to be told the grounds for our being stopped, let alone any search, arrest or detention. In the overwhelming majority of criminal investigations, the police cannot hold a suspect in detention for more than four days without bringing criminal charges – at that point they must justify the deprivation of the liberty of the citizen. We assume these rights as part and parcel of living in Britain. In other countries – China, Egypt or Syria, for example – dissidents and government critics live in constant fear of being arrested and arbitrarily detained, with minimal checks on the use and abuse of police powers.

Article 39 also bans serious punishment 'save by the lawful judgment of his peers or by the law of the land', while Article 38 prevents royal officials prosecuting an individual 'without producing faithful witnesses in evidence'. These guarantees formed an early basis for the common law model of a fair trial – including the presumption of innocence and the right to elect trial by jury when faced with a serious punishment. If the state wishes to imprison or otherwise punish an individual – depriving him of his liberty – it must prove the criminal case against him beyond reasonable doubt. It is for the state to demonstrate guilt, not for the individual to prove his innocence. Whether the accusation is illegal parking or a bank robbery, a court will throw out on the first day of trial a case brought without the evidence to back it up.

Likewise, the right to trial by jury remains relevant today. In criminal cases, the right to elect a jury – twelve members of the public rather than a single judge – provides a check against both over-zealous prosecutors and the kind of bad law that even a functioning democracy may pass from time to time. People prosecuted for offences that they believe to be harsh, unjust or just trivial – such as dropping an apple core on the street, or selling groceries in ounces and pounds rather than kilograms – still rely on trial by jury today to challenge unfair law enforcement, putting their faith in the common sense of twelve members of the public. These are fundamental safeguards built into our common law system – and manifestly absent from continental European principles of law and justice.

The second relevance of Magna Carta to the modern debate on rights lies in its constitutional character. Replete with quid pro quos, it is premised on the coupling of rights with responsibilities, balancing the interests of the king and his subjects. Magna Carta was framed as a social bargain, explicitly designed as a contract between the king and the barons – ruler and ruled – requiring reciprocal respect. The conception of liberty, or more accurately certain specifically defined liberties, was spelt out through a series of rights that sought predominantly to check the overwhelming or arbitrary exercise of power by the monarch. The barons intended to restrain the meddling of the king in their affairs, and Magna Carta's overarching aim was to protect their freedom from the Crown, rather than obliging the monarch to do anything in particular for them.

Magna Carta represented a compromise of competing interests, rather than any coherent blueprint for liberal democracy. According to Churchill, the barons 'groped in the dim light towards a fundamental principle', which they found in the 'only half understood' idea that 'Government must henceforward mean something more than the arbitrary rule of any man, and custom and the law must stand even above the King.' Those early freedoms from royal interference subsequently developed into a range of fundamental liberties demarcating the state's ability to interfere in the lives of its citizens – including freedom from arbitrary arrest and prolonged detention without charge – and outlined the broader contours that would define the relationship between the citizen and the state. Rooted in our history, this basic idea of placing checks on the power of the state, thereby preserving the freedoms of the citizen from interference, are at the heart of the current debates on the limits of state surveillance, the reach of database state, the right of the police to take and retain DNA on innocent people and safeguards on the use of the ever-present coverage provided by CCTV cameras.

The initial constitutional cast set by Magna Carta developed piecemeal, over the following eight centuries, into a model of liberal democracy. Unlike many other countries, Britain's constitution is not codified in a single overriding document, but made up of a patchwork of laws and conventions that have developed steadily over time. The Petition of Right in 1628 added constitutional bars on taxation without the consent of Parliament and the use of martial law in peacetime. Inspired by Sir Edward Coke – who held the posts of Attorney General and Chief Justice before standing for Parliament – the Petition of Right also provided the earliest protection of individual privacy. Coke's famous maxim that 'a man's house is his castle' informed the drafting of Article VI, which protected private homes from being forced by the Crown to house soldiers, a longstanding grievance. This established one of the first legal protections against intrusions into the home, on which later common law privacy protections were incrementally built.

Today, we expect that the sanctity of the home will only be breached in the most exceptional of situations warranted by the strict necessity of law enforcement or public safety – not on the whim of some civil servant, quango or local official. Similarly, we expect the state to respect the privacy of our correspondence, internet access and email exchanges, unless there are strong security grounds for interception or monitoring. We recognize the need for the state to gather some information on us, but only on a limited – need-to-know – basis, in order to help fight serious crime and terrorism. Few are comfortable with the idea of giving the state *carte blanche* to collect, retain and share our detailed, personal and sensitive information. The state is meant to be accountable to the citizen, not the reverse.

Like Magna Carta, the Bill of Rights, passed in 1689 in the aftermath of Civil War and the Glorious Revolution, was another straightforward, unpretentious text addressing in clear and concise terms a catalogue of widespread grievances. A dozen constitutional gripes were followed by thirteen general remedies, as well as redress for particular issues of contemporary concern. The Bill of Rights built on earlier rights. Fair trial safeguards were added, strengthening the independence of jury selection from bias, and requiring the prior conviction of a criminal offence before the imposition of fines or the forfeiture of property. Article 20 of Magna Carta had stipulated that 'For a trivial offence, a free man shall be fined only in proportion to the degree of his offence, and for a serious offence correspondingly, but not so heavily as to deprive him of his liveli-hood'. The underlying idea was that criminals should get their just deserts, pay the price for their offence, but that the punishment should fit the crime. There must be a limit on the right of the ruler to punish those subject to his rule. The Bill of Rights added to this the requirement that 'excessive bail ought not to be required, nor excessive fines imposed ...'. These early constitutional innovations marked out the British idea of justice as firm but fair. Today, debates about crime and punishment still focus on these basic ideas, whether it is the debate about honesty in sentencing or consideration of the proportionality of criminal punishments.

The same clause of the Bill of Rights added a ban on the inflic-tion of 'cruel and unusual punishments', an early precursor to the modern ban on torture. Today, the legal standards applied in the UK, European and UN human rights law developed from this early definition, set out more than three hundred years ago. Students, journalists, political activists and others challenge or protest against the government, confident that they will not be persecuted for their views or political activities, as they are elsewhere. There would be widespread outrage in this country if the state engaged in the kinds of murder or torture of its citizens that take place in many other parts of the world – including Russia, Iran and Sudan. Allegations of torture by British troops in combat are investigated seriously, and UK cooperation with foreign agencies accused of practising torture attracts intense scrutiny.

The Bill of Rights also contains one of the earliest guarantees of freedom of speech, declaring that 'the freedom of speech, and debates or proceedings in parliament, ought not to be impeached or questioned in any court or place out of parliament'. The freedom to think and say what we like, without inciting violence or harming others, is fundamental to the idea of liberty in this country. This right – and the related freedoms of worship, conscience and peaceful protest – developed from the early struggle for religious freedom during the Reformation into the modern rights we enjoy today.

From the moment we wake up in the morning and pick up a newspaper, we take it for granted that a full range of competing views and perspectives will be presented on any issue of the day. We expect to hear every conceivable criticism of government and politicians. Consciously or not, we form our own views on the basis of the plethora of information and views regurgitated through an exceptionally free and exuberant media. It is difficult to imagine what it must be like to live under the blanket censorship that hides what is really going on in countries like North Korea. British protection of freedom of speech is also stronger than in many other democracies. In France, for example, there are legal restrictions on the media reporting of the private peccadilloes – and more serious improprieties – of politicians that would be unthinkable in Britain.

The scope for freedom of speech exploded with the advent of radio, television and, later, the internet – the modern medium for social interaction and popular debate, allowing individuals, groups, campaigners and businesses to exchange ideas and opinions twenty-four hours a day, seven days a week, across the world. We take these freedoms for granted in Britain, whereas others cannot. In China, for example, the government censors the internet. So, if you Google the Falun Gong, the banned spiritual movement, the Chinese service provider will direct you to those hits that provide negative commentary. China also restricts internet content on Tibet and those calling for democratic reform. Closer to home, even Turkey, an aspiring candidate for membership of the European Union (EU), censors internet criticisms of Kemal Atatürk, the founder of the country's modern secular republic, an action that would be unheard of in this country.

From the freedom of speech inside Parliament, under the Bill of

Rights, developed our freedom of speech and the right to peaceful protest outside Parliament. For the politically active, peaceful protest – from a single demonstrator through to mass rallies – serves as a means of voicing concerns, grievances or criticisms of the government. It is particularly important during periods of political controversy to allow the ventilation of strongly held views. Governments cannot satisfy everyone. But they can – and should – allow the expression of a full range of competing views. People in this country take pride in the right to peaceful public protest. Even the politically disinterested generally expect the right to be tolerated, however obscure or unappealing we may find the views of particular protesters. It is inconceivable that the tanks could roll into Trafalgar Square to crush peaceful protests against the war in Iraq, as they did in Tiananmen Square during the brutal crackdown on protesters in 1989 that left hundreds of students dead, or that Britain could routinely jail and intimidate peaceful protesters, as Chinese police did to silence democratic voices of dissent during the 2008 Beijing Olympics, at the 2012 London Olympics.

While fundamental rights began to emerge from the thirteenth century, and would become one of the pillars of our liberal democracy, they were not conceived in isolation – they were not the only pillar in the nascent democratic architecture. Magna Carta built on the emerging common law system, created by Henry II in the twelfth century and based on uniform and consistent courts respecting 'precedent' – the rulings laid down in previous cases. The common law underpins the rule of law in the UK – with the exception of Scotland, which operates a civil law system – but is also inextricably interwoven with the idea of freedom under law. It is based on a unique and powerful presumption of liberty, the presumption that the individual is free to do anything that has not been expressly forbidden or restricted by law.

The Bill of Rights reinforced the rule of law, by entrenching law-making power in Parliament and restraining the exercise of legislative power by the Crown. It also helped mould a separation of powers between government, Parliament and the courts – a system of checks and balances to prevent any one branch of the state from dominating the others or abusing its power. The Act of Settlement 1701 later reinforced the separation of powers, bolstering both the role of Parliament and the independence of the judiciary.

Above all, the development of freedom under law and democracy in Britain went hand in hand, preserving the liberty of the individual and decentralizing power to the people. The Bill of Rights declared: 'That election of members of parliament ought to be free', and required that 'for redress of all grievances, and for the amending, strengthening and preserving of the laws, parliaments ought to be held frequently'. The constitutional design was based on the election to Parliament of those mandated to make the law of the land. Slowly but surely, the number of people entitled to vote in elections expanded. A series of reforms, starting with the Reform Act of 1832 and culminating in the Representation of the People Act 1983, widened the electoral franchise. Women first received the vote in 1918, in recognition of the sacrifices made during the First World War, and the threshold age for men and women was eventually lowered to eighteen in 1969. The Parliament Acts of 1911 and 1949 further consolidated the power of the directly elected House of Commons, at the expense of the House of Lords.

In this way our fundamental rights were originally designed to support, reinforce – but also respect – the other building blocks of our democracy: the rule of law, separation of powers and parliamentary democracy. 'Rights' were not something separate from democracy, but part of it. It is a worrying feature of the modern debate that the expansion of new human rights increasingly runs against the grain of the rule of law and the principle of democratic accountability for law-making.

Civil war served as a powerful catalyst and, from the seventeenth century onwards, these constitutional developments both reflected and inspired an emerging tradition of liberal British thinkers. At first blush, Thomas Hobbes appears an unlikely liberal. A royal tutor, cynical about human nature and a determinist, Hobbes advocated firm governmental authority to rescue mankind from its natural, brutish and anarchic state. Nevertheless, he was one of the first to secularize the concept of political authority, resting it on the notional consent of the people rather than divine right. He developed the idea of a social contract, between ruler and ruled, at a critical juncture in our history. He represents an early pioneer of the principle of government by consent of the people – the basic idea underpinning all subsequent theories of democracy.

John Locke built on Hobbes' early insights. He was the first British thinker to articulate a meaningful conception of freedom under law. He did not define with precision the list of freedoms he had in mind, let alone their content, but his general direction was clear enough: '[A]ll men may be restrained from invading others rights.' In particular, no one is permitted, unless for the purpose of giving effect to justice, to 'take away, or impair … the life, the liberty, health, limb or goods of another'. Those words left their historical mark, providing the formula adapted by Thomas Jefferson to the 'unalienable Rights' of 'Life, Liberty and the pursuit of Happiness' set out in the United States Declaration of Independence. If Magna Carta and Bill of Rights strengthened the protections of the citizen from government, Locke extended this idea to include protection of our fundamental freedoms from other threats to individual liberty – whether from repressive laws duly passed in Parliament, or wider abuse from intolerant quarters of society. Today, whether it is taking a stroll round the block, voicing displeasure at politicians or just exercising the typically British prerogative of keeping oneself to oneself, we are taking advantage of this basic idea of liberty inherited from Locke.

Locke's ideas on personal freedom were not set in a vacuum, but tied to his theory of social contract, woven together by his views on political constitution. He wrote: '… freedom of men under government is to have a standing rule to live by, common to everyone of that society, and made by the legislative power erected in it; a liberty to follow my own will in all things where the rule prescribes not; and not to be subject to the inconstant, uncertain, unknown, arbitrary will of another man'.

For Locke, liberty was inextricably linked to the rule of law. He recognized that government, Parliament and the courts were all capable of abusing their powers. He justified a separation of powers precisely 'because it may be too great a temptation to human frailty apt to grasp at power, for the same persons who have the power of making laws, to have also in their hands the power to execute them'. So, too, the rule of law needed 'indifferent and upright judges, who are to decide controversies by those laws'. Locke was one of the first to foresee the importance of maintaining a balance between the powers of government, Parliament and the courts.

Britain may not have a written constitution, and there is no formal or rigid separation of powers, but as a senior judge in the House of Lords has described: '[it] is a feature of the peculiarly British conception of the separation of powers that Parliament, the executive and the courts each have their own distinct and largely exclusive domain'. In recent years, that basic constitutional division of labour has come under increasing strain. Outspoken judges have been more and more critical of government policy. Ministers in turn have issued scathing remarks about the criminal sentences handed down by the courts. The Human Rights Act has blurred the lines of responsibility between all the three branches of the state. And the government has regularly been accused of marginalizing Parliament, particularly with respect to the conduct of foreign policy and the loss of parliamentary law-making powers to the EU.

If Locke is the point of departure for modern liberalism, John Stuart Mill developed his conception of individual liberty two centuries later, strengthening the case for protecting the citizen from the 'tyranny of the majority' as well as that of the state. Mill's central principle remains relevant today: '[T]hat the only purpose for which power can be rightfully exercised over any member of a civilised community, against his will, is to prevent harm to others. His own good, either physical or moral, is not a sufficient warrant.'

Mill warned against the 'despotism of custom' and embraced the 'diversity of character and culture'. His vision was a pluralistic society where individuals experiment as they wish with ideas, beliefs, practices and the general business of running their own lives. His defence of liberty was based on both its value to the individual and to society, as he directly identifies one with the healthy development of the other: '[I]t is important to give the freest scope possible to uncustomary things, in order that it may in time appear which of these are fit to be converted into customs.'

When Mill defends particular liberties, such as the freedoms of thought, religion and speech, he also has firmly in mind a wider benefit, beyond the individual, that comes from guaranteeing the expression of competing views. His comment, '[h]e who knows only his side of the case, knows little of that', shows his concern with the ossifying of lazy, untested opinions into dogmatic truths. Mill explicitly links the competition of ideas – made possible in a vibrant, free society – with human development and social progress. His instinctive hostility to paternalism remains an enduring influence on the modern debate about limits of interference by the nanny state in our daily lives, whether it is the smoking ban, rules on parents smacking their children or the introduction of compulsory ID cards.

Mill's idea of freedom was built on a mistrust of government, even the democratic kind. He recognized that a free country needs more than just elections. It needs to preserve and protect individual liberty. As the American Founding Father Benjamin Franklin quipped: 'Democracy is two wolves and a lamb voting on what to have for lunch. Liberty is a well-armed lamb contesting the vote.'

If Mill acknowledged the limitations of formal democracy, it was Isaiah Berlin who was honest about the limits of liberty. An Oxford don for most of his professional life, Berlin was born and raised in (what was then) Russia until the age of twelve. He witnessed the Russian Revolution and, as a Jew, felt keenly the horrors of German fascism. His hometown, Riga, was situated along one of the battle lines of the Cold War. Berlin rejected the idea that there was a single coherent theory of life, history or human meaning. He described the belief that 'there is a final solution' to the great philosophical questions in life – with the theories that underpinned both communism and fascism firmly in mind – as bearing the greatest responsibility for 'the slaughter of individuals on the altars of the great historical ideals'. He recounted Immanuel Kant's adage that 'from the crooked timber of humanity no straight thing was ever made'. From this conception of history and life, Berlin made the case for pluralism and liberty. He defined and defended 'negative freedom', which he associated with fundamental liberties and collectively characterized as 'the area within which a man can act unobstructed by others'. But he was not dogmatic, recognizing that the precise parameter of an individual's rights was a 'matter of argument, indeed haggling'.

Berlin was just as clear about the limitations of relying on liberty. Responding to the classic riposte that freedom so narrowly defined means nothing to the poor peasant or starving child, he readily agreed: 'Liberty is not the only goal of men' – and might not mean much to those living in poverty or squalor. Nevertheless, Berlin argued, it was preferable to discount the relevance of liberty – as an inadequate answer to social inequality – than confuse it with some wider mission to achieve social justice, let alone try to expand its scope to incorporate the latter: 'Everything is what it is: liberty is liberty, not equality or fairness or justice or culture or human happiness or a quiet conscience.'

Berlin defended the British idea of liberty, but he kept it in perspective. He acknowledged the need to weigh liberty against other aspects of the public interest – today brought into sharper focus by the demands on law enforcement in fighting crime and terrorism. Perhaps most importantly, Berlin recognized that liberty is not the only – or even the most important – thing we value in life. You cannot pay the mortgage with habeas corpus or raise a family standing on a soap box at Speaker's Corner in Hyde Park. Most of us will never need to rely on the safeguards that make a criminal trial fair. Berlin defended liberty as a pillar of our liberal democracy, but was under no illusion that it could somehow eradicate social inequality, cure cancer or stop global warming. At a time when every gripe and grievance in modern life can be dressed up as a violation of someone's human rights, Berlin reminds us of the risks of inflating rights and presenting them as a panacea for every ill in the world.

These, and many other influential thinkers, contributed to the philosophical, historical and constitutional development of a unique British model of liberal democracy, a model in which freedom under law supports and reinforces a system of parliamentary democracy. Our civil and political liberties represent the first and fundamental freedoms we enjoy as citizens of this country. They are the crown jewels of our liberal democracy, carving out an area of autonomy, free from the interference of the state, which is enjoyed by every individual as of right.

We take advantage of British liberty without thinking about it. We spend most of our waking lives preoccupied with making a living, paying the bills, spending time with friends and family and pursuing the range of things that give value and meaning to our lives. Yet, in an increasingly apathetic age, it is worth recognizing the extent to which such carefree indifference is the privilege of living in a free country. The ability to dislocate ourselves from politics, public debate and the prying eye of the state is a testament to freedom under law, which has traditionally been protected in Britain and is now under threat. Even if we take our freedoms for granted, much of what we do on a daily basis is dependent upon liberty, or would soon vanish without it.

The freedom to switch off and get on with our lives unmolested is not something that happened by accident. The apathy option was won through great sacrifice. It took seven hundred years of inspiration, perspiration and, above all, struggle to crystallize the British idea of – and commitment to – liberty, in clearer and sharper form. As one historian summed up, it 'cost blood, and took centuries'. In 1939, Churchill characterized and inspired Britain's lonely defiance of the totalitarian menace sweeping Europe in terms of:

> a war, viewed in its inherent quality, to establish, on impregnable rocks, the rights of the individual … a war to establish and revive the stature of man.

During that war alone, hundreds of thousands of British soldiers and civilians died, an immense sacrifice for the liberties we leisurely enjoy today. While the British commitment to liberty withstood the assault from fascism, it faced another serious – and more sustained – onslaught, this time from the authoritarian left.

Writing around the same period as Mill, Karl Marx was contemptuous of the idea of liberty evolving in Britain in the nineteenth century. For Marx, rights epitomized a corrupt egoism, separating the individual from his real identity, absorbed as part of society: 'Liberty, therefore, is the right to do everything that harms no-one else … It is a question of the liberty of man as an isolated monad withdrawn into himself.'

Marx argued that the individual would only be free once he conceived himself in terms of a wider collective. Marx criticized rights as purely formal legal constructs, divorced from any real or meaningful content – a right to property is meaningless to the homeless, free speech of limited value to the starving. In fact, liberty was worse than irrelevant because it crystallized unjust – middle-class – privileges at the expense the working class. As Lenin claimed: 'Freedom in capitalist society always remains about the same as it was in ancient Greek republics: Freedom for slave owners.'

Marx's theory of class struggle was based on the imperative to realize the *real* needs of humankind rather than the artificial attachment of a liberal and bourgeois elite to an arbitrary selection of formal rights that perpetuate an unjust status quo.

Fellow communists like Engels asserted – somewhat counter-intuitively – that 'Freedom is the recognition of necessity'. The logical implications for the individual were sobering. Individual worth must be subordinated to the overriding imperative driving a Marxist society towards inevitable class struggle and revolution. Real freedom can only be achieved by recognizing and participating in that emancipation of the downtrodden from the shackles of capitalism.

Built on these philosophical foundations, socialism and communism were constructed in direct and aggressive antagonism to individual liberty. Marxism is all too willing to sacrifice the individual for the collective good. Communist revolutionaries were thereby given ample ideological justification for repressing individual liberty, captured by Lenin's cold observation that: 'Liberty is precious – so precious that it must be rationed.'

Armed with this moral justification, communist governments across the world routinely engaged in the most egregious human rights abuses throughout the twentieth century. This dogmatic ideological commitment to the collective allowed the most basic individual liberties to be easily brushed aside. It is estimated that the Soviet regime killed almost sixty-two million over a seventy-year period in the name of the socialist revolution, twenty million of whom died under Stalin. Some were executed, some died during famines precipitated by coercive Soviet economic policy and others perished in the gulag or working on slave-labour construction projects. Communist China's Great Leap Forward, between 1958 and 1962, created mass famine that killed between twenty and thirty million. Yet neither Stalin nor Mao could match the Khmer Rouge for pure ferocity. The Khmer Rouge slaughtered two million out of eight million Cambodians – a quarter of the entire population – in an effort to purify Cambodia of all bourgeois influences and drag the country towards the mirage of communist utopia.

Subsequent communist governments recognized the atrocities of earlier regimes, perpetrated in the name of socialist revolution. Deng Xiaoping declared that Mao had only been 70 per cent right and Khrushchev criticized Stalin's reign of terror. But such abuse of power was explained as a misapplication of socialism. Ironically, Khrushchev blamed the individualism of the Stalinist cult – rather than the totalitarian state – for 'mass repressions and brutal acts of violation of Socialist legality'. Stalin's excesses did not give grounds for an ideological shift – Marxism and liberty remained incompatible and irreconcilable – leaving intact the ideological weapon with which to attack personal freedoms.

During the Cold War, communist governments also relied on the Marxist conception of freedom to avoid signing up to human rights treaties. Two international human rights lawyers summarized the relationship between socialism and human rights: 'Since the State by definition represents the interests of the people, the citizens can have no rights against the State ... The socialist State expresses the will of the mass of the workers, and the individual owes it absolute obedience.'

Throughout this period the Soviet Union and other communist governments relied on their very different conception of freedom, and their cynical view of individual liberty, to avoid assuming any international human rights obligations under the guise that they would 'interfere with domestic affairs' and 'sovereignty'.

However, the spread of socialist ideas beyond the Soviet bloc generated a number of treaties providing for social and economic rights, a more subtle reflection of the Marxist critique that civil and political liberties did not address people's real needs. The International Covenant on Economic Social and Cultural Rights 1966 included rights to work, a fair wage, healthcare, education, the right to take part in cultural life and the right to enjoy the benefits of scientific progress. In reality, the Covenant reflected aspirations not rights. These new rights could not be judicially enforced in domestic courts in the way that, for example, illegal detention can be challenged or the right to protest asserted in specific cases.

This attempted compromise, coupling civil and political liberties with other 'rights', was reflected in the approach of continental European governments, which had historically, philosophically and culturally been much more susceptible to socialist influence. The development of social democratic movements on the continent can be seen as an attempt to forge a compromise between the two conceptions of freedom that otherwise stand in clear and unequivocal conflict with each other. The influence of this attempted synthesis – between Marxism and liberalism – has extended beyond domestic politics, to the development of a common European identity through the supranational institutions of the Council of Europe in Strasbourg and the EU in Brussels.

In Britain these twin strands of socialism lay beneath the surface of the New Labour project that swept Tony Blair into power in 1997. Both ran against the traditional grain of British liberty. Marx had a less powerful, but nonetheless enduring, influence in Britain. New Labour had successfully concealed, rather than extinguished, the orthodox brand of socialism, and Tony Blair managed formally to dislocate the Labour Party from the dogma of public ownership of the means of production during his famous 'Clause Four' moment in 1994. Nevertheless, the Labour Party's updated constitution still stubbornly described it as a 'socialist' party.

Looking around the table at Tony Blair's new Cabinet of Ministers in May 1997 and more broadly across the corridors of power in Whitehall, a surprising number of ministers and key advisers, including John Reid and Peter Mandelson, were formerly Communist Party members, allies or associates – including two Home Secretaries, until recently the cabinet minister responsible for the Human Rights Act. Other cabinet ministers with previous communist or Trotskyite connections include Charles Clarke, Stephen Byers and Alan Milburn. Marxism had been a key influence on them during their formative years, and once in power they were not passive bystanders. They propelled the New Labour agenda and rose rapidly through the ministerial ranks. Given the Marxist antagonism towards individual freedoms, they were unlikely to provide an instinctive defence of British liberty, and more likely to join – if not drive – the imminent assault.

If what one commentator has called the 'liberty reflex' was replaced with a Marxist disposition amongst a leading cabal in government, there was a further – more surreptitious – thread running through the New Labour machine, most notably Tony Blair, which would further erode the British tradition of liberty from an altogether different direction. The new Prime Minister was determined to 'lead in Europe', putting Britain at the vanguard of European policy-making after years of Conservative foot-dragging. While successive administrations had sought to ignore the growing irritant created by adverse rulings, and the increasing rate of dubious case law, from the European Court of Human Rights in Strasbourg, the incoming government took active steps to increase the flow by enacting the Human Rights Act in 1998, thereby incorporating the European Convention and all its case law directly into UK law. The government was palpably relaxed about the prospect of importing the European approach to human rights, grounded in the social democratic tradition. It ignored the risk of diluting the British liberal tradition through an expansive European approach to human rights that pursued social and economic justice, exponentially extending the scope of 'rights' and inflating – rather than restraining – the role of the state.

While ideological baggage and European strategy boded ill for British liberties, New Labour tactics would only make matters worse. Tony Blair, Gordon Brown and the other architects of New Labour correctly calculated that winning back public confidence in the Labour Party meant seizing the centre ground of politics. In order to achieve this, a policy of triangulation was constructed. In crude terms, the electoral plan of attack involved dumping the most obvious outward trappings of the party's socialist heritage, outflanking the Conservative Party by matching, if not surpassing, its tough stance on crime and security and promising Labour's grassroots supporters a step change in investment in public services – a more subtle and publicly palatable means of redistributing a large volume of the nation's wealth than a sustained programme of nationalization.

The second element in this equation would tempt the government, time and time again, to embark on grandiose security gestures that rode roughshod over fundamental liberties with negligible countervailing benefits in terms of public safety. The third element, massive additional spending on public services, would harness the expansion of the idea of human rights, well beyond anything previously recognized in Britain, as a visible vehicle for claiming credit for fighting the social injustice that New Labour claimed to have inherited from the Thatcher years.

The outcome of the election in May 1997 added a further practical consideration, which strengthened the government's hand in the looming assault on liberty. Having secured a landslide overall majority of 179 seats in the House of Commons, the new administration was well placed to force through virtually any legislation without serious risk of defeat. The sheer volume of new criminal law and security measures, introduced by the new government over the course of a decade, would displace the common law presumption in favour of personal freedom that held sway in this country for centuries.

In this way, a constellation of disparate factors gathered that would pose the most serious threat to the British legacy of liberty in post-war history. Built from scratch, nurtured and defended – through periods of monarchical despotism, civil war and attempted foreign invasion – ancient British freedoms found themselves under siege from an unconventional and unscrupulous wolf in sheep's clothing. The previous rough consensus on the minimum fundamental rights of the citizen – shared more or less by successive Conservative and Labour governments – was cast aside, as the new Labour administration prepared to embark on a relentless and historically unprecedented assault on British liberty.

PART II

WHERE DID RIGHTS GO?

2

Security versus Liberty

'We must plan for freedom, and not only for security, if for no other reason than that only freedom can make security secure.'

KARL POPPER

Since New Labour came to power Britain has suffered a sustained attack on its tradition of liberty, with the government regularly claiming that stronger measures are justified to strengthen our security and make us safer. This unprecedented assault on our fundamental freedoms has been waged on diverse fronts, with justifications clustered around three principal rationales.

First, the government has argued that decisive action is needed in response to a unique danger, namely the terrorist threat posed by al-Qaeda and related fanatical groups. Second, it has justified its actions in the sphere of law enforcement and criminal justice on the basis of the overriding imperative to cut crime and tackle anti-social behaviour. Third, it has massed a range of powers to watch, intercept and gather private details on its citizens on the basis that such inroads on our privacy will make the individual, and our society as a whole, safer. The common denominator is the assumption that, when push comes to shove, security can be traded for – and should be prized above – liberty, a tough but necessary choice that many, at least at first sight, may intuitively be inclined to accept.

The difficulty with this analysis is that liberty and security are rarely stark alternatives or juxtaposed choices. The government has assumed the existence of a hydraulic relationship between freedom and security, a zero-sum game in which we have a genuine choice to pay a price in terms of our personal freedom, in order to yield a security dividend that provides greater public protection against violent crime and terrorism. But is the real world that straightforward, and does this paradigm provide more than a simplistic gloss, a political crouch that obscures a more complex picture? Draconian measures will always undermine liberty. But there is scant evidence that they have made us safer.

An alternative assessment, supported by a growing body of evidence over the last eleven years, is that the government's attack on our core freedoms has not yielded any clear, significant or demonstrable security dividend; indeed, it has often had the reverse effect, jeopardizing rather than strengthening our security.

In the field of counter-terrorism, the government's approach has fixated on a number of high-profile gestures, including extending detention without charge for terrorist suspects, introducing control orders and pressing ahead with ID cards, amongst a package of other authoritarian measures. While the government has moved to raise the limit on pre-charge detention sixfold since 2003, the rate of home-grown radicalization and the numbers involved in terrorist-related activity have only grown faster, at a current rate of 25 per cent per year according to MI5 – hardly the symptoms of successful policy.

When it comes to fighting crime, the government has created more than three thousand new criminal offences and attacked fundamental pillars of British justice, including the presumption of innocence and the right to trial by jury. Yet, at the same time, violent crime has nearly doubled, the UK has the second highest crime rate in Europe and fatal stabbings and gun violence have surged.

Nor has the exponential increase in surveillance powers by the state improved public safety. Eighty per cent of CCTV footage is not fit for purpose. The government loses personal data on a regular basis, exposing those it is charged to protect to unnecessary risk. And, far from helping police to crack down on fraud, one Chief Constable predicts the government's flawed proposals for ID cards will set the 'gold standard' target for criminal hackers.

As one commentator, Jenny McCartney, characterized the approach:

> A pattern is emerging in the way that Britain deals with any kind of threat ... It acts like a terrified but sieve-brained householder who tries to foil prospective burglars by putting expensive, complicated locks on the top windows while frequently leaving the back door swinging open ...
>
> The Faustian bargain that New Labour has traditionally offered the public is that we should submit to ever more intrusion in exchange for greater security. What we are getting now is intrusion and insecurity – and even Faust managed a more attractive deal than that.

Time and time again since it came to power in 1997 the government has presented tough measures that infringe fundamental liberties as a price worth paying to make the public safer. The serious charge to be laid against this government is that its confused approach has been driven as much by considerations of PR as national security. The government has deployed increasingly dramatic rhetoric with each new announcement, heralding serious inroads on our fundamental freedoms, with precious little improvement in public protection to show for it. Far from offering a finely balanced trade-off, or even a Faustian bargain, the government's approach has turned out to be a straight con – leaving us both less free and less secure.

We have become accustomed to national security being regularly cited as one of the main grounds for sacrificing individual liberty, particularly in the aftermath of 9/11 and subsequently the 7/7 attacks in London. Yet Britain has faced serious threats to its national security before, without knee-jerk resort to such far-reaching, unfocused and permanent measures that seek to redefine the fundamental balance in the relationship between the citizen and the state.

During the Second World War identity cards and internment were introduced in the face of global war and direct military attack. In 1940, faced with the Blitz and the real prospect of a Nazi invasion, the government interned a range of 'enemy aliens', principally Italian and German civilians living in Britain. Around eight thousand were detained although most had been released by 1942 and the legal basis was revoked at the end of the war. Yet, as A. C. Grayling notes, from 1940, faced with an imminent invasion by Nazi Germany, temporary measures were taken that undermined individual liberty. In contrast today, 'in face of a far lesser threat', Britain is 'enacting *permanent* legislation of even more draconian kinds'.

Churchill only reluctantly introduced temporary wartime measures that infringed individual liberty, removing them once the immediate exigencies allowed. When Oswald Mosley, the notorious Nazi sympathizer, was released from internment in 1943, Churchill sent a telegram to the Home Secretary justifying the decision in the following terms:

> [T]he great privilege of habeas corpus, and of trial by jury, which are the supreme protection invented by the English people for ordinary individuals against the State ... The power of the Executive to cast a man into prison without formulating any charge known to the law and particularly to deny him the judgement of his peers – is, in the highest degree, odious and is the foundation of all totalitarian governments ... Extraordinary powers assumed by the Executive with the consent of Parliament in emergencies should be yielded up, when and as, the emergency declines ... This is really the test of civilisation.

Faced with a very real threat to national life, in one of the darkest moments in British history, the government of national unity took finite and temporary measures to meet the specific, overwhelming and undeniable threat.

Since then, our fundamental freedoms have come under periodic strain, most regularly in the context of the struggle against terrorism. The conflict in Northern Ireland lasted for around thirty years and cost 3500 lives, including more than 1800 civilians. Britain undoubtedly faced a real and sustained terrorist threat, and the government took measures against IRA terrorism that incurred human rights challenges and political controversy – including, most notably, the use of internment and Diplock courts (the latter allowing criminal trial of those accused of terrorist suspects without juries). Nevertheless, over a thirty-year period, internment lasted for only four years and withstood legal challenge at the European Court on Human Rights, which accepted that it had been required by the exigencies of an emergency situation. In practice, internment proved a disaster – fuelling the resentment and violence it was introduced to contain – and was replaced for the rest of the conflict with a maximum limit of seven days' pre-charge detention, a fraction of the maximum period now in place in Britain.

Equally, Diplock courts were used between 1973 and 2007 because of the clear and serious threat of witness intimidation amidst the sectarian conflict, which successive governments – of both main parties – accepted was undermining efforts to bring criminal prosecutions against those accused of paramilitary violence. While a judge replaced the jury as the trier of the facts in these cases, the measure applied to paramilitary groups on both sides of the conflict, trials remained public and were subject to appeal.

The conflict threw up a range of other human rights controversies – including miscarriages of justice arising from police misconduct (such as the Birmingham Six and Guildford Four) and criticism of the shooting by British special forces of three IRA members in the course of trying to set off a bomb in Gibraltar.

Beyond the conflict in Northern Ireland, the Spycatcher episode arose out of the government's attempts to ban the publication of a book written by Peter Wright, a former MI5 officer, between 1987 and 1988. The book was published in the US and Australia and the government was eventually defeated in its attempt to prevent publication and bring related claims against the *Sunday Times* and *Guardian*.

No previous government can claim a perfect record on civil liberties, yet it is difficult to avoid the impression that the deliberate and concerted assault on liberty throughout the last decade has been without precedent – of a different order of magnitude to the *ad hoc* incursions that preceded it.

While the new government introduced a range of repressive new measures from 1997, the most serious attack on fundamental liberties in the name of national security took place after 9/11, when the government sought to introduce indefinite detention without charge for foreign terrorist suspects, and gathered momentum with its hastily put together response to the London bombings in July 2005. At a press conference less than a month after the dust had settled on the attacks in central London that left fifty-two people dead and many more seriously injured, Tony Blair reacted with a list of twelve new security measures, announcing a radical change of approach: 'Let no one be in any doubt, the rules of the game are changing.'

With this dramatic gesture before an audience of journalists, the then Prime Minister ostentatiously signalled that the struggle against terrorism would no longer be shackled by the traditional safeguards that protect those suspected – but not yet convicted – of involvement in any crime. In the years that followed, the government would introduce a range of measures that would undermine British liberty in the name of fighting terror. Proposals for ninety-day detention without charge, control orders amounting to house arrest, compulsory ID cards and a slew of measures that stifle free speech were proposed as the necessary means of countering the rising threat of al-Qaeda-related terrorism in Britain.

New laws were rapidly formulated and presented by a government desperate to find a legislative way to demonstrate its security credentials in the wake of two terrorist attacks on the capital. Reactive legislation was broadly – and poorly – drafted, often rushed through Parliament under pressure of time that prevented proper scrutiny. Almost inevitably, the new powers were widely construed, without clear focus, which both blunted their operational effectiveness in countering terrorism and left them susceptible to abuse by law enforcement officers acting under operational pressures.

Looking back at Tony Blair's press conference in August 2005, it is instructive to note the fate of the twelve-point plan he announced, each measure of which was hailed as 'either being taken now, immediately, or under urgent examination'. Many of the eye-catching measures rushed out were quietly abandoned or rendered unworkable – Hizb ut-Tahrir has not been banned, grounds for deportation have been restricted not expanded, the idea of a maximum time limit on extradition dropped and border controls remain porous.

Equally, while the most repressive measures proposed – control orders, the offence of glorification of terrorism and extending pre-charge detention – have generated political controversy and threatened or undermined individual liberty, they have subsequently proved to be of minimal security value, if not outright counter-productive.

Of the string of measures announced, none posed a greater danger to British liberty than the new proposals to extend detention without charge, a serious threat to the ancient right of habeas corpus. In 2003, the previous seven-day limit on detention without charge – which had proved adequate for dealing with Irish terrorism for the past twenty years – was doubled to fourteen days, in response to the terrorist attacks on 9/11. While all other serious criminal cases remained subject to a four-day limit (including drug trafficking, organized crime and complex fraud cases), in 2005 Tony Blair sought to extend the time limit in terrorism cases to ninety days, offering no credible evidence as to why yet another massive increase was necessary to protect the public. In November 2005 the ninety-day proposal was rejected, Blair's first ever parliamentary defeat, but the limit on pre-charge detention was increased to twenty-eight days – as an extraordinary emergency power to be used only in the most exceptional of circumstances.

While the proposals were rushed through without an opportunity for thorough scrutiny, evidence made available since suggests that some increase in the powers of police detention beyond fourteen days was necessary to deal with the increased terrorist threat and the growing number, and increasing complexity, of cases under police investigation. Basic details of the number of suspects and volume of evidence in police counter-terrorism investigations demonstrate some of the operational pressures on police and prosecutors. This was backed up by public briefings from the Security Service, MI5. In 2006, the Director General of MI5 spoke publicly of thirty terror plots threatening Britain and 1600 individuals under surveillance. By 2007, her successor had revised that risk assessment – the Security Service was now monitoring at least two thousand individuals thought to be involved in terrorism – and estimated that there might be a further two thousand they were unable to track.

Nevertheless, the government also increasingly relied on the shroud of secrecy that covers the work of our counter-terrorism authorities to avoid explaining the reasons for extending the powers of the police to hold suspects without charge. And while it has demonstrated an insatiable political appetite for extending the maximum period still further – beyond twenty-eight days – it has not offered any convincing evidence to demonstrate that such a step is necessary.

Between 2005 and 2008 the government put forward numerous proposals to extend the detention without charge beyond twenty-eight days. Seemingly plucked out of the air, proposals for fifty-six, fifty-eight, ninety days and even indefinite detention without charge were all mooted – with the government settling on forty-two days in the face of widespread scepticism from Parliament and the wider public. Despite some indications that Gordon Brown might prove less cavalier as Prime Minister than his predecessor, he made clear his intention to press ahead soon after taking office in June 2007. The government forced the legislation through the House of Commons on 11 June 2008 by nine votes, despite a major revolt by Labour backbenchers and amidst widespread reports of reticent MPs being bullied or offered financial inducements to silence their dissent. One estimate put the price tag on securing the vote as high as £1.2 billion. In October, the forty-two days proposal was subsequently mauled from all sides in the House of Lords. The Home Secretary reacted by accusing all those opposed to forty-two days of ignoring the terrorist threat and withdrawing the proposal from the Counter-Terrorism Bill. Yet at the same time, she published a separate new proposal, with even wider powers to extend pre-charge detention to forty-two days, and threatened to force it through Parliament in the event of another terrorist attack – an irresponsible display of sublime political brinkmanship.

While the government cites police support for forty-two days, the equivalent of a short prison sentence, it has failed to articulate any persuasive justification or present any evidence to back up its case. Nor has it explained why other less repressive measures would provide inadequate alternatives. Instead of presenting a compelling case on the merits, the government has relied on popular nervousness after the 7/7 bombings and the – increasingly abused – public trust that the government would not seek additional security powers unless it was absolutely necessary.

So what is the strength of the case for extending detention without charge in Britain beyond twenty-eight days? A cursory comparison with international practice is revealing. At twenty-eight days the UK already has by far the longest period of pre-charge detention amongst comparable democracies. In Europe, France permits only six days' pre-charge detention and Germany only two. While the continental justice systems operate differently, these represent the limits on the period of detention without formally laying charges before an accused. In common law countries with a justice system more closely comparable to our own, Australia allows twelve days' pre-charge detention, New Zealand two and Canada just one day. In the US, after the horrors of 9/11 – and two terms of President George W. Bush's war on terror – two days' pre-charge detention has proved more than adequate in dealing with ten recent complex terrorism investigations. Outside the democratic world, Russian law only allows the police to hold suspects for five days, Zimbabwe only allows twenty-one days' detention and even China only allows police detention of suspects for thirty-seven days. Britain, once a beacon of liberty, now has the longest period of detention without charge in the free world.

If international comparisons suggest that forty-two days is excessive, experience at home points to the same conclusion. While the security environment in Britain has changed in recent years, none of the counter-terrorism investigations in the UK to date have demonstrated the need for a longer period. Twenty-eight days was enough to comfortably deal with the most complex terrorism case we have ever faced, the plot to blow ten transatlantic airliners out of the sky at Heathrow in August 2006. If successful, it would have been the worst terrorist attack in British history, almost certainly causing a greater number of casualties than the attacks in the US on 9/11. Operation Overt, the police investigation that followed, was certainly complex – involving close cooperation with international partners, sifting large amounts of evidence (including computer hard drives and forensic analysis) and reviewing a wide range of suspects. It was held up, on both sides of the debate, as the litmus test case for scrutinizing whether the police can cope with a twenty-eight-day limit.

During Operation Overt, twenty-four suspects were arrested and seventeen were charged with terrorism offences. Of the twenty-four arrested all of those charged with the more serious offences of conspiracy to murder and conspiracy to blow up aeroplanes were charged within twenty-one days of arrest. Five were detained on lesser charges of 'acts preparatory to terrorism' (and other related offences) to the maximum limit of twenty-eight days.

The five held for twenty-eight days formed the crux of the government's case for an extension of the time limit. Ministers claimed the police were coming perilously close to having to release terrorists, because they were running out of time to gather the necessary evidence to charge them. But do the facts back this up? Of the five held for twenty-eight days, three were released without any further conditions. They were not placed under any restrictions on release. They were not subject to a control order, or any other related measure, limiting their movements or activities – the clearest indication that, by that point, they were now believed to be entirely unconnected with any terrorist activity relating to Operation Overt. So, the three innocent suspects released after twenty-eight days do not provide evidence that the government needs a longer period of detention to prevent real terrorists from walking free.

However, two of the five suspects were charged at the end of the twenty-eight-day period. But, in both cases, the Metropolitan Police and Crown Prosecution Service subsequently confirmed that the evidence relied upon to charge them was obtained within four and twelve days of arrest respectively. Furthermore, both suspects were subsequently bailed, which no court would conceivably have allowed if they posed a threat to public safety. The Home Secretary, Jacqui Smith, and the Minister for Security, Tony McNulty, both persistently denied these facts when they were presented to them in the House of Commons. At best, they failed to test the evidence presented to them by the police with the rigour to be expected of ministers. At worst, they disregarded – and then denied – key facts that they found inconvenient as they struggled to make the case for forty-two days. Either amounts to a serious dereliction of ministerial duty. The fact remains that, in the most challenging terrorism investigation the UK has ever had to deal with, police obtained all the evidence necessary to charge all the suspects within twenty-one days – not twenty-eight let alone forty-two days. There was never any risk that the police would have to release a serious terrorist suspect – posing a threat to the public – as a result of the twenty-eight-day limit.

On the contrary, as the Director of Public Prosecutions (DPP) made clear for all counter-terrorism investigations carried out under the twenty-eight-day limit, the law enforcement authorities coped comfortably. Far from being 'up against the buffers' operating within the twenty-eight-day limit, as one senior police officer would later irresponsibly claim, the twenty-eight-day maximum limit gave the police ample time to gather the evidence required to make the decision to charge or release, even in the most exceptional of cases. There has been no other evidence or cases – suggested or adduced – that support the case for extending detention without charge beyond twenty-eight days.

This explains why senior law enforcement officials have refused to back yet another extension of the maximum limit – including the DPP, the senior prosecutor at the Crown Prosecution Service, Lord Goldsmith, the former Attorney General, and a range of senior police officers. While the Commissioner of the Metropolitan Police sought to justify the move, his support was based on a 'pragmatic inference' that cases are getting more complicated, rather than any particular evidence drawn from police operations.

Further insights into the operational challenges faced during Operation Overt would emerge later at the end of the first trial of eight of the central suspects, which concluded on 9 September 2008. None of the suspects were convicted of conspiracy to blow up aeroplanes, although three were convicted on the more general charge of conspiracy to murder. In the aftermath of the trial, recriminations began to emerge from police, prosecutors and Whitehall, dismayed about the failure to convict anyone of the specific plot to blow the transatlantic airliners at Heathrow out of the sky. Reports trickling through the media suggested that police had been forced to arrest the suspects pre-emptively, by nervous US officials scarred by the experience of 9/11. The arrests were carried out earlier than planned, before the plotters had purchased airline tickets and obtained new passports, which would have provided valuable additional evidence of the specific plot. If this is accurate, and pre-emptive arrests prevented the police and MI5 from catching the plotters red-handed, then no amount of pre-charge detention would be able to rectify that evidential opportunity lost.

In the wake of the verdicts, Andy Hayman, the former officer who ran Operation Overt, went public with a withering critique of the organization of counter-terrorism policing in Britain. He criticized the lack of effective cooperation between local police forces and the Metropolitan Police's national counter-terrorism command, and went on to highlight a list of operational police failings that were impeding the counter-terrorism effort:

> … the present arrangements are frequently clumsy: IT and communication systems are not always joined up; surveillance teams, armed response units and scenes-of-crime officers vary in expertise and capability; the lines of command and control become stretched … These factors are serious enough but they pale into insignificance compared to funding arrangements.

Hayman called for an overhaul of counter-terrorism policing. He was a supporter of ninety days' pre-charge detention in 2005, yet in his post-mortem of Operation Overt he did not once mention the twenty-eight-day limit amongst the problems he had encountered during that investigation, or more widely.

Lacking any compelling evidence from Operation Overt or any other previous terrorism investigations that could justify an extension beyond the twenty-eight-day limit, the government shifted tack and speculated that Britain could conceivably face multiple attacks, each on the same scale as the Heathrow plot in 2006. This nightmare scenario envisaged five simultaneous attacks in Britain, each equivalent to 9/11. The scenario presented was entirely hypothetical. There was no evidence that it reflected a genuine risk analysis. Nor was there any explanation of how such elaborate, compound and complex plots could be hatched on British soil without alerting the police or security services well in advance.

Curiously, in its zeal, the government had overlooked its own legislation which already provides sweeping powers to deal with genuine national emergencies on that scale. The Civil Contingencies Act 2004 was explicitly designed to deal with terrorist threats, amongst other national emergencies. It allows the government to extend pre-charge detention beyond the twenty-eight-day limit by additional, and renewable, thirty-day periods. The extensions are subject to judicial review and parliamentary approval. If the government really needs this power, it must publicly state that there exists an emergency which makes it necessary to use it. If there existed a plot to blow fifty planes out of the sky – the hypothetical scenario posed by the government – there could be little doubt that there would exist a genuine emergency. It would also be both impossible and irresponsible to try to conceal the real situation for more than a few days. In practice, any public statement on the emergency would not need to be made in the immediate midst of a crisis. The government would just be required to make its statement before the expiry of the existing twenty-eight-day pre-charge detention limit. So, even on this hypothetical scenario, there was no need to extend the current twenty-eight-day limit – a reserve power was already in place, subject to robust safeguards.

Even human rights groups like Liberty and barristers, including David Pannick QC, confirmed that such broad emergency powers could be used, removing any conceivable justification for a further extension of the twenty-eight-day limit, even under the worst nightmare scenarios conjured up by ministers. However, the government rejected this analysis on two grounds. It suggested that there were technical difficulties in using the 2004 Act in this way. It also claimed that declaring an emergency would create panic. It is difficult to take either argument seriously. If there are technical difficulties in applying the 2004 Act, they could presumably be addressed through a minor legislative amendment providing the clarity required. Equally, the British public are not known for their disposition to panic, whether during the Blitz of 1940, the campaign of IRA violence, the London bombings in July 2005, in the aftermath of the terrorist plot at Heathrow in August 2006 or during the attacks in Glasgow and London in 2007. On the contrary, British public reaction has been consistently characterized by composure and resolve. Furthermore, the government itself has hardly been shy about publicly briefing blood-curdling assessments of the terrorist threat. MI5 now regularly briefs on the thousands of terror suspects operating in the UK and the Metropolitan Police Commissioner referred to the future terrorist threat as the coming 'epidemic'. The government's refusal to consider its existing powers under the 2004 Act, and insistence on draconian new powers, demonstrates its preference for placing Britain under a permanent undeclared state of emergency – rather than a temporary and transparent one, if and when the strict necessity should arise.

Finally, faced with mounting opposition in 2008, the Home Secretary based her proposals for a forty-two-day maximum limit on what she referred to as a 'precautionary principle'. The precautionary principle is derived from environmental law, which presents a rather different set of challenges to counter-terrorism. There has been no explanation of why this environmental principle is relevant or what it might mean in the context of terrorism. It appears little more than a thin veneer to allow the government to keep returning to Parliament for additional police powers on the basis of an unspecified threat that may or may not materialize at some indeterminate point in the future.

While there is not a shred of hard evidence to support the case for extending detention without charge beyond twenty-eight days, the government has encouraged a common, but wholly misleading, assumption that extending pre-charge detention would help deal with the classic 'ticking bomb' scenario – that we need longer than twenty-eight days to hold terrorist masterminds or suicide bombers who might otherwise abscond to launch a terrorist attack. In fact, experience suggests the opposite. The key players in a terrorist plot are, in practice, the least likely to be held for the maximum period of detention without charge, because they are the suspects that tend to be questioned and investigated first. During Operation Overt, all the alleged ringleaders were arrested and charged within twenty-one days. It was only those either subsequently released (without further suspicion) or charged with lesser offences that were held for twenty-eight days.

This case illustrates an emerging trend: it is precisely those most likely to be innocent or least involved in a terrorist conspiracy who are most likely to be held for the longest period of detention. Far from being necessary to deal with imminent threats to public safety or terrorist masterminds, extensions of pre-charge detention are generally used to follow up secondary leads and suspects. Each extension of the maximum period of detention risks exacerbating this trend – delaying the point at which the police need either to charge or release those on the fringe of their investigation. It is often said that those with nothing to hide have nothing to fear, but the reality of police investigations suggests that those with nothing to hide may be most at risk from extensions of pre-charge detention.

If an innocent person is detained for weeks or months, the consequences can be personally disastrous, even if he is eventually released. The case of Lotfi Raissi demonstrates the devastating impact that prolonged detention without charge can have on a wholly innocent individual. Raissi was an Algerian-born pilot living in London. He was arrested in Britain after 9/11, because he had attended the same flying school as the bombers. US authorities accused him of having taught the 9/11 bombers to fly the planes that crashed into the Twin Towers in New York. The FBI quickly realized that this was unlikely to be true. However, the British police held Raissi in pre-charge detention awaiting extradition to the US on the flimsiest basis. He was not held on suspicion of terrorism offences but on trivial grounds, including that he had lied on his pilot's licence by failing to reveal previous knee surgery – an allegation that was subsequently proved false as well.

It appears that the US authorities were still interested in questioning Raissi, but no longer thought it likely that he was involved in 9/11. The Court of Appeal in Britain later criticized both the US and UK authorities for deploying this 'device' to keep Raissi in detention without charge for over four months. The court went on to criticize the British police and the Crown Prosecution Service for 'serious defaults' in allowing this abuse of process. The court exonerated Raissi of all allegations, delivering a judgment that paved the way for him to seek compensation. The case shows how, in the wake of a terrorist attack, the police can come under considerable pressure to bend the law at the expense of a suspect who may prove to be entirely innocent.

In this instance an innocent man's life was left in ruins. Raissi was twice stabbed by prisoners during his period of detention, because of allegations that he had links to the 9/11 terrorists. He suffered two nervous breakdowns under the strain and did not sleep properly for seven years. He lost his job and found himself blacklisted from finding a new one. He became entirely dependent on his family, although in the wake of his arrest both his wife and his brother's wife also lost their jobs.

If extending pre-charge detention would undermine a fundamental freedom, with severe consequences for the innocent that are imprisoned – as half of all those held for twenty-eight days have been – there is an increasing number of warnings that, far from making us safer, an extension to forty-two days may actually jeopardize our security. In addition to criticisms by human rights lawyers and NGOs, a growing chorus of security experts have publicly declared their opposition to forty-two days – on the basis that it is either irrelevant as a security measure or actually risks making the terrorist threat worse.

While the government has consistently cited evidence from MI5 on the growing numbers involved in terrorism to bolster its case for forty-two days, it is striking that the current and previous two heads of MI5 have either criticized or refused to back an extension beyond twenty-eight days. In an interview in July 2007, the former head of MI5, Stella Rimington, made clear her opposition to an extension: 'It behoves us all to question when governments want to bring in increasingly draconian measures.'

This was followed by further, more recent, criticism from her successor at MI5, Baroness Manningham-Buller, who declared she could not support the extension to forty-two days 'on a practical basis or on a principled one', arguing that the measure was both disproportionate and unworkable. The current Director General of MI5, Jonathan Evans, also refused to publicly back forty-two days. The subsequent riposte from ministers – that MI5 is not responsible for pre-charge detention – flies directly in the face of its regular reliance on MI5's assessments, not to mention Tony Blair's public claim in August 2005 that MI5 had then asked for an extension. The reality appears to be that MI5 positively backed an extension beyond fourteen days – but refused to back an extension beyond twenty-eight days.

There is further disquiet within the ranks of the police. Chief

Constables and other senior officers have expressed their opposition or reservations in private, with senior officers at the Metropolitan Police letting it be known that the forty-two-day proposal is unworkable, and therefore either irrelevant or counter-productive as a security measure.

Other experts warn against two specific risks generated by prolonged detention without charge. First, the disproportionate effect on innocent young Muslim males risks creating widespread resentment and serving the twisted narrative that extremists and terrorists thrive on – Britain targeting Muslims at home as well as abroad in Iraq and Afghanistan. Such draconian measures alienate whole communities, nurturing the friendly sea within which terrorism thrives. In short, a further extension beyond twenty-eight days risks serving as a recruiting sergeant for terrorism.

During the debate on ninety days, Lord Condon, former head of the Metropolitan Police, raised this concern in explicit terms: 'If we now go back and make it look like we are going to challenge yet again the point of 28 days that we have reached, I fear that it will play into the hands of the propagandists, who will encourage young men and women … to be misguided, brainwashed and induced into acts of martyrdom.'

More recently, Lord Dear, former Chief Constable of West Midlands Police and a former Chief Inspector of Constabulary, delivered an even starker warning:

> Make no mistake, extending pre-charge detention would most certainly be a propaganda coup for al-Qaida … The immediate danger if we travel down this road is that we will lose the battle for hearts and minds abroad, and particularly in the minority groups in this country, whose long-term support is vital if we are to counter and remove the threat of terrorism.

Even the government's own Security Minister, Lord West, expressed concerns about extending pre-charge detention before being forced to retract them by the Prime Minister:

> I want to have absolute evidence that we actually need longer than 28 days. I want to be totally convinced because I am not going to go and push for something that actually affects the liberty of the individual unless there is a real necessity for it. I still need to be fully convinced that we absolutely need more than 28 days and I also need to be convinced what is the best way of doing that.

A growing list of security experts, with front-line experience in the fight against terrorism, are warning that extending pre-charge detention will aggravate, not mitigate, the terrorist threat level.

The second security risk in extending pre-charge is that it will cut off the flow of human intelligence to the police. In 2007, the head of counter-terrorism at the Metropolitan Police, Peter Clarke, made the case publicly that improving public understanding and trust represents the greatest current challenge we face in addressing the terrorist threat. While Clarke supported the Metropolitan Police's line in favour of forty-two days, he has also pointed out that very few terrorism prosecutions originate from 'community intelligence' – namely members of local communities coming forward to the police with information or cooperation about suspected terrorist activity. This is in marked contrast to the high level of cooperation and intelligence derived from local communities in France and other countries. Clarke warned that: '… the lack of public trust in intelligence is in danger of infecting the relationship between the police and the communities we serve. Trust and consent are two concepts that lie at the heart of the relationship between the British police and the public.'

It is increasingly evident that the disproportionate impact of police powers on the Muslim community risks undermining their confidence in and cooperation with the police and security services. This has a direct bearing on our operational capability, choking off vital 'community intelligence', which is critical to counter-terrorism investigations. Even the government's own impact assessment, accompanying the proposal for forty-two days, acknowledges this: 'Muslim groups said that pre-charge detention may risk information being forthcoming from members of the community in the future.'

The real risk is that further extending pre-charge detention will not just sacrifice the fundamental freedoms of the citizen but also harm our security, both by increasing the radicalization of disaffected young Muslim men, and alienating the local communities whose active cooperation is pivotal to the counter-terrorism effort. Far from involving a delicate balance between collective security and individual liberty, as a security measure forty-two days' pre-charge detention is unnecessary, if not counter-productive. That is not a trade-off – it is just lose-lose.

In contrast, senior counter-terrorism officers report that one of the most positive developments, helping to combat the climate in which radicalization thrives, has been the recent string of criminal convictions in terrorism cases. Nervous Muslim communities were alarmed by the armed raid in Forest Gate, London, in 2006, which was based on mistaken intelligence relating to a potential chemical bomb attack. Wild conspiracy theories circulated suggesting that the raid was part of a propaganda exercise to hype up the public perception of the terrorist threat. As spurious as these claims were, the subsequent public conduct of trials in other terrorism cases – and the convictions that followed – helped demonstrate, to even the most sceptical quarters, that the UK's struggle against terrorism is all too real. That in turn has improved the confidence of, and cooperation from, Muslim communities. Peter Clarke argues:

'The series of terrorist convictions in recent years has been a victory for the rule of law and sends out a strong, positive signal to all communities.'

Again, it is striking that the open and transparent conduct of these criminal cases – through a British justice system that respects fundamental rights – has not only resulted in the long-term incarceration of dangerous terrorists, but also had a positive impact on the climate in which police counter-terrorism operations take place.

It is a popular myth that we now face the dilemma of weighing security considerations against the liberty of the individual. In fact, the publicly available evidence on both sides of this debate points broadly in the same direction. Sustaining the fundamental liberties every individual enjoys in this country as of right provides one of our most important tools in refuting propaganda from Islamic radicals and terrorists. Protecting the fundamental freedoms of all British citizens is critical to puncturing the myths propagated by extremists and ensuring cooperation between local Muslim communities and the police, which is in turn vital to the UK's counter-terrorism capability.

In addition to these security risks, the government's fixation on pre-charge detention has also distracted its political focus and energies from a range of other much needed measures, which could strengthen our operational counter-terrorism edge. If the government had expended a fraction of the political capital that it has squandered on forty-two days on these measures it could have strengthened national security without sacrificing British liberties.

Take just three examples. First, removing the ban on using intercept evidence in court would help the police gather evidence that could be used in trial proceedings. Almost every other country in the world has overcome security concerns to allow the use of intercept evidence in court to prosecute terrorists. In the UK, intercept evidence can be used in deportation proceedings, control order cases and applications to court to freeze terrorist assets. But despite numerous reviews, British prosecutors – virtually alone in the world – are still banned from using intercept evidence to convict terrorists in court. In its obsession with forty-two days, the government has neglected a valuable tool that would put terrorists behind bars without undermining the freedom of the innocent.

Second, allowing police to question terrorist suspects after they have been charged would take some of the pressure off the police during the pre-charge investigation period. There have been calls for the introduction of post-charge questioning for several years, but the government inexplicably delayed until 2008 before making any formal proposals in this regard.

Third, one of the arguments used to support the case for extending pre-charge detention is that evidence on computer hard drives may be encrypted and take time to decipher. In response, Parliament created a criminal offence for withholding encryption keys and computer passwords, allowing prosecutors to charge and imprison suspects for obstructing an investigation in this way. By the time of the vote on forty-two days in 2008, there were still no convictions under this new power, despite repeated reliance by the government on the volume and encryption of computer data in terrorism investigations as part of its case for extending pre-charge detention.

The lack of commitment to these kinds of practical measures reveals serious shortcomings in the government's security strategy. Equally, while the government has been all too willing to deploy senior police officers to try to make its case for forty-two days, it has failed to listen to – let alone act upon – the operational concerns now being expressed publicly by senior officers like Andy Hayman. In its obsession to force through controversial extensions of pre-charge detention, the government has neglected or overlooked valuable law enforcement measures capable of attracting political – and a wider national – consensus.

The presentation of a crude trade-off between security and liberty is at odds with the basic facts. The government's sustained assault on the right of habeas corpus has exacerbated the terrorist threat rather than reduce it, and distracted it from other practical counter-terrorism priorities. Fifty-four per cent of those asked in 2008 said that the government's main motivation for pressing its proposals on forty-two days was 'to look tough on terror' rather than national security. That is not a balance or a trade-off – but rather a hijacking of security policy for political ends. If the government is eventually successful in its stubborn attempt to extend pre-charge detention to forty-two days, it would set a dangerous precedent – with nothing to stop it from returning to seek yet further extensions in the future.

This pattern is mirrored more widely in the recent approach to counter-terrorism in the UK. The government has passed broad powers with inadequate safeguards and checks, which are prone to overuse or abuse in practice. Stop and search, under new terrorism powers, is running at 41,900 cases per year. Between 2001 and 2007 there were 1228 arrests on suspicion of terrorism. The rate of convictions over the same period remains, at forty-one, comparatively low in terms of overall numbers, although the proportion of terrorism prosecutions resulting in a conviction is now over 90 per cent.

A broad brush approach is open to abuse. It was disclosed that during one month in 2007 police at Gatwick airport conducted hundreds of random searches outside the (already wide) rules, without the required ministerial authorization. And the wider the powers, the greater the risk that innocent people will be caught in a security net so widely cast. In one case, in 2005, Sally Cameron, a thirty-four-year-old property developer from Dundee, was arrested and detained for four hours as a terrorist suspect. Ms Cameron, who used to walk to work to keep fit, was arrested under the Terrorism Act. Two police cars were called to apprehend her merely for walking along a cycle path restricted to cyclists under security regulations – even though there was no visible signpost indicating any restrictions on access to the pathway.

In another episode, a disabled twelve-year-old boy and his parents were detained under the Terrorism Act, police accusing his mother of people-trafficking her mixed-race son. The family were surrounded by ten police officers and detained for two hours, until officers resolved the misunderstanding.

Other security measures have undermined liberty, with minimal countervailing security gains. The government has been forced to continuously fend off legal challenge to its control order regime, rushed through Parliament in 2005 after the House of Lords struck down its attempt to detain foreign terrorist suspects indefinitely without charge. The control order legislation created wide powers that allow severe restrictions to be placed on those merely suspected of involvement with terrorism. While an order made by the Home Secretary must be confirmed by a judge, it can be imposed on people who have not been proved guilty of any criminal offence. The orders may include controls on who a person can meet with or speak to, bar access to the internet or telephone and impose restrictions on when a person can leave his home and where he can go – amounting to virtual house arrest for up to sixteen hours per day.

Control orders impose what amounts to a criminal punishment, but circumvent the basic rights of an accused to a proper trial. This deliberate evasion of one of the most basic foundations of British justice not only undermines liberty, but also generates acute resentment amongst the local community affected, with little extra security guaranteed in return. Only thirty individuals have been placed on control orders – while MI5 estimates that four thousand people pose a terrorist threat in Britain. Paradoxically, as the terrorist threat rose, the government's reliance on control orders declined. There were eighteen control orders in force in 2006, fourteen in 2007 and just eleven by the first quarter of 2008. This trend suggests that, for all the ministerial hype, control orders have proved to be a relatively ineffectual tool in practice – otherwise the government would have made greater use of them as the terrorist threat level rose.

This inference is supported by wider experience. A fifth of those placed on control orders have escaped. A recent government review found that control orders were only suitable for a 'small number of cases, in the absence of a viable alternative for those few instances'. Lord Carlile, the government-nominated reviewer of the control order regime, has acknowledged the difficulties in monitoring and enforcing control orders, even suggesting that anti-social behaviour orders (ASBOs), used by the police to tackle yob culture, might work just as well in practice. Other measures, to strengthen border controls and intelligence are likely to achieve far more in terms of public protection, at far less cost to individual liberty. The government should focus more on bolstering law enforcement through the courts – by using intercept evidence and post-charge questioning – not weakening safeguards designed to protect the innocent.

The government introduced legislation providing for a national identity register coupled with compulsory identity cards with similar enthusiasm. The proposals epitomize its clumsy, authoritarian approach to security.

In 2003, the government announced its plans for ID cards amidst great fanfare, another eye-catching initiative designed to portray a

Labour administration taking tough measures to improve security, at the cutting edge of modern technology. The proposals involve taking nearly fifty categories of personal information on each and every citizen, to be stored on a Home Office database and shared with other government departments, agencies and even foreign governments. Privacy campaign groups like Liberty and NO2ID warn that the ID cards will intrude into our privacy, enabling government departments and companies liberally to share masses of our personal data – including name, date of birth, addresses, identity records, photographs, signature and fingerprints – allowing the state and businesses continuously to track the movements and transactions of every citizen. While the government has sought to give assurances about privacy protection, safeguards and limits, the ID cards legislation gives the Home Secretary wide powers to extend the scope and remit of the ID cards regime by order, adding a further risk of mission creep once the system is fully operational.

Privacy concerns have been further exacerbated by growing doubts about the government's ability to implement the ID cards project. Fear of wide state powers to collect data on the citizen have only been made worse by the reality that careless and unaccountable civil servants will be charged to run the system. Government-managed databases have an appalling track record when it comes to protecting personal data (see Chapter 4), which means ID cards threaten to make us less – not more – safe.

At a more fundamental level, compulsory ID cards reverse the traditional relationship between the citizen and the state in this country. While historically in Britain the state has been accountable to the citizen, ID cards mark a significant shift, making it the presumption – rather than the exception – that the state has the right to peer into an individual's private life and keep tabs on every citizen. Information Commissioner Richard Thomas, a privacy watchdog, has expressed 'increasing alarm' that ID cards are: '…

beginning to represent a very significant sea change in the relationship between the state and every individual in this country'.

Ministers have tried to overcome widespread concern by touting ID cards as a way of solving benefit fraud, illegal immigration and terrorism. Yet, one by one, the government's claims for ID cards have dissolved under examination. First, it was claimed that ID cards would tackle benefit fraud. However, the overwhelming majority of benefit fraud involves people lying about their personal circumstances – only a fraction of cases involve misrepresentation of identity. Besides, the technology ID cards use is itself highly vulnerable to cloning and, therefore, fraud. So, far from protecting against scams, Microsoft's National Technology Officer has warned that ID cards could trigger 'massive identity fraud on a scale beyond anything we have seen before'.

Next, it was said that ID cards would prevent illegal immigration. This was difficult to sustain in light of the exemption from ID cards for all short-term visitors (under three months) to the UK. Even if that loophole was closed, independent tests have shown that the IT used in both biometric passports and ID cards can be cloned within minutes, a vulnerability that those profiting from illegal immigration are bound to exploit.

Finally, it was claimed that ID cards would help prevent terrorism. This assertion proved equally flawed since the vast majority of terrorists do not hide their identity, but rather actively seek notoriety. Spanish ID cards did not stop the Madrid bombers in 2004, Turkish ID cards did not stop the Istanbul bombers in 2003 and German ID cards did not stop the Hamburg terrorist cell that planned 9/11. In Britain, ID cards will do little to stop British-based bombers since it will not be mandatory to carry and produce the card on request. Nor could ID cards protect Britain from foreign terrorists – because short-stay visitors will not be required to hold one. Ministers have now openly conceded that ID cards will do little to prevent terrorism or crime, the Home Office website listing, as popular 'myth', that 'ID cards can stop global terrorism and crime'. As the Home Office's Security Minister candidly accepted: 'Perhaps in the past the Government, in its enthusiasm, oversold the advantages of identity cards. We did suggest, or at least implied, that they may well be a panacea for identity fraud, for benefit fraud, terrorism, entitlement and access to public services.'

Unsurprisingly, as the ongoing debate has exposed the flaws in the government's plans, public enthusiasm for, and confidence in, ID cards has plummeted – with support dropping from 78 per cent in 2003 to 43 per cent in 2007, with 48 per cent of those asked opposed.

In response to widespread criticisms, Home Office ministers decided to phase the roll-out of ID cards. Revised plans announced in 2008 will first target airport workers, then foreign nationals and subsequently students and other sections of the population. Rather than cancel an increasingly discredited policy, the government has shifted its approach, looking to introduce a national system by stealth.

ID cards were presented as a trade-off that would create a small amount of inconvenience but make us all much more secure. The evidence shows that the policy is a fraud – ID cards will impinge on individual liberty and jeopardize our personal security. Given these flaws, and independent estimates that the programme could cost up to £19 billion, the government should scrap its plans for a national ID card register and focus on practical security measures – including improving the integrity of the biometric technology used in visas and passports.

In addition to inroads on habeas corpus, the erosion of the presumption of innocence and reckless intrusions into personal privacy, national security has been used as a pretext for a further government assault on free speech and peaceful protest.

Freedom of speech dates back to the Bill of Rights of 1689. It has been protected by the common law in Britain for centuries, and serves as one of the hallmarks of liberal democracy. In the words of Thomas Jefferson, 'the liberty of speaking and writing … guards our other liberties'. Nevertheless, freedom of speech has never justified violence. Mill's classic exposition of liberty explicitly acknowledged that the exercise of individual rights can be limited where it would involve doing harm to others. In short, liberty tolerates those expressing obnoxious or offensive views, but not those who stir up violence or otherwise direct harm against other people. This distinction marks the dividing line in a free society that tolerates free speech but outlaws incitement to violence. In marked contrast, since 1997 the government's contorted approach has curtailed legitimate free speech on spurious security grounds, but ignored – or been slow to act against – those posing a real threat, such as fanatics who preach extremism and call for violent jihad against Britain.

Widely drawn new security legislation has been over-zealously enforced by police officers against soft targets like peace activists, students and other peaceful protesters in a wholly unnecessary and disproportionate manner. New powers were used to fine the sellers of 'Bollocks to Blair' T-shirts (£80 per offence) and arrest, search and eject Walter Wolfgang, a refugee from the Holocaust and member of the Labour Party, who heckled 'nonsense' at the Foreign Secretary as he was making the case for the war in Iraq during his speech at the 2005 Labour Party conference.

New security laws have also been used to stifle free speech and protest within one kilometre around the Houses of Parliament. Originally introduced as a precaution against security threats or disorder close to such a sensitive location, new legislation has been relied upon to suppress peaceful protest no matter how small the number of people involved. In May 2006, the Metropolitan Police spent £110,000 raiding and removing Brian Haw's one-man anti-war protest against British operations in Iraq. The same legislation was used to prosecute and convict two anti-war protesters who read the names of British soldiers killed in Iraq at the Cenotaph on Whitehall. In response to widespread opposition, the government announced a review of the legislation in March 2008, but left it unclear what security restrictions on free speech will remain in place.

ASBOs have also been used to muzzle free speech. Philip Howard, a street evangelist who regularly preached on Oxford Street, was ASBOed in 2006 by Westminster Council after receiving complaints. Mr Howard became famous for his quirky religious catchphrases – such as 'Don't be a sinner, be a winner' – and was generally tolerated by passers-by shopping in central London. His public preaching may have irritated a few people, but was harmless. The use of ASBO legislation by local authorities to silence him is yet another abuse of new law enforcement powers at the expense of free speech.

In 2005, the government again cited security as the basis for its efforts to enact a crime of 'glorifying' terrorism. It introduced legislation that aimed to ban public expression of views that indirectly give encouragement to or condone terrorism. The offence was challenged by opposition politicians and civil liberties groups, on grounds of free speech, because it went well beyond even indirect incitement to terrorism. The final law was watered down from the original proposal, so much so that it has never been used in practice. However, critics insist that existing law for prosecuting incitement to violence is perfectly adequate, and that the new definition risks stifling legitimate debate – with legal experts arguing that the new offence is broad enough to prosecute people commemorating the anti-apartheid movement in South Africa or the Easter Rising of 1916 against British rule in Ireland.

In a further round of government proposals aimed at prohibiting offensive language being used against minorities, ministers brushed aside objections on the grounds of free speech to produce proposals to outlaw inciting religious hatred. Accused of excessive political correctness, the government was originally defeated when it sought to ban incitement to religious hatred with a definition so broad that it risked having a chilling effect on legitimate topics of religious debate. A diluted version of the law was eventually adopted in 2006. It avoids criminalizing language which is merely abusive or offensive, and requires an intention to threaten another person on religious grounds – which would already render the language unlawful under existing law. However, the dilution of the new criminal offence has not stopped the police from trying to prosecute those engaging in legitimate public debate about religious and political opinions. In one ludicrous case, police issued a summons to a fifteen-year-old boy, threatening prosecution under the Public Order Act, for attending a peaceful demonstration holding a placard describing the Church of Scientology as a 'cult'.

What makes the government's position so alarming is that, while taking repressive action against those airing legitimate opinions, it has at the same time cosseted those preaching vitriol and violence. In 2007, the *Dispatches* documentary 'Undercover Mosque' revealed the homophobic, sexist and intolerant preaching of extremist Muslim clerics at the Green Lane mosque in Birmingham. The documentary showed preachers referring to homosexuals as 'filthy dogs', justifying the 7/7 bombings and explicitly calling for the death of those who convert from Islam. West Midlands Police recommended to the Crown Prosecution Service that it consider a prosecution – not against the preachers, but, rather, the filmmakers for allegedly misrepresenting the views of the clerics and undermining community relations. Even when it became clear that there was no evidence to back up this unfounded allegation, police and prosecutors still referred allegations against the programme to Ofcom, the media watchdog. Ofcom threw out the complaint, finding that Channel 4 and *Dispatches* had produced the documentary accurately and responsibly. Channel 4 and *Dispatches* responded by suing the police and the CPS for libellously suggesting that the documentary had been selectively edited in order to distort the views of the preachers. The police and CPS were forced to issue a public apology and pay a six-figure sum by way of compensation. The case demonstrates how broad public order powers, coupled with a culture of excessive political correctness, can lead to flagrant lack of respect for legitimate free speech, while simultaneously tolerating fanatical extremism – a naïve approach with dangerous consequences both for our security and our freedom.

In another case, a whistle-blower, Derek Pasquill, disclosed sensitive Foreign and Commonwealth Office (FCO) documents which appeared in newspapers, exposing FCO engagement with extremist Islamic groups, such as the Muslim Brotherhood in Egypt, some of whose members have connections with terrorism. Far from forcing an embarrassed FCO to reconsider its policy on engagement with radical Islamic groups, the government's reaction to this controversial exposé was to press for a prosecution against Mr Pasquill for breaching the Official Secrets Act. The prosecution's case collapsed when senior FCO officials admitted that a prosecution could not succeed, because Pasquill's actions were actually beneficial – encouraging a constructive debate on a serious matter of public interest.

It is remarkable, too, how, having stifled peaceful protest and closed down legitimate debate in the most harmless of circumstances, government policy has been so tolerant of those who stir up extremism and violence. In February 2006, demonstrations were held in London against the publication of Danish cartoons depicting the Prophet Mohammed in a manner that many Muslims found offensive and insensitive. Around five hundred protesters were involved in the protests that followed, and a small number of people carried placards calling on Muslims to 'bomb' the US and Denmark, 'massacre those who insult Islam' and urging 'whoever insults a prophet, kill him'. Four protesters were prosecuted and convicted of soliciting murder in July 2007. As David Perry QC, the prosecuting barrister argued, the words used were plainly criminal: 'If you shout out, "Bomb, bomb Denmark; bomb, bomb USA", there is no doubt about what you intend your audience to understand … The prosecution case is that the defendant was clearly encouraging people to commit murder – terrorist killing. This was not simply a demonstration about cartoons. It was a recruitment for terror.'

The court agreed and convicted the accused. Notwithstanding the criminal prosecutions, it is difficult to understand the police decision to allow protesters to proceed with their demonstration in the first place, carrying banners that openly incited violence. The Metropolitan Police said they had allowed the protest to continue for fear of public disorder – itself an astonishing sop to extremism, at the expense of law enforcement. But they then waited a further six weeks before making any arrests. In contrast, the government was quick to condemn the Danish cartoons, which, though offensive to many Muslims, did not incite violence.

In another notorious case it took years to prosecute the extremist preacher Abu Hamza, who was eventually found guilty of giving speeches that solicited murder and sentenced to seven years' imprisonment. Hamza had been based at the Finsbury Park mosque since 1997 and investigated by the Metropolitan Police on several occasions from 1999 onwards. He was not, however, arrested until 2004, following a US request for extradition on terrorism charges. In the meantime, Hamza was left free to preach vitriol and violence against Britain – which he described as 'like the inside of a toilet' –

and openly encourage violence against Jews and other non-believers, or 'kaffirs'. In response to criticism of its inaction, the government suggested that it did not have enough grounds to prosecute Hamza under existing law. Yet when he was eventually prosecuted, he was convicted of six counts of soliciting murder under the Offences Against the Person Act 1861 – passed under Lord Palmerston's premiership. Even after his arrest, Hamza managed to buy a £220,000 property, despite orders to freeze his assets by the Treasury, enacted in accordance with United Nations counter-terrorism resolutions. The consequence of this lax approach was to allow a hotbed of extremism to fester at a time of growing radicalization in Britain.

This lax approach has extended to government policy on visas and entry clearance. In 2008, Ibrahim Moussawi, front man for the terrorist organization Hezbollah, was allowed to enter the UK on a speaking tour. Another extremist who advocates suicide bombing against civilians, Yusuf al-Qaradawi, was granted a visa to visit Britain on several occasions before eventually being refused in 2008 in response to mounting political and public pressure. In 2004, a year before the terrorist attacks on London, the Mayor, Ken Livingstone, hosted – and physically embraced – al-Qaradawi, later likening him to a pope.

These cases speak volumes about the government's respect both for liberty and the law. It has clamped down hard on harmless – often eccentric – protesters who seek to make their point peacefully, but sent an altogether more ambiguous and dilatory message to those inciting violence on the streets of Britain. While the government's overly broad security legislation has paved the way for intolerant policing of public demonstrations, a timorous approach to those promoting terrorism and excessive political correctness have obscured the reasonably clear distinction between what counts as liberty and what breaks the law. We now live in a country where a boy of fifteen is threatened with prosecution on the spot for making a peaceful protest, but violent extremists are left at large for years.

No matter how hard the government tries to convince us otherwise, it has produced scant evidence of a hydraulic trade-off, whereby sacrificing a degree of liberty can make us commensurably – or even significantly – more secure. If anything, experience suggests the opposite. Repressive measures are often counter-productive in practice, a fig leaf designed to generate the impression of government action or a distraction from focusing on less eye-catching practical measures that would strengthen our counter-terrorism capacity.

Perhaps the greatest risk of all is that draconian measures, taken in the name of security, do the terrorists' job for them. Al-Qaeda and its affiliates have made it their declared purpose to replace democracy across the world with a strict form of sharia law. Terrorist attacks are designed to inflict mass panic and elicit a reactionary response, including knee-jerk anti-terrorism legislation that stifles individual liberty, a first step towards undermining our democracy. For all the rhetoric of the 'war on terror', a real show of strength would be to refuse to bow to terrorism by resisting draconian over-reaction to terrorist outrages – and take a public stand in defence not just of our security, but also the very values that the terrorists seek to destroy, values that have been hard won and bitterly defended by this country for centuries.

3

Short-circuiting the Justice System

'Trial by jury is more than an instrument of justice and more than one wheel of the constitution: it is the lamp that shows that freedom lives.'

LORD DEVLIN

If the debate on terrorism has thrust into the limelight the competing claims of security and liberty, the government has also engaged in a secondary – altogether more clandestine – assault on liberty, targeted at the criminal justice system.

British justice is designed to be firm but fair. Yet, since 1997, the government has tarnished many of its hallmarks. It has introduced forty-five criminal justice laws – more than the total passed in the previous century – creating more than three thousand new criminal offences, each one said to be necessary to tackle crime. Far from respecting the basic safeguards built into the justice system to protect the innocent, it has undermined them. In an effort to tackle spiralling yob culture, anti-social behaviour orders were introduced in 1998, eroding the basic principle that someone is innocent until proven guilty. From 2001, the government rolled out a widespread expansion in the use of spot fines, originally designed for parking and speeding offences, but now deployed to punish a range of both trivial and more serious crimes – circumventing the courts, allowing police and council officials to act as judge and jury and using the justice system as a means of raising revenue. This was followed in 2003 by the first in a series of concerted attempts to remove the ancient bulwark against arbitrary punishment by the state – the right to trial by jury. In the meantime, extradition rules have been relaxed so that British citizens can be surrendered for trial abroad on the basis of weak evidence, even where the alleged behaviour is not a crime under UK law.

For all the tough talk, the government has junked basic checks on the powers of the state, without delivering on its bold pledges to improve public protection. Following an enormous injection of public resources, Britain spends more on law and order – both as a proportion of spending and of GDP – than any of the other twenty-nine countries in the Organisation for Economic Co-operation and Development. Yet few are willing to swallow the government's over-spun claims to have cut crime – 65 per cent of people believe crime is rising. While some categories of crime have fallen, such as burglary and car theft, this is largely because improved technology allows people to take more effective measures for themselves, to protect their homes and properties. For other crime, which requires state intervention, the record is dismal. Since 1997, police-recorded violent crime has risen by almost 80 per cent. We now have over four hundred serious knife crimes each week and injuries from gun crime have soared nearly fourfold. Rising numbers of police officers have not boosted detection rates – with just one in four crimes detected by the police, and detection rates for violence against the person actually falling from 82 to 57 per cent since 1997. International comparisons are equally bleak. Britain has the second highest crime rate in Europe, and is the worst for anti-social behaviour, leading *Time* magazine to the conclusion that 'An epidemic of violence, crime and drunkenness has made Britain scared of its young'. One thing is clear – the attack on our justice system has singularly failed to make Britain safer.

The rule of law, presumption of innocence and the right to a fair trial form part of the British liberal tradition dating back to the thirteenth century. These fundamental rights provide basic safeguards that prevent the state from punishing the innocent through law enforcement, criminal punishment and – ultimately – imprisonment. They protect our liberty and have traditionally been conceived as negative rights – limitations on the state's ability to interfere with the individual. However, they also require the state to set up, fund and maintain independent courts that guarantee the core elements of due process necessary to make a criminal trial fair. The current system of courts is largely based on legislation enacted in the last 150 years, but reflects a much deeper historical evolution. It stands as a pillar of our liberal democracy, critical to the protection of freedom under law and a shield against the arbitrary exercise of power by government and legislators.

The criminal justice system in this country was not perfect before 1997. In terms of law enforcement, there was, and remains, a strong case for harnessing technology to strengthen the effectiveness of the police, and streamlining the work of the courts. Criminal re-offending rates have remained stubbornly high under successive governments, and the prison regime has called out for reform for years – to better prepare offenders for release into the outside world. Equally, there were criticisms of the fairness of British criminal justice well before 1997. Human rights lawyers took issue with abuses of police power, criticized the inequality of arms between prosecution and defence lawyers and questioned the oversight mechanisms for police misconduct and miscarriages of justice. Other commentators lamented the lack of a clearer separation of powers, the emasculation of the judiciary and the increase in the discretionary powers of the police. On all sides, constructive criticism called for improving and modernizing the system.

What marks out the approach over the last eleven years is the government's decisive intention to sidestep or abandon – rather than strengthen – fundamental components in the justice system. The prejudices of the old left and the dictates of New Labour tactics combined to produce a government with little respect – if not outright disdain – for the basic principles of British justice. Traditional socialists had been nurtured by Marxism to regard the justice system as a bourgeois instrument for working-class suppression – dismissing the attendant rights of due process as an insidious cosmetic cover. Closer to home, Will Hutton's *The State We're In*, which provided inspiration to New Labour, added the judiciary to the list of partisan, illiberal institutions in cahoots with an inherently conservative Establishment. Hutton directly associated the judiciary with an almost indivisible Conservative enemy. He accused the judges of 'being more executive-minded than the executive … with the law providing almost no refuge from the Conservative Party', and bemoaned the fact that defects in the separation of powers were compounded by: '… the judiciary and Conservative Party hierarchy largely sharing an education, culture and outlook. Judges appoint other judges in their own image, while the criminal justice system is increasingly involved in maintaining public order.'

J. A. G. Griffiths went even further, with an excoriating leftist critique of the political bias of the post-war judiciary:

My thesis is that judges in the United Kingdom cannot be politically neutral, because they are placed in positions where they are required to make political choices which are sometimes presented to them, and often presented by them, as determinations of where the public interest lies; that their interpretation of what is in the public interest and therefore politically desirable is determined by the kind of people they are and the position they hold in our society; that this position is part of established authority and so is necessarily conservative and illiberal.

He added:

In both democratic and totalitarian societies, the judiciary has naturally served the prevailing political and economic forces … The confusion arises when it is pretended that judges are somehow neutral … there are innumerable ways – through the development of the common law, the interpretation of statutes, the refusal to use discretionary powers, the claims to residual jurisdiction and the rest – in which the judges can fulfil their political function and do so in the name of the law.

If Marxist dogma and contemporary critiques had inured the incoming government to treat the justice system as a covert ally of the right, and enemy of the left, the politics of triangulation convinced the architects of New Labour that persuading the public that it was 'tough on crime, tough on the causes of crime' was pivotal to their electoral success. It fuelled a media strategy that thrived on a relentless stream of half-baked initiatives, hyperactive law-making and a perpetual focus on the short term. Wide and ill-thought through laws forced through Parliament were susceptible to overuse, and abuse, by police striving to meet the latest central government target. Government action plans and gimmicks, like the 2006 Respect Action Plan, were rolled out and regularly re-announced by ministers for media consumption, with little consideration of how they could be delivered in practice to achieve their stated goals. The overriding imperative, of manufacturing a public perception that the government was taking action, would time and time again tempt ministers and policy-makers to take short cuts with the most basic components of British justice, in the latest forlorn attempt to offer up some visible – albeit illusory – sign of leadership on law and order.

The Crime and Disorder Act 1998 was one of the earliest laws passed by a government desperate to burnish its tough anti-crime credentials. The very first measure introduced by Section 1 of the Act was the concept of an anti-social behaviour order. ASBOs involve the application of varying restrictions on the liberty of individuals who have engaged in minor level crime or been a persistent nuisance in their community. They were designed – and touted – as a robust measure to restore some order on the streets and yank into line youths and young adults who spread litter, graffiti public property, harass or abuse others, take drugs or get drunk and start fights. In practice, however, ASBOs have proved to be neither firm nor fair.

The new ASBO abandoned basic checks designed to protect the presumption of innocence on which the British criminal justice system is built. Police and local authorities do not need to prove the anti-social behaviour beyond reasonable doubt (the criminal standard of proof), but only demonstrate that complaints of anti-social behaviour are more likely than not to be true – on the balance of probabilities (the civil standard of proof). Equally, ASBOs can be ordered relying on 'hearsay evidence' – a second-hand account of facts provided by a witness – which is normally excluded in criminal trials. Despite these short cuts, breach of the ASBO restrictions can result in a criminal punishment, including up to five years in prison. So, it is a device explicitly designed to allow the attachment of a criminal punishment without going to the bother of proving guilt to the normal evidential standard, short-cutting a basic safeguard designed to protect the innocent and ensure those accused of criminal behaviour get a fair trial.

The definition of anti-social behaviour is so widely drawn that ASBOs are susceptible to abuse by over-eager police and local authorities. They have been excessively relied upon and used in totally inappropriate situations. For the most part they have been targeted at children between the ages of ten and seventeen, which carries the risk of stigmatizing many young people as criminals at an early age – sometimes for relatively trivial behaviour, and on the basis of weak proof. One fifteen-year-old boy received an ASBO for pinching newts from a neighbour's pond, and another was threatened with an ASBO for throwing a toy at a social worker.

There is further concern that ASBOs are being disproportionately used to penalize – rather than treat – children (and adults) with mental disorders. Research by the British Institute for Brain Injured Children in 2007 found that over a third of children on ASBOs had mental health disorders, such as autism, attention-deficit hyperactivity disorder (ADHD) and other learning difficulties. One teenager with ADHD was given an ASBO for jumping over a neighbour's fence; another with Tourette's syndrome for swearing, the primary symptom of the disorder. In an adult case, Kim Sutton was ASBOed in 2005 after several attempts to commit suicide in the River Avon. The ASBO's response to her serious personality disorder was to ban her from jumping into any river or canal.

The use of ASBOs has not been confined to problem children, but expanded by petty-minded local officials to cover a whole range of different – often trivial – cases, diverting precious resources from dealing with real crime. An ASBO was imposed on a harmless street-corner preacher, in order to shut him up, stifling his legitimate – if eccentric – exercise of freedom of speech. In 2007, a thirty-nine-year-old mother of two was ASBOed after a neighbour complained to the council about her singing Gary Glitter classics in the bath. She subsequently breached the ASBO. After a trial lasting over a week – costing the taxpayer tens of thousands of pounds – the case was dismissed by Lincoln Crown Court, Judge Machin criticizing the council's absurd waste of time and money on such a trivial case: 'I cannot emphasise too strongly that the cost of all this is really completely out of all proportion to any public interest that might be served.'

In another bizarre case, a shepherd in Gloucestershire was ASBOed for exercising his five-hundred-year-old right to graze his sheep in the Forest of Dean. The local authorities claimed that Jeremy Awdry could not control his sheep. On receiving the ASBO, Mr Awdry complained that the allegations were unsubstantiated and based on 'hearsay'. But he accepted the order anyway, because he could not afford to contest it in court. Common sense suggests that many of these situations should be dealt with through other informal means, not law enforcement. In this case, the individual concerned complained that the charges were based on inadequate evidence, but also that he was pressured by the financial risks into accepting the punishment.

Nevertheless, some erosion of the basic checks in the justice system might be regarded as worthwhile if it delivered safer streets and more secure homes. Yet while ASBOs side-step safeguards for the innocent, they have proved an ineffective tool for cracking down on anti-social behaviour. ASBOs are so poorly enforced that 55 per cent are breached, with over a third breached on five or more occasions. Research by the Youth Justice Board in November 2006 found that, far from deterring youth crime, ASBOs were regarded by young offenders as a 'badge of honour' – something to aspire to – making a mockery of government claims that they have dramatically improved public order.

Rather than review or scale back the use of this unfair and

ineffective approach, the government has rapidly extended it as a model to address a whole range of new scenarios. Similar orders have now been devised to deal with gangsters, violent criminals and even terrorist suspects. At the other end of the spectrum, in 2008 the government announced a further drive to focus ASBOs on naughty children as young as ten, who are to be targeted with so-called 'Baby-ASBOS' in an effort by the state to control their behaviour.

Building on its short-lived media success with ASBOs, the government passed legislation in 2001 giving the police and local authorities new powers to issue penalty notices for disorder, and rapidly increased its reliance on them along with the power to issue fixed penalty notices and conditional cautions. They allow police and council officers to issue on-the-spot fines. These were designed to punish anti-social behaviour, without all the hassle of taking a criminal prosecution through the courts.

Like ASBOs, spot fines provide a diluted form of justice, which is neither firm nor fair. They were intended as devices to pressure those apprehended to accept a modest fine (between £50 and £80), and avoid the time, cost and effort of challenging the punishment in court – in return for avoiding a heavier punishment, ranging from an increased fine to imprisonment, and a formal criminal record. The explicit aim is to short-circuit the entire court process by allowing the police or council officials to investigate, prosecute, try and punish criminal offences – without any judicial check or consideration.

For an individual threatened with such a penalty, the incentive to avoid a criminal record and a heavier fine, or even prison, exerts heavy pressure to accept the fine – irrespective of guilt – rather than challenge it in court, which undermines the most basic principles of due process. An over-reliance on spot fines also rides roughshod over the separation of powers between the proper role of the police (an arm of government) and the courts. It is a fundamental principle of justice that the same person or authority should not both make criminal allegations against an individual and decide whether or not they are upheld.

Spot fines may be a reasonable, cost-efficient way of dealing with minor offences, such as speeding or parking offences, and there may be limited scope to extend such penalties to other less serious offences. However, the broad new powers – and their increasing deployment – have created a real risk of abuse, which has been magnified as they are applied to more and more serious offences.

The growing reliance on these measures also places the traditional role of the police officer under increasing strain. In the nineteenth century, Sir Robert Peel, the founder of modern policing in Britain, articulated the principle that: 'Police should always direct their action strictly towards their functions, and never appear to usurp the powers of the judiciary.'

Peel argued that a strict demarcation of law enforcement functions was necessary to ensure the independence of the police and sustain public confidence. The increasing use of spot fines by police and local authorities, to deal with the most trivial of allegations, threatens both. In one case, Zoe Watmough, a young mother of two, was fined by council environmental officers for putting out her rubbish the day before it was due to be collected. Ms Watmough contested the charge in the magistrates' court but was forced to pay an increased fine of £265 – including a £15 victim surcharge, even though it was a victimless offence.

Since there is no need to prove an offence has taken place before issuing a spot fine, there is little to stop jobsworth local officials from abusing their authority. Kate Badger, a young mother of three, was accused of dropping an apple core from her car window in Wolverhampton town centre. A council warden issued her with a £60 spot fine. Ms Badger vigorously denied the charge of 'knowingly causing the deposit of controlled waste, namely an apple core, on land which did not have a waste management licence'. She stubbornly refused to pay £60 for such trivial and unproven accusations and opted to contest the charges in the Crown court before a jury, risking a heavier fine of up to £20,000 or even six months' imprisonment. While Ms Badger was successful, and the case was kicked out of court for lack of evidence, the majority of people are not prepared to challenge the penalty in court, given the costs and risk of a much heavier punishment – including the possibility of a prison term. Gordon Williams, a fifty-eight-year-old self-employed decorator, was given a £30 spot fine for smoking in his van, because it was technically classified as a place of work. His wife paid the fine, rather than kick up a fuss, because she was worried that the council would double the amount.

The risk of abuse is particularly high for the vulnerable and the elderly. In one harsh incident, a traffic warden issued a £35 fine to a disabled eighty-two-year-old, who was lawfully parked in a disabled bay. Mrs Raine, who suffers from Parkinson's disease, was fined as she dozed in her car because her disabled parking disc was upside down on the car windscreen. South Lakeland council defied common sense by rejecting the appeal, its spokesperson saying that: 'Guidance notes issued with the badge and parking disc clearly state that it should be clearly and correctly displayed at all times'. In another absurd case, a grandmother was fined when her twenty-month-old grand-daughter dropped two crisps on the pavement. Barbara Jubb, from Crawley in Sussex, kicked the offending crisps into the gutter, at which point she was immediately issued with a spot fine for £80 by council officers.

In many of these cases, far from being used to curb crime or tackle anti-social behaviour, there is growing public concern that spot fines are being used by local authorities and police forces as a ploy to tax generally law-abiding members of the public. These concerns have been exacerbated by the introduction of personal commission for law enforcement officers in an effort to raise the number of fines and the level of revenue. For example, in Peterborough council wardens receive £35 commission for each spot fine administered, even though the actual fine may only be £50 if it is paid on time. The Chief Inspector of the Crown Prosecution Service – the prosecution watchdog for England and Wales – has warned that 'the power to fine is now vested in many authorities and brings the risk that over zealous use may lead groups of citizens to believe that they are in reality the subject of a revenue raising initiative … This may cause substantial damage to public confidence.'

The excessive use of spot fines is not just petty-minded. The increasing reliance on them has detracted from the punishment of more serious crimes. The government has encouraged the use of spot fines for a growing list of offences – including assault, drugs offences and shoplifting – in order to inflate its statistics on the number of 'criminals' being brought to justice. Spot fines effectively condone pay-as-you-go-hooliganism and punish shoplifters with a glorified parking ticket, reducing criminal justice to little more than an administrative means of taxing – rather than punishing and deterring – criminal and anti-social behaviour.

As a result of this approach, many more offenders do not even reach court, where judges have greater powers of punishment that are suitable for more serious crimes. By 2007, less than half the total number of 'offenders brought to justice' actually received a criminal punishment following a conviction in court, neatly coinciding with the dramatic rise in the number of spot fines being dispensed by police and councils as a substitute. The government claims that spot fines for hooliganism and drunken disorder allow police to give yobs a short, sharp, shock without the time, effort and resources required to go through the courts. This has proved shortsighted in practice – with a mere half of Penalty Notices for

Disorder being paid without resort to court, undermining both the criminal justice and financial rationales for their excessive use. Although limited data has been made publicly available, anecdotal evidence suggests that it is the generally law-abiding citizens who are paying the spot fines issued for the more trivial offences, while the more serious offenders casually ignore the half-hearted attempts to rein in their criminal behaviour.

The courts themselves have also expressed serious concern about the government's attempt to cut them out of the process of criminal punishment, reducing both the safeguards for the innocent and the sentencing powers for serious crimes. The head of the body representing magistrates' courts has publicly complained about the 'inappropriate use' of 'out-of-court disposals for offences that are too serious', lamenting the concerted effort to 'take more offenders out of court', criticizing the blurring of the line between the proper responsibilities of the police and the courts: 'How far do you go in having punishment handed out by police and prosecutors? I think that's a really important constitutional point that ought to be debated. But it's being ducked at the moment.'

Rather than debate or review the use of spot fines, ministers have promoted their wider use. As with ASBOs, the government's growing reliance on spot fines demonstrates a short-cut mentality. Far from providing a potent deterrent for anti-social behaviour, spot fines are eroding both British justice and effective law enforcement – and the public's trust along with them.

Duly emboldened by the illusion of action conjured by its steady chipping away at the justice system, from 2003 the government launched a fresh assault, this time on the right to trial by jury – seeking to remove it from fraud trials, coroners' inquests, other complex criminal trials and cases where there is a risk of jury tampering. In each case, when presenting their proposed new laws, ministers cited the legal complexity of trials or some security threat to try to justify assuming a power to remove the jury. In reality, each attempt to displace the role of juries has signalled a law enforcement or security shortcoming – none of which can be cured by attacking this ancient British safeguard. The real danger is that these attempts to remove juries – each specific instance justified as a wholly exceptional measure – will lead down the slippery slope towards a much more general erosion of this fundamental right.

The right to trial by jury dates back to Magna Carta, when it replaced trial by ordeal of fire or water, by which guilt was determined on the basis of torture by drowning or being burnt alive. The introduction of juries was intimately bound up in the wider struggle for liberty and freedom from persecution by the state and the Church. They provide a vital safeguard, ensuring that the ordinary individual gets a fair deal out of the complex machinery of criminal justice. Where juries believe that an accused is getting a raw deal – either because of lack of evidence or because 'the law is an ass' – they will acquit.

Throughout British history controversial accused have relied upon their right to a jury trial in high-profile political cases. When William Cobbett, campaigning for social and political reform in the 1830s, was put on trial – accused of whipping up civil unrest – the jury acquitted him. More recently, in 1985, a jury acquitted Clive Ponting, a Ministry of Defence official prosecuted for disclosing documents about the sinking of the *Belgrano*, an Argentine warship sunk in controversial circumstances during the Falklands War. Mr Ponting's disclosures contradicted the government's public statements on the episode, creating political embarrassment and public disquiet. Mr Ponting was cleared despite both evidence that he had breached the Official Secrets Act and the directions of the trial judge – because the jury thought punishing him would be unfair in light of all the facts in the case and the public interest in knowing about the information he had disclosed.

Endowed with a rich historical legacy, the fundamental case for trial by jury today is basically the same. Twelve fellow citizens are better placed than a single judge to make sure that someone accused of a serious criminal offence – and therefore at risk of a serious punishment – will not be unfairly convicted. Twelve has the obvious numerical advantage over the idiosyncratic views of a single judge – a jury can provide a more balanced assessment of the facts of a case than the judge, however legally expert he may be. Juries reach their verdict by unanimity, or a majority vote of at least ten to two, which sets a high threshold for a criminal conviction in serious cases that may involve imprisonment. Individual jurors are drawn from all walks of life, classes and backgrounds, providing an important democratic element in the justice system. The former judge (and later politician) Lord Simon characterized the modern jury as 'a microcosm of society'. In controversial or complicated cases, juries connect the intricate mechanism and convoluted procedures of justice with the ordinary, everyday life of the public. The option to elect trial by jury is a safeguard designed to protect the innocent, but twelve jurors drawn at random from the public also add an important element of democratic oversight to the justice system.

It is not just political activists and whistle-blowers who put their faith in the ancient British right to trial by jury. Ordinary members of the public, going about their daily business, continue to rely on juries as protection against the abuse of power, whether by local authorities, central government or even the EU. In February 2008, a seventy-four-year-old man was found not guilty of criminal damage by a jury, despite clear-cut evidence. Iorwerth Jones had climbed onto the roof of Dynefor council headquarters and smashed tiles with his hammer, causing £30,000 worth of damage.

He defended his actions as part of his campaign for a public enquiry into the establishment of a lorry park, authorized by the council, near the home he was building himself outside Llandovery. He claimed it had only been moved to the vicinity of his home because residents living near an alternative location had complained. He did not deny destroying the tiles and threatening further damage to council property if the council continued to ignore his plea for a review. Despite these admissions, the jury sympathized with Mr Jones and refused to convict. After the verdict, the judge urged the council to come to an agreement with him.

As well as delivering 'sympathy verdicts', juries serve as a valuable check on trivial or spurious punishments, including the arbitrary expansion in the use of spot fines. When Kate Badger was fined for allegedly dropping an apple core from her car window, the right to opt for jury trial allowed her to successfully call the council's bluff, by appealing to the common sense of twelve members of the public to protect her from frivolous prosecution. The case against her collapsed as soon as it was put to the test in court.

Around the same time Janet Devers, a sixty-four-year-old woman who runs a fruit and veg stall in the East End of London, was charged with twelve criminal offences for selling her produce in pounds and ounces, in defiance of UK legislation implementing EU law – although even EU officials say they never intended to criminalize traders using imperial measures. The local authorities seized her scales and initiated a prosecution. Hackney council secured a conviction in the magistrates' courts on eight counts, including for selling scotch bonnets, pak choi and okra in bowls – rather than by the kilo. But Mrs Devers was able to opt for trial by jury in the Crown court to challenge four more serious counts. While the magistrates' court expressed some sympathy, giving her a conditional discharge, she now has a criminal record, cannot visit family in the US and must pay around £5000 in costs. The jury trial is scheduled for 2009 and, if convicted, Mrs Devers faces a fine of up to £65,000 and financial ruin. Despite the risks, she pleaded not guilty and exercised her right to a jury trial, saying: 'I am much happier about having a jury trial because you won't get 12 people on the jury who will find me guilty.'

These cases are testimony to the enduring relevance of the right to trial by jury. Ordinary British citizens still put their faith in juries, when they believe that unjust law or abuse of power is allowing the state to infringe the liberties that matter to them. The offences alleged are often minor, with council officials trying to intimidate, meddle or intrude into the private lives and daily business of honest, hard-working and generally law-abiding citizens. When Mrs Devers was interviewed about the case on her stall in June 2008, a local Hackney official tried to gag her, claiming cameras were not allowed on the market under local regulations. He promptly scurried away when friends of Mrs Devers pointed out the exemption for news broadcasters and that, in fact, he was breaking the rules by trying to wield local powers without wearing the standard council-issue bib.

Pettiness aside, the cases point to a wider concern that limited law enforcement resources are being wasted on soft targets and trifling offences. As Mrs Devers told the *Wall Street Journal*: 'We have knifings. We have killings. And they're taking me to court because I'm selling in pounds and ounces.'

Notwithstanding the modern relevance of – and reliance on – the right to trial by jury, the government in 2005 took the unprecedented step of proposing a new law to allow its removal in fraud cases. Ministers claimed that complex fraud cases were too complicated, long and costly to retain juries, blaming them for the collapse of a number of high-profile trials.

However, the role of the jury is particularly important in fraud cases, which can result in heavy punishments, including substantial prison sentences. As Harriet Harman, a Justice Minister when Parliament debated the proposals, previously argued, but has apparently now forgotten: 'Any offence serious enough to carry a sentence of imprisonment is serious enough to justify allowing the defendant to choose trial by jury. Someone who may lose his liberty as a result of being found guilty is entitled to choose to "put himself on his country". And that means twelve of his fellows, not appointees of the Lord Chancellor.'

Perhaps the single most important responsibility that the jury has in fraud trials is the determination of 'dishonesty', which is pivotal to the prosecution's case. The legal test involves deciding what an ordinary member of the public would regard as dishonest. This is a highly subjective judgement on which an individual's liberty will often ultimately rest. Amidst the mass of complex evidence and technical detail in fraud cases, the court has to make this fine – and intuitive – judgment. Twelve individuals drawn from the wider public will provide a more balanced assessment than a single judge, who may well be more predisposed, based on experience in countless previous cases, to believe the prosecution's version of events.

In the course of protracted parliamentary debates on the proposal, the government rehashed its line of argument, contending that complex fraud cases were too long, wasted too much money and were beyond the comprehension of ordinary jurors – suggesting that the trials were too sophisticated for twelve humble individuals, picked up off the street, to keep up with. Yet precious little evidence has been presented to back up such arrogant assumptions. In practice, juries discipline lawyers on both sides to present their case in a clear and intelligible manner. It is a good way of keeping the esoteric legal work of judges and barristers in touch with the real world.

The debate culminated after the collapse in 2005 of the long-running Jubilee Line fraud trial. Again, it was claimed that the jury had been unable to follow the proceedings. However, that line of argument was presented and roundly rejected in the review that followed. The report by the Chief Inspector of the Crown Prosecution Service stated: 'The size and nature of the case was not such as to make it intrinsically unmanageable before a jury … This outcome was not a systemic failure of the criminal justice system or the nature of jury trial.'

The Attorney General conceded this point at the time. Rather than blame the jury, the report laid out the shortcomings in the methods of the prosecuting authorities and the court, including the lack of fraud expertise of the prosecutors (rather than the jurors), over-charging and poor case management – criticisms that call for a strengthening, not abandonment, of the system. Nor does wider evidence support the government's contention that juries hamstring the delivery of justice in fraud cases. The Serious Fraud Office's (SFO) Annual Report in 2007 showed that 71 per cent of those prosecuted by the SFO were convicted – around average compared to other types of case – and all of those convicted were sentenced to terms of imprisonment.

Even the Bar Council was prepared to accept that lawyers – rather than juries – were to blame for long drawn-out cases, summing up the weakness in the government's case: 'The problem of long trials is not juries, but their management by professionals in the prosecution, defence and court service. What's more, removing juries might lead to the introduction of even more complex evidence, which would make trials longer and more expensive.'

If there is a case for speeding up fraud cases, it needs to be done by strengthening – not undermining – the justice system. There are a number of practical measures that could expedite fraud trials. The rules on disclosure, selection of charges and case management could be tightened up. There is a case for investing in greater fraud expertise in the Crown Prosecution Service, specific judicial training and better use of IT to save time. The Lord Chief Justice introduced a protocol to streamline heavy and complex cases in 2005. The effectiveness of these reforms should be reviewed and, where necessary, strengthened.

Equally, fraud trials are not the only complex cases to go through the courts. Murder, terrorism and other serious crimes present equally tricky issues, involving hotly debated, complicated, forensic and scientific evidence, so if juries are removed in fraud cases the government may well be tempted to extend the precedent to other categories of trial. Yet in all of these cases, the lawyers, judges and expert witnesses get well paid to present the case in a manner that is understood by ordinary people – including the accused, the jury and the wider public. That way justice is done and seen to be done. When the legislation to remove juries from fraud trials was opposed in the House of Lords in 2007, ministers vowed to press ahead regardless.

There are further signs of a broader effort to undermine the role of juries in the justice system. The Criminal Justice Act 2003 provides general powers for the removal of the jury where there is a risk of jury tampering. In February 2008, prosecutors applied to court to use these powers for the first time to remove the jury in a drug-trafficking case, claiming that the police could not prevent interference with the jury. The judge rejected the request, but it is a worrying sign that prosecutors are now willing to resort to such an extreme measure. No official explanation has been offered as to whether or not the risk of nobbling juries is in fact greater now than ever before, or why, if that is the case, the risk cannot be properly managed, as before, through police protection.

The government has not stopped there. In 2008, it proposed to give the Home Secretary the power to remove juries from coroners' inquests. These inquests are set up to ensure an independent, impartial and transparent enquiry when an individual has died in suspicious circumstances – including in the care or custody, or as a result of actions, of the British state. The inquest process is designed to ensure a public and impartial review of the circumstances of death. The jury is an important part of the procedure of ensuring public scrutiny, which is especially important where the state may bear some responsibility for the death of one of its citizens. In spite of this, the government claimed that it would sometimes be necessary to remove the jury, in order to introduce sensitive and secret security information into the inquest process – which ordinary jurors are not be allowed to see. The proposals announced would allow the Home Secretary to remove the jury, appoint the coroner and hold proceedings in secret, not just on grounds of national security, but also where there are other – much broader – 'public interest' considerations. Such overt political interference cuts straight across the independence and transparency of the inquest process. The government presented no evidence to show why such measures were necessary, nor why the existing procedures for dealing with sensitive issues of national security are inadequate.

In the meantime, leaked Home Office documents encouraged widespread press speculation that the government was rushing the measures through Parliament to allow two forthcoming controversial inquests – into the shooting of Jean Charles de Menezes and the 7/7 bombings – to be held in secret, in order to avoid political embarrassment. In these cases, there had been serious allegations of failures by the police and security services and extended delays in setting up the inquests. Concerns about transparency and accountability were compounded by efforts by the Defence Secretary – including a failed legal challenge – to gag the coroners, after a spate of criticisms of the Ministry of Defence during inquests into the deaths of British soldiers on active service in Iraq and Afghanistan. Ministers have failed to offer a persuasive explanation to dispel the suspicion that its real aim is to conceal the potential for political embarrassment created by transparent inquests.

In none of these instances has the government provided a convincing justification for its attack on one of the ancient pillars of our justice system. Far from being warranted on grounds of national security or law enforcement, respective attempts to remove juries have revealed shortcomings in the prosecution of fraud cases (rather than their consideration by jurors), weaknesses in the system of witness protection and concerns that inquest juries would be sidelined to hide security failings. The government has treated juries with disdain, as an outdated obstacle and a convenient scapegoat for its own failings. Yet the attack on the jury system comes at a time when more and more people are relying on it to protect them against the arbitrary exercise of state power, and the inquest system is providing an important layer of transparency where innocent life is lost during counter-terrorism or military operations. Juries provide a reality check on the state – stopping unjust prosecutions, highlighting government mistakes and helping to sustain public confidence in the system. If the steady erosion of the role of juries continues, it will lead to more innocent people being criminalized, more government negligence going undetected and a consequent loss of public trust in British justice.

If British justice has been subtly and steadily eroded at home, the government has acquiesced in a further assault from abroad. Since 9/11, it has sacrificed key safeguards under UK law that protect British citizens from extradition requests to face spurious prosecution in foreign countries. On the pretext of facilitating international cooperation in terrorism cases, the UK government has relaxed the basic checks that prevent UK nationals from being whisked away to face trial abroad on flawed charges or minimal evidence.

The UK now allows extradition to a range of countries without them having to demonstrate a prima facie case – i.e. present preliminary evidence to make the case – that the individual pursued has committed any crime. So, in the NatWest Three case, the US authorities only had to provide sufficient information that would justify arresting three British bankers in relation to allegations of fraud involving the bankrupt US energy giant Enron. This was enough to allow their fast-track removal to face a Texan court, where they promptly felt compelled to plead guilty in return for a much reduced sentence and potential return to serve their time in a UK jail. The British government cannot extradite US suspects to face charges here with such relative ease, because of protections guaranteed to American citizens by the US Constitution, so the arrangements are inherently lopsided.

The dilution of the standard of proof required to extradite British citizens has been extended throughout the EU by the European Arrest Warrant (EAW), the implementation of which was also forced through Parliament by the government in the aftermath of the September 11 attacks in the US. The EAW further dumbs down British safeguards designed to protect the innocent. Standard extradition procedure in Britain requires 'dual criminality', so that a citizen cannot be extradited for alleged crimes in Bulgaria, Belgium or any other European country, unless the alleged conduct is also a criminal offence under UK law. However, the EAW allows thirty-two exemptions to that rule, not just to deal with terrorism, but also to allow fast-track extradition for a range of other loosely defined offences including 'swindling', 'computer-related crime' and 'racism and xenophobia'. Austrian prosecutors availed themselves of these convenient arrangements to issue an arrest warrant for Professor Gerald Töben, an Australian historian, as he passed through Heathrow airport, for publishing material that denied the existence of the Holocaust. Yet Holocaust denial is not a crime in Britain or Australia (where the offence was allegedly committed), because of the common law tradition that free speech should be tolerated – however offensive – unless it incites violence. That way, such contemptible views can be aired – and roundly repudiated – in public, rather than making martyrs of cranks and crackpots by putting them on trial. The EAW was rushed into UK law as a counter-terrorism measure, but is now being used to prosecute those who set foot on British soil for thought crimes that would not pass muster under British law. The dilution of fundamental safeguards in the extradition process is both unfair and goes well beyond anything required for national security.

4

Surveillance Society

'Knowledge without integrity is dangerous and dreadful.'

SAMUEL JOHNSON

The assault on liberty and the erosion of justice have been compounded by intrusive inroads made by the increasingly omnipresent and prying eye of the state into the private lives of British citizens. Since 1997, the government has pioneered the rise of Big Brother government, the database state and – increasingly – a surveillance society.

There were complaints before 1997 of inadequate protection of privacy in Britain. Lawyers and commentators in the 1980s bemoaned the lack of regulation of electronic eavesdropping, police surveillance, and media intrusion into the private lives of the royal family, celebrities and others caught in the public eye. However, the intrusions by the state into personal privacy over the last eleven years dwarf those that preceded them, despite the enactment of the Human Rights Act creating a new overarching right to privacy under UK law.

Since 1997, the state has sanctioned a dramatic increase in

bugging and given free rein to other forms of spying – not just to help the police and MI5 to fight crime and terrorism, but also allowing hundreds of councils and quangos to spy on local residents on relatively trivial grounds. It now has hundreds of powers to force its way into the home. It has accumulated vast amounts of private information on mammoth databases, but runs them so recklessly that countless security breaches have put millions of people at risk. Far from learning the lessons, its imminent ID cards scheme threatens even worse to come. The hoarding of personal information, by the state on the citizen, has not made us safer. If anything we are more exposed than ever – our private lives to state surveillance, and our personal data to careless civil servants and criminal hackers. The government has spent millions of taxpayers' money collecting the largest DNA database in the world and littering Britain with more CCTV cameras than in any other country, but its dysfunctional approach has undermined the privacy of innocent people with only the most meagre impact on levels of crime and anti-social behaviour.

In 2004 the Information Commissioner, Richard Thomas – the UK's privacy watchdog – warned that the creeping jurisdiction of the state was undermining our liberty, turning Britain into a 'surveillance society'. Two years later, he issued the following stark assessment:

> Today I fear we are in fact waking up to a surveillance society … As ever-more information is collected, shared and used, it intrudes into our private space and leads to decisions which directly influence people's lives. Mistakes can also easily be made with serious consequences – false matches and other cases of mistaken identity, inaccurate facts or inferences, suspicions taken as reality, and breaches of security. I am keen to start a debate about where the lines should be drawn. What is acceptable and what is not?

Another two years on, the government has ducked any serious public debate, with the reach of the state expanding ever further. The government is not passively acquiescing in developments beyond its control. Nor can its serial failures be discounted as a series of unrelated mishaps. They are driven by a broader strategy – both naïve and reckless – designed to reverse the traditional accountability of the state to the citizen, which has historically characterized Britain's liberal democracy.

Gordon Brown has been a powerful influence on government strategy, first as Chancellor and then as Prime Minister. Sir David Varney, one of his close advisers, was personally appointed to drive through the reform of public services. Varney published a detailed report in December 2006 setting out a broad strategic vision, in which he urged ministerial departments to drive through 'transformational government', focusing on the 'totality of the relationship with the citizen', 'identity management' and – ominously – the establishment of 'a single source of truth' on each and every citizen. The report implored government to coordinate and pool personal data on the individual to enable cost savings. It suggested that the risks would largely be shielded from view, because 'The public do not see this process. They experience only public services packaged for their needs.' The report characterized the introduction of identity cards as the nadir of this grand, centralizing, project.

The Varney Report highlighted a range of IT opportunities for public services, but neglected protections, safeguards and liabilities. It is striking that, within two years of the report, most of the pioneering successes cited have turned sour. The report praised NHS online for its growth of 74 per cent in a single year. Yet in 2007 database failures at nine NHS Trusts led to the loss of 168,000 patient details. This followed separate security errors on the new NHS training website, which exposed the personal details –

including sexuality, ethnicity and mobile phone numbers – of hundreds of junior doctors. The Varney Report also extolled the Department of Transport's introduction of online vehicle licensing. Yet, just a year later, it emerged that the same department had lost the personal details of three million applicants for driving licences. The report went on to acclaim improvements in public service delivery derived from the introduction of a new non-emergency '101' number. Within a year, the Home Office had cut all funding, despite the millions of pounds already invested.

As for Sir David Varney, the author of the report, a year after stepping down as Chairman of HM Revenue and Customs (HMRC) in 2006 the department paid tribute to his strategic vision – by losing the child benefit records, including a wide range of personal information on twenty-five million people, having tried to send them to the National Audit Office by regular post. The HMRC fiasco was the result of basic naïvety about the risks involved in the retention, storage and sharing of personal data by the state. It exposed the millions involved to serious risk of fraud and other criminal abuse. In the wake of this massive security breach, 73 per cent of people asked said that it had undermined their trust in the government's ability to protect their confidential information. Nor was it an isolated lapse – but, rather, the latest in 2110 security breaches at HMRC in a single year.

The intrusions into personal privacy, and string of database fiascos, are the practical reality of New Labour's creeping authoritarianism, which yearns to harness cutting-edge technology to expand the reach and control of the state. For all his recent talk of Britishness, Gordon Brown's blueprint for the country stands in direct conflict with centuries of this country's history.

The development of legal protection for individual privacy in Britain dates back to Sir Edward Coke's famous quip that 'a man's house is his castle'. It informed the drafting of the Petition of Right in 1628, which established legal protections against intrusions into the home, marking an early line in the sand to defend individual privacy from intrusions by the Crown.

Following a surge in legislative hyperactivity over the last decade, by 2008 the state had amassed over a thousand separate legal powers to intrude into the home – the first and foremost realm of a British citizen's privacy. The multitude of powers derive from EU as well as UK law, with almost a third having entered into law through regulations rather than a properly debated Act of Parliament. As well as police officers, councils and other quangos can rely on these powers, only a quarter of which require prior notice to be given to the residents targeted. Force can often be used to gain entry to the home, with penalties for non-compliance rising up to a fine of £5000 or even a prison sentence.

Government and local officials can wield these powers to force their way into the home, not just to pursue criminal fugitives or terrorist suspects, but also on a wide range of additional – relatively trivial – grounds: on the one hand, to check health and safety standards, television licences and seize documents disclosing official secrets; and at the other extreme, to conduct rabbit control, check baby-sitting credentials and pursue ill-gotten gains plundered from shipwrecks. There are further powers of entry to inspect potted plants for pests, check the regulation height of hedgerows and monitor the environmental credentials of refrigerators. The proliferation of the grounds of entry, the wide discretion granted, the lack of safeguards for the citizen and inconsistent record-keeping on the use of such powers has left the individual wide open to arbitrary abuse by the state, without any serious justification on the grounds of law enforcement or national security.

As well as forcible intrusion into the home, covert surveillance – including the bugging of telephones, monitoring of emails and interception of post – has expanded dramatically. The government passed the Regulation of Investigatory Powers Act (RIPA) in 2000. While it was designed to equip the police and security services for the fight against crime and counter-terrorism, it was so widely drafted that hundreds of public bodies can avail themselves of these powers. By 2008, there were more than a thousand interception operations initiated under RIPA every day in Britain, and more than six hundred public bodies entitled to monitor intercepted communications data – over three-quarters of which are local councils, rather than branches of the police or the security services.

Over three-quarters of those granted these powers are not using them, suggesting both that they are being provided when they are not strictly necessary and that they are excessively relied upon by a relatively small proportion of public bodies. While publicly available information is limited, the annual reports from the Prime Minister to Parliament reveal that this expansion has led to a regular and increasing misuse of the powers available – with 1088 errors made in the exercise of interception powers in 2006 rising to 1182 in 2007.

In addition to bugging of communications, other forms of surveillance have been extended by stealth under RIPA's broadly drafted powers. Between 2005 and 2008 there were between 28,000 and 32,000 authorizations each year for other forms of 'directed surveillance' – or spying – of which over a third were granted to local councils and other public bodies, rather than the police or security services. This means that councils and quangos are initiating around a thousand surveillance investigations every month, with the rate almost doubling between 2006 and 2007. It marks a serious shift of power in our society. In 2000, covert surveillance was limited to twenty-eight categories of public authority. By 2008, there were fifty-nine categories – with a total of 792 separate public bodies using the powers, over half of which are local councils.

Unsurprisingly, the growth in the availability of surveillance power has led to its use in a range of novel – and unforeseen – scenarios. Whereas undercover surveillance used to be the preserve of MI5, Special Branch and a limited number of other law enforcement agencies, they are now used to investigate unlawful dog-fouling, ensure compliance with planning regulations and spy on those suspected of fly-tipping.

In one case, it emerged that Poole council had spied for almost three weeks on a young family who had applied to a local primary school. Council officials relied on surveillance powers to track the family in order to check whether they fell within the catchment area, despite having given assurances to the parents that the application for their daughter was in order. Mother of three Jenny Paton complained:

> I was quite horrified. My children were named directly as targets for surveillance. They literally followed us.
> …
> My daughter is still having trouble sleeping. She's asking if there is a man outside watching us.

The council may well have violated the law, because RIPA should only be used for directed surveillance 'for the purpose of preventing or detecting crime', but officials remained unrepentant despite the absence of any evidence to suggest that the parents had lied on the school application form. The investigation was not an isolated case. The powers are regularly used, including to snoop on whether fishermen at Poole harbour are complying with shellfish regulation, with significant public resources devoted to what the council viewed as a criminal investigation.

Elsewhere, a similar pattern emerges. Councils in Derby, Bolton, Gateshead and Hartlepool use surveillance powers to investigate dog-fouling. Bolton council also rely on RIPA to investigate littering. Kensington and Chelsea council have conducted covert surveillance to check the legitimate use of a disabled parking badge. Conwy council spied on a person found to be working while claiming to be off sick.

Even the Chief Surveillance Commissioner, who reports directly to the Prime Minister, has criticized the excessive use of RIPA by local authorities, lambasting a majority of councils for compliance failures, which he blamed on the 'inexperience' of local officials, 'a serious misunderstanding of the concept of proportionality' and 'poor oversight'.

RIPA contains intrusive powers that should be confined to dealing with relatively serious crimes and threats to national security, and subject to stronger safeguards. It is a skewed security strategy that allows local councils to check intercepted email and phone records to investigate trivial misdemeanours – like breaches of dog quarantine and storage regulations – but bans our prosecutors and courts from using intercept as evidence to convict terrorists. The use of intrusive security powers by neighbour spies impinges on the liberties of local residents, but also squanders precious local revenue – at a time of rising council tax bills – that could be better spent by police forces on tackling more serious crime and antisocial behaviour.

If central government and local authorities have increased their powers to gather information on the individual, it is no surprise that they have sought to increase their capacity to store and share the information gleaned from their snooping. The onset of a surveillance society has been accompanied by the growth of the database state, as the government has sought to facilitate its ability to cut crime – and control its citizens – through automated processes made possible by the IT revolution. Yet the government's track record of running databases and registers is dreadful, exposing the public to huge vulnerabilities. Government advisers, like David Varney, and ministers have naïvely assumed that databases will all but run themselves, ignoring the need for competent management with disastrous consequences. The periodic government response to systematic failures is to hang out to dry some lacklustre junior civil servant for failure to follow procedure, ignoring the need for managerial expertise and a proper system of oversight for which ministers will take responsibility.

Take the Home Office, which is specifically tasked with protecting public safety, over the last few years. In May 2006, the Criminal Records Bureau wrongly labelled 2700 innocent people with criminal records, leading to court ushers, children carers and students being wrongly identified as pornographers, thieves and violent robbers. Applicants for jobs and university places were turned down as a result, while others had to be fingerprinted at local police stations to prove their innocence. A system designed to protect the public from criminals has been so poorly run that it penalizes the innocent. It also puts the public at risk. The following year, the Sex Offender Register lost track of more than three hundred serious criminals because loopholes in the system allowed offenders to avoid giving a specific address to the authorities monitoring them. In the same month, it emerged that the Home Office had left criminal records of 27,000 British nationals convicted abroad – including murderers, rapists and paedophiles – sitting in files at the department, when they should have been registered on the Police National Computer.

These systemic failures continued in 2008, with Home Office contractors losing a computer file containing private details on the entire prison population and thousands of other prolific offenders and priority criminals, a major security breach which risked the taxpayer picking up a legal bill for Home Office liability to the UK's criminal fraternity. Worryingly, the same contractor has also been engaged by the Home Office to implement the ID cards scheme.

Because of the current high risk of the state mismanaging the data it collects, there is an inherent danger in relying on public sector databases. In 2002, school caretaker Ian Huntley murdered the ten-year-olds Holly Wells and Jessica Chapman in Soham, Cambridgeshire. This tragic case might have been prevented but for a string of database failures. Cracks in the systems and the negligent management of police and social service databases scuppered the vetting process at the school that employed Huntley and prevented police from taking earlier action. Amongst the long list of mistakes made, Humberside Police failed to keep a proper record of Huntley's criminal past, even deleting a warning that he was a 'serial sex attacker'. The Bichard Report in 2004, commissioned in the wake of the Soham murders, recommended sweeping reforms, but the government's follow-up has been dogged by delays and inertia – most notably it has failed to follow through on the key recommendation of a national police IT system to link up police intelligence.

In another case in 2008, Levi Bellfield was found guilty of murdering two women. Bellfield had been recorded ninety-two times on police computers, between 1996 and 2004, including for various assaults and sexual offences. Police computer records were in disarray and overlooked by investigating officers, allowing Bellfield to remain at large for so long despite a sustained campaign of violence against women.

This track record is a far cry from the promise of 'transformational government' to revolutionize public services. While IT can strengthen law enforcement and wider security, it comes with inherent frailties. Government cannot be run robotically from Whitehall and databases are no panacea for the responsible handling of sensitive information. The government's flawed strategy combines incessant centralization of power with blind faith in IT to deliver public services through sprawling systems that collate vast quantities of data in an unfocused, unchecked and unaccountable manner. A dearth of government expertise and experience means that the initial scrutiny of IT and database projects lacks the necessary rigour to conduct the most elementary risk assessments, in order to ensure basic protective safeguards to prevent – and contingency planning to mitigate – the serial system failures that result in regular security breaches. As a result, in addition to privacy concerns arising from the steady accumulation of private information by the state, the weak management of disparate and unwieldy databases has exposed the public to greater risk.

Recent database fiascos are a fraction of the risk presented by the government's ambitious plans for the future, including a national identity register coupled with compulsory ID cards. In addition to privacy concerns and criticisms that ID cards will not be able to deliver the protection that the government claims – from illegal immigration, benefit fraud and terrorism – Microsoft's UK Technology Officer has warned that ID cards will create a specific risk to the public. He calls it the 'honey pot' effect, whereby clustering masses of personal data in a single, acutely vulnerable place will tempt fraudsters – and possibly terrorists – to hack into that database in order to access, copy or clone other people's identities. The national identity register is a sitting duck for creative criminals.

It is not just the precarious design of the database that is flawed. ID cards rely on biometric technology, such as fingerprints, yet tests show that biometric passports can be cloned with a gadget costing as little as £100 and there is now a flourishing UK market in stolen identities. Further studies by the Biometric Assurance Group, which reviews government biometric projects, have warned that relying on fingerprints to identify people could lead to tens of thousands of false matches – which risks innocent people being arrested or denied entry into Britain. That risk is particularly acute for the elderly, because their fingerprints are less easy to verify. Contrary to the Hollywood image of ID cards monitoring dangerous criminals at every turn – carefully cultivated by ministers – under-developed technology deployed by slapdash officials presents a massive potential liability for the future.

The government's own advisers have warned about these risks. Sir James Crosby was specifically commissioned by the Prime Minister to review the 'identity management' programme in 2006. The Crosby Report 2008 set out a range of principles to try to help introduce identity cards in a safer and more reliable manner, drawing on recent experience in the private and public sectors. It recommended establishing a governance structure independent of Whitehall, minimizing the range of personal data stored, limiting the sharing of data between government departments (without the consent of the individual) and providing swift and effective remedies in cases of breach of security or confidentiality. In contrast, the ID card project remains government-run, will store vast amounts of personal data on a single database and allows widespread access across government departments. Ministers show every sign of making Sir James's prediction – of 'failure to secure advantage' while 'locking in disadvantage' – a reality.

In May 2008 the government announced further plans for a Communications Data Bill based on an EU Directive, which would take every telephone, email, internet and mobile phone record in Britain and store it on a single government-controlled database to which a range of public bodies would have access for – as yet loosely defined – counter-terrorism and law enforcement purposes. While the government's track record casts serious doubts over its ability to protect this mass of personal data, the scheme proposed would mark a paradigm shift in the relationship between the state and the citizen – replacing the presumption that the state needs exceptional grounds to intrude into our private lives with an automatic presumption in favour of state access to a range of detailed personal information.

In parallel with its half-cocked pursuit of a revolution in identity management, the government has massively expanded the use of the police DNA database, first set up in 1995. The aim was to enable police to collect, store and reference DNA sampled from crime scenes and individuals, in order to assist them with law enforcement – by helping identify those involved in crimes under investigation, and strengthening the evidence available for prosecution in court.

Since 1997 the DNA database has grown rapidly by stealth, brushing aside concerns about individual privacy on the untested premise that merely increasing the number of samples on the database will itself cut levels of crime. Before 2001, the police could take DNA samples – including fingerprints, mouth swabs and hair – gathered during an investigation, but had to destroy them if they related to suspects who were not subsequently convicted of a criminal offence. In 2001, the government changed the rules to remove that requirement and later expanded the scope of the database, so that DNA could be taken from anyone arrested. Ministers regularly claim public support for this approach, yet when in 2008 a government advisory body, the Human Genetics Commission, launched a 'citizens enquiry' to explain the DNA database and test public opinion, it found that a majority of people believed that the DNA of innocent people should not be retained.

As a result of this expansion, by 2008 there were nearly 5 million DNA profiles stored on by far the largest DNA database in the world, more than ten times the size of its US equivalent (in terms of the proportion of the population covered). There are signs that the government is not finished there, but is looking at ways to expand the database even further, while there have been calls from within the ranks of the police to put every UK resident on the database to give it universal scope.

These developments have generated widespread unease. The DNA database has suffered from all too familiar, basic management flaws: 26,000 police-collected samples were left off the DNA database, an estimated 13.7 per cent of the profiles on the database are duplicates and a further half a million entries have been wrongly registered.

Then there are the more fundamental flaws of design. The DNA database has not been properly debated in Parliament or by the wider public. As a result, there are no statutory basis, criteria or safeguards and wholly inadequate oversight. At the most elementary level, this haphazard approach has skewed any sense of ordered priorities. On the one hand, DNA samples have been taken from over a million innocent people – including 100,000 children – who have never committed any crime. On the other hand, not all of those convicted of serious crimes and sent to prison have been recorded on the database, and terrorist suspects subject to control orders have also been left off.

This arbitrary approach has inflated the size of the database, potentially paving the way for a universal database registering the DNA of every British citizen. The growing range of uses for the database includes searching for relatives of suspects, otherwise unconnected with any police investigation, and genetic research. These broadening functions infringe personal privacy, and raise wider questions about the government's real intentions as the role of the database is gradually extended beyond policing.

It also reverses the presumption of innocence that normally applies in this country. DNA can be found at a crime scene for a range of arbitrary reasons totally unconnected with participation in a criminal offence. However, the matching of such samples against others on the database will raise suspicions and the police may feel the need to require those matched to explain themselves in order to demonstrate their innocence – even though a quarter of those entered onto the database were not convicted of any offence. The steady accumulation of samples of innocent people risks turning Britain into a nation of police suspects, further reversing the relationship of accountability between the state and the citizen, at the expense of the latter.

The database's increasingly wide net has captured a range of anomalous cases. Sixteen-year-old Caitlin Bristow from Cheshire was attacked by a gang while walking in a local park. When she reported the incident, those accused blamed her for provoking them. Despite protests from her family, the police acted on the allegations and took Caitlin's fingerprints and DNA samples. Her DNA will be stored on the database for life even though she was not even charged with a criminal offence, let alone convicted. Frustrated by the police reaction, Caitlin said:

> I don't trust the police now. I have lost faith in them and would not go to them for help if it happened again. I want to clear my name and don't want a black mark against me. It worries me that they've got hold of my personal details and that this may affect my future. Your DNA makes up who you are and the police have stolen it from me. This could happen to anyone who reports something to the police. I did nothing wrong but they have tried to criminalise me by putting me into the system.

This kind of experience is becoming increasingly commonplace. A person is violently assaulted and reports the attack. The person accused levels a counter-accusation and, however spurious, the original complainant also finds himself arrested by officers, because of pressure to meet government targets and a politically correct culture that considers it unfair not to treat both sides the same where conflicting allegations have been made. For the innocent party to the fracas, this means his DNA will be taken and retained for life even after police clarify the true version of events.

In another recent case, police arrested and took DNA from a student accused of dodging a £2.40 train fare. Jared Ahmed, studying English and Culture at Salford University, complained that there was no conductor on the train so he had no opportunity to buy a ticket. British Transport Police refused to accept or check his version of events and justified taking a DNA sample as 'standard procedure'. In this way, DNA samples are collected and permanently retained on the flimsiest of grounds.

Wider concerns have been expressed about the disproportionate impact of this arbitrary approach on ethnic minority groups. In November 2006, Trevor Phillips, then chairman of the Commission for Racial Equality, expressed unease that the automatic storing of data of those who come into any contact with the police risked undermining race relations and public confidence. His comments followed findings that 77 per cent of young black males in England and Wales had their details registered. He said:

> Stop and search statistics suggest that black males are more likely to be stopped simply because they are young black males ... This database figure is just perpetuating this stereotype, and does nothing to instil confidence in a measure that seeks to serve all members of our community. It is provocative, unfair and unjust and will do little to reduce crime ... It would be fairer to have a database that restricts itself to storing the DNA profiles of those who are convicted, rather than this fast and loose approach, which opens up the potential for discrimination.

So, what are the countervailing law enforcement benefits to outweigh the inroads being made on personal privacy and the presumption of innocence? And would a universal DNA database including all innocent British citizens and residents, as well as those convicted or arrested pending trial, dramatically cut crime?

While popular television programmes give the impression that infallible technology can lead the police straight to dangerous criminal fugitives, the reality is not so straightforward. Ministers have consistently, and knowingly, exaggerated the law enforcement impact of DNA in order to enlist public support and avoid addressing questions about the increasing size – and function creep – of the database. On 17 June 2008, in response to criticism of the database, Gordon Brown made a speech staunchly defending the retention of the DNA of innocent people, boldly claiming that without the change in the rules eight thousand individuals – including 114 murderers, 116 rapists and 68 other sexual offenders – would have got away with their crimes. The figures were trashed as false and misleading in a stinging nine-page rebuttal issued by GeneWatch, an NGO that monitors developments in genetic technology. The figures relied upon by the Prime Minister were not real cases at all, but the result of an elaborate, speculative – and flawed – extrapolation from general estimates about the numbers of DNA samples previously removed from the database, before the change in the rules on retention of DNA on those acquitted of criminal charges. In particular, GeneWatch noted, 'It is not possible – let alone probable – that 114 murderers would have walked away if DNA profiles from innocent people were not kept.'

Similarly, some commentators on the left, including *The Times*' David Aaronovitch – himself a former communist – justify taking the DNA of innocent people on the grounds that they include what he calls the 'guilty who haven't been to prison', a telling indication of his disregard for the presumption of innocence. He claims that 'many of us are prepared to trade our contested rights to anonymity in order to reduce the agonies of those whose kids or siblings are the victims of unfound killers or attackers'. He all too readily swallows the government's blithe assumption that our security and our freedoms are tradable commodities – as if the heartache of the latest knifing in London can be automatically lifted by measures that impinge upon individual liberty, such as a universal DNA database.

The reality is that the ambitious expansion of the DNA database needs to be put in some kind of law enforcement perspective. DNA profiles are only taken in a fraction of the total number of cases of police recorded crimes – less than 1 per cent – because DNA is often not available at the crime scene. While DNA collection can assist with investigating some sexual or violent offences, there is no evidence that the expansion of the UK database has improved crime-solving rates overall. The proportion of recorded crimes detected using DNA did not increase between 2003 and 2008, despite the expansion of the database. Equally, Scotland's clear-up rate using DNA from crime scenes is higher than in England and Wales, even though under Scottish law most people have their samples removed if they are not subsequently found guilty of an offence.

While graphic or tragic criminal cases may generate calls for a universal database, they rarely withstand close scrutiny. Aaronovitch cites, as examples of the value of a universal DNA database, the cases of Steve Wright and Mark Dixie. In 2008, Steve Wright was found guilty of murdering five prostitutes, based on DNA evidence gathered by the police. However, it was matched with an existing sample on the database taken pursuant to Wright's previous conviction for theft. As in many serious cases, Wright's criminal behaviour had got worse over time, his earlier conviction for a comparatively minor offence providing the vital DNA later relied upon by police. At around the same time, there were similar calls for comprehensive DNA sampling following the conviction of Mark Dixie for murdering the young model Sally Anne Bowman. Again, Dixie had sixteen previous criminal convictions (albeit before the DNA database was established), and, critically, police had not taken his DNA when he was deported from Australia, where he was linked to at least two sexual offences. The Wright and Dixie cases support the swabbing of DNA of past criminals, not the innocent.

The government's strategy has focused on increasing the volume of DNA profiles, when improving the systems for managing the database might yield greater law enforcement dividends, in terms of solving and preventing crime. In 2008, it emerged that careless officials at the Crown Prosecution Service had mislaid for almost a year a disc containing four thousand samples from convicted criminals, including murderers and rapists. The disc had been sent by the Dutch authorities to check the profiles against the UK's DNA database. Before the disc was eventually found, allowing the DNA to be checked, eleven further crimes had been committed in Britain by offenders sampled on the Dutch disc.

While enlarging the database is not a silver-bullet solution for solving crime, there are additional risks involved in an over-reliance on DNA. In February 2007 it emerged that up to two hundred criminal cases were being re-examined by the UK Forensic Science Service, because of concerns about the reliability of DNA evidence. Later that year, one of the biggest murder cases in British history collapsed following a £16 million investigation leading to a trial that hinged on the reliability of DNA evidence. Sean Hoey was acquitted of the murder of the twenty-nine people who died during the Omagh terrorist attack in 1998, because of doubts arising both from the forensic reliability of the Low Copy Number DNA technique and the serious mishandling of DNA samples by the police.

The exponential growth in the DNA database over the last eight years has been disproportionate to the corresponding gains in law enforcement. Recent practice suggests that improving the handling of samples and the integrity of the database – as opposed to more comprehensive sampling – would be of greater value in terms of law enforcement. At a more fundamental level, we need a serious public debate about the priorities, proportionality and safeguards for the database, including the criteria for sampling DNA and the compelling case for removing the DNA samples of innocent people who have not been convicted of any crime.

While the government's approach to the storage of DNA is arbitrary, it is surpassed for sheer dysfunctionality by the haphazard roll-out of closed-circuit television (CCTV). As the head of CCTV at the Metropolitan Police fumed in 2008:

> CCTV was originally seen as a preventative measure. Billions of pounds has been spent on kit, but no thought has gone into how the police are going to use the images and how they will be used in court. It's been an utter fiasco: only 3% of crimes were solved by CCTV. There's no fear of CCTV. Why don't people fear it? [They think] the cameras are not working.

Since 1997 the government has invested heavily in the deployment of CCTV cameras, making the British public the most watched in the world. Yet basic failures overlooked by ministers, from design through to implementation, have blunted CCTV's use as a crime-fighting tool, leaving the British citizen with the worst of all worlds – spied on, unprotected against intrusions into personal privacy, no safer on the streets and left to foot the bill for hundreds of millions of pounds so poorly invested.

Because of its underlying disregard for the liberty of the individual, coupled with pervasive technological ineptitude, the government has failed to test the business case for CCTV deployments.

CCTV provided a very visible sign of government action, for which it could – at least in the short term – claim credit. However, effective CCTV requires a coordinated approach, linking local authorities, police, commercial operators, prosecutors and the courts. Ministers eager to score political points had neither the expertise, patience nor the long-term perspective to examine carefully and test whether the enormous public funds invested were actually making Britain safer. The onset of a surveillance society is less a conspiracy of malevolent secret police in jackboots and more the consequence of the government's instinctive indifference to British liberty, coupled with the most basic ministerial incompetence.

First introduced in the 1980s and expanded during the following decade, central government invested £38.5 million in CCTV between 1994 and 1999. The injection of public investment into CCTV took place in a climate of public anxiety following the murder in 1993 of the toddler James Bulger, whose ten-year-old murderers were caught on haunting CCTV footage. CCTV was subsequently promoted as a popular means of visibly deploying modern technology to prevent such shocking crimes. From 1997, the government initiated a step change in investment, injecting £170 million between 1999 and 2003. Additional funds followed, with an estimated total of £500 million of taxpayers' money invested in CCTV since 1997. Public sector investment has been matched by private sector deployment, with a majority of CCTV cameras in the UK now commercially operated.

It is not clear exactly how many cameras there are in Britain, but experts estimate around 4.2 million. That means there is one camera for every fourteen people, with the average individual in London being recorded by three hundred different cameras every day. Britain now has more security cameras than any other country – around a fifth of the world's CCTV.

While CCTV undoubtedly has some law enforcement value, it

raises a number of questions about personal privacy. Are there limits on the state's – and businesses' – powers to snoop on the citizen? What happens to the footage after it has been retrieved, how long is it kept and who can it be shared with? And, perhaps most importantly, who watches the watchers? What oversight and accountability do we have to ensure public confidence in the state's monitoring of the individual going about his daily life?

CCTV was originally designed to help tackle crime, anti-social behaviour and terrorism. It is now being used to enforce speed limits, parking laws and bus lanes, channelling law enforcement resources away from serious crime and generating complaints that it is being used to raise revenue for local authorities.

In January 2008, it emerged that CCTV cameras linked to the DVLA driver database were being widely used to monitor entry to rubbish tips by local residents, to enforce local regulation on dumping waste – a further symptom of function creep. Further plans to extend the role of CCTV include deploying cameras to film children sitting exams to check for cheating. There has been little debate about the limits on what CCTV can and should be used to monitor, and where we draw the line. The human rights group Liberty has warned that the increasing omnipresence of visual surveillance risks a 'chilling effect' on the confidence of people to take part in public activities.

Concerns about CCTV surveillance are not limited to public spaces. In one case, CCTV council operators in Sefton, Liverpool, filmed a young woman undressing and taking a bath, displaying the pictures on a plasma screen at their control centre. Although those responsible were prosecuted, such cases raise questions about levels of unreported abuse of privacy and the level of accountability for such abuse. In another case, security guards at the Welsh Assembly were caught pointing CCTV cameras on nearby homes and hotels. Although disciplinary action was taken by their employers, they claimed there was no breach of privacy and there was no criminal investigation by the police.

The existing oversight and accountability for the deployment and use of CCTV rests with data protection legislation and the watchdog role of the Information Commissioner. The current arrangements lack teeth: no one knows how many CCTV cameras there are, there is no central register of cameras, guidance on CCTV is not legally enforceable and the Information Commissioner has limited powers to address serious abuse or wrongdoing.

So, given the huge cost to the taxpayer and the intrusion into individual privacy, how much safer has CCTV made our lives? Government ministers heap praise on CCTV as a linchpin in their law enforcement agenda. When concerns about both privacy intrusions and the effectiveness of CCTV were raised by the Conservative MP David Davis during his 2008 by-election campaign, Home Office ministers circulated a briefing paper misrepresenting his criticisms as outright opposition and calling on party activists to publicize this in the media. The Labour Party Briefing document from Home Secretary Jacqui Smith and Security Minister Tony McNulty described CCTV as: '... a powerful crime-fighting tool. It has proven effectiveness time and again in tackling crime and disorder and plays a vital role in the fight against terrorism and in helping communities feel safer.'

In case there was any doubt, ministers concluded: 'CCTV makes our streets safer.' Such bald assertions are difficult to reconcile with the effectiveness of CCTV reported to the same ministers through the Home Office's own detailed assessments. A departmental evaluation of CCTV programmes in 2005 found that CCTV 'had little overall effect on crime levels' – cutting crime in only 7 per cent of deployments. There was further evidence of displacement, rather than deterrence of criminal behaviour. CCTV was found to 'have played no part in reducing fear of crime' and, in fact, 'public support for CCTV decreased after implementation by as much as 20 per cent', as residents realized it was having minimal impact. These figures were subsequently backed up by senior officers, who say that CCTV has done little to prevent late-night violence in town centres.

At first sight these findings are surprising. The reasons became clearer as a result of a further joint study by the Association of Chief Police Officers and the Home Office in 2007. The report's findings describe how CCTV has been rolled out on a massive scale without thinking through the priorities, implications or costs – and without any consistent standards against which to measure its effectiveness. As an example of partnership across the criminal justice system and between government, councils and business, the deployment of CCTV has been a shambles.

A wide net of CCTV cameras have been cast across the country – capturing as much of people's daily lives as possible – with little thought given to the time, effort, expertise and resources required to store, retrieve and analyse the footage so that it can be used for intelligence purposes or as evidence in court. At the most basic level, the report found that CCTV had been deployed without thinking through the police resources required to analyse CCTV footage, the costs of storage and the need for standardized technology between operators and other users. Even when camera footage is retrieved by the police, 80 per cent of it is of such poor quality that it cannot properly identify suspects, defeating the whole point of CCTV in the first place.

At a strategic level, the report points to striking conflicts between the contradictory objectives CCTV is being deployed to achieve. CCTV cameras are mainly aimed at cutting the level of persistent, minor crime – the so-called 'volume crime'. But given the relative seriousness of each of the numerous individual crimes involved, this places a huge drain on police time and the resources required to retrieve and analyse the CCTV footage. In contrast, while the cost of retrieving CCTV for more serious crimes – such as terrorism – is much less, as a proportion of the overall costs in this kind of police investigation most CCTV cameras are in the wrong place to catch these very different patterns of criminal behaviour. At the most basic level, the law enforcement aim conflicts with the financial case for CCTV – and yet no one in government appears to have anticipated, or acted upon, such a simple and obvious flaw in the way CCTV has been deployed.

The report lists a range of other elementary problems. A single camera may be required to monitor a static location, like the entrance to a shop (which shopkeepers prefer). But this prevents it from following moving suspects (which may be more useful to the police). Equally, while crime patterns change over time and criminal conduct may be displaced, many CCTV cameras have remained static.

One of the central aims of CCTV is to help prosecute criminals, yet perhaps the most worrying disconnect, highlighted by the report, is between the police and the criminal justice system. The police, prosecutors and courts do not use compatible technology, so CCTV footage often needs to be copied – necessitating more time, cost and effort – in order to be used as evidence. Even then, the 'presentation of CCTV evidence at the majority of courts continues to be a problem'. In this way, the impact of CCTV in prosecuting crime has been diluted at every step of the process. Basic failures to think through the aims and costs in rolling out CCTV have resulted in half a billion pounds of public money being squandered on surveillance since 1997 which often cannot properly be used by the police.

These government reports pose serious questions about the current effectiveness of CCTV as a law enforcement tool. After fifteen years and the investment of so much taxpayers' money, 'This uncertainty extends to where the cameras are, if they are deployed and covering the correct areas, if the images they produce are fit for purpose and whether they are being used effectively by the police.'

One of the most striking illustrations of these serial failures followed the fatal shooting of Jean Charles de Menezes, who was mistakenly identified as a terrorist suspect, by armed police in July 2005. None of the CCTV cameras covering the tragic incident – from the bus Mr de Menezes caught, the tube he entered or Stockwell underground station – provided any footage to assist the subsequent review conducted by the Independent Police Complaints Commission (IPCC). As a result, while the IPCC concluded that the footage had not been deliberately tampered with, defective CCTV left serious questions unanswered about the shooting of an innocent man.

Far from being deterred by these systematic failures, however, the government is looking to expand the use of CCTV still further. Not content just to watch British citizens, UK CCTV will now also talk to them. Technology piloted in London and Middlesbrough detects anti-social behaviour and transmits an oral warning. As Orwellian as this may sound, it is another poor substitute for real policing. These talking cameras risk ridicule, if not physical damage, from the kinds of trouble-maker they aim to deter.

A report on CCTV by the Society of Royal Engineering in 2007 concluded that 'the available studies fail to provide evidence that surveillance brings significant benefits, or that any benefits it brings outweigh the limitations it imposes on individual rights'. The report's author, Professor Nigel Gilbert, warned about the vulnerability of CCTV to abuse and hackers, calling for a moratorium on new CCTV deployments until the case for them can be more clearly demonstrated.

Again, despite popular misconception, the justification for erosions of privacy proves thin in practice. David Aaronovitch colourfully defends CCTV because of the misery of residents living in a local housing block where 'somebody's been taking a dump every night in their lift'. He continues: 'Do they feel spied upon? No. They don't feel spied upon. They feel that this is some way of maybe trying to catch the person who takes a dump in the lift.'

Yet the idea that we can trade being 'spied upon' with ridding ourselves of such anti-social behaviour is a myth – at least based on the experience to date. If anything, in answer to Aaronovitch's question local residents eventually feel let down by the mirage of yet another intrusive measure paid for through soaring council tax bills, but which leaves them no safer as they go about their daily lives.

While CCTV can strengthen law enforcement, the current scatter-gun approach serves neither personal privacy nor security. We need a far more rigorous, critical and focused approach to the investment in, and planning of, CCTV deployment, while strengthening the systems for accountability and sanctions to protect innocent members of the public from privacy intrusions.

There are worrying signs of a further, growing threat to personal privacy from the EU. The EU, driven by the European Commission and pro-integration member states, is rapidly seeking to increase its control and authority in the field of Justice and Home Affairs. As a result, the British government has subscribed to a series of EU schemes devised by law-makers in Brussels for the retention and sharing of personal data – including fingerprints, DNA, car registration details and email, internet and mobile phone usage.

Since Britain stockpiles five times more DNA on its national database than the rest of the EU, international police DNA checks are likely to result in far more matches against the British DNA database than any other. That means that the British police will share the DNA of British citizens far more widely than any other

EU country. Aside from the lack of reciprocity and the distraction of police time in dealing with such requests, it will also have the effect of sucking a disproportionate amount of innocent British nationals – as well as some guilty ones – into European police investigations, including as criminal suspects.

At the same time, the difficulties in protecting personal data in the UK will inevitably be aggravated, if exchanged across twenty-seven EU member states. If the government cannot protect our personal data shared across Whitehall, what chance when it is sent to Bucharest?

The UK is not a reluctant contributor to this agenda. It has been at the vanguard of EU efforts to pioneer a pan-European data-sharing regime, leading a £13 million project to test the interoperability of electronic identity systems, known as Project Stork. While the government has denied any move towards European-wide identity cards, the trade group representing the government's contractors would only concede that 'Stork is not intended to replace passports in the short term', and further details of the scheme remain murky.

Wider international comparisons provide additional perspective on the scale of surveillance in the UK. In 2007, Privacy International, an NGO that monitors privacy around the world, categorized Britain as an 'endemic surveillance society'. It ranked UK privacy protections joint forty-third out of the forty-seven countries surveyed globally – and with the worst record in Europe. The UK ranking was on a par with Singapore, and only marginally better than Russia and China. Privacy protection in Scotland, which has devolved authority in this area, was found to be significantly better than in England and Wales.

The inroads on personal privacy in this country have had a significant impact on public confidence. An ICM poll in February

2008 found that 53 per cent of those questioned were not confident that government, councils and banks would protect their personal information. Seventy-seven per cent worried more about the safety of their personal details than they used to, with 72 per cent saying they felt powerless to protect such data.

As public trust ebbs away, longer-term questions remain about the direction in which Britain is heading. We are still far from a British equivalent of Oceania, Orwell's nightmare society depicted in *1984*. Big Brother is the name of a television programme and state-monitored CCTV does not yet extend into the home. Nevertheless, broad surveillance powers, ill-thought-through government schemes, recklessly run databases and the drip feed of EU regulation are changing the relationship between the state and the citizen. Whereas the idea of British liberty has traditionally held the state answerable to its citizens, and made interference with our private lives the exception, the individual is now increasingly accountable to the state and privacy intrusions are becoming the norm.

A report in 2006, commissioned by the Information Commissioner, offers a disturbing vision of Britain in 2016. It depicts a society in which shoppers are scanned as they enter stores, with their purchase profile and marketing data instantly accessible (through sophisticated and rapid data mining), enabling shop assistants to evaluate the potential value of a customer and prioritize customer service accordingly.

The report envisages global satellite navigation providing twenty-four-hour comprehensive police monitoring of all vehicles – tracking more intrusively selected cars. Ubiquitous and highly sensitive CCTV cameras – now fitted with microphones as standard – zoom in on suspicious activity and conversations. Facial recognition systems will monitor the movements of each citizen, using cameras embedded in lampposts and walls, tracked by aerial drones. Diverse information on each citizen can be rapidly collated and scanned for early warning of suspicious or high-risk behaviour – to allow the authorities to intervene well before any potential threat, disorder, infraction or undesirable behaviour occurs. Genetic details and school, work, leisure and other behavioural patterns are analysed for early warning signs. Holidaymakers and other travellers will be able to get quicker access and better service through airports if they are prepared to give up detailed sensitive biometric information, which can then be shared globally within seconds. Customs officers will conduct virtual strip searches on individual passengers, using state-of-the-art scanners. Employees will be subjected to biometric as well as psychometric tests, with health and lifestyle information conditioning opportunities, terms of employment and remuneration packages. The risks to children will be closely controlled through CCTV, ID cards and strict limits on their location, diet, internet access, email communications and other activities – as well as omnipresent surveillance of their movements. The elderly will find themselves increasingly isolated from human contact, as sensors and cameras – and remote monitoring – become a substitute for care at nursing homes and visits from social services.

Whether this forecast proves remotely accurate or not remains to be seen. In one respect at least it actually appears over-optimistic, since it assumes the efficient operation of government IT and databases, and ignores the enormous scope it offers to exploitation by hackers, fraudsters and even terrorists.

In any event, the surreptitious expansion of surveillance in Britain has already taken huge strides, and shows no sign of abating. There is a growing chorus of concern at the extent of state snooping on the citizen in this country, without adequate safeguards or accountability. Claims that intrusive surveillance is making us more secure are over-blown, given technological vulnerabilities, a dearth of the most basic government planning and deficient operational management. There are undoubtedly law enforcement benefits to be had from the use of new technology, including DNA and CCTV. However, it is increasingly evident that the current unfocused and arbitrary approach has both undermined individual privacy and proved costly and counter-productive in practice. Few doubt the need to incorporate technological advances into the fight against crime and terrorism. In his valedictory speech as DPP in 2008, Ken MacDonald urged:

> We need to take very great care not to fall into a way of life in which freedom's back is broken by the relentless pressure of a security State ... Of course modern technology is of critical importance to the struggle against serious crime and, used wisely, it can and will protect us. But we need to understand that it is in the nature of State power that decisions taken in the next few months and years about how the State may use these powers, and to what extent, are likely to be irreversible. They will be with us forever. And they in turn will be built upon. So we should take very great care to imagine the world we are creating before we build it. We might end up living with something we can't bear.

Britain now needs a proper, public debate about the limits on state surveillance and its impact on our society. We need clearer criteria and stronger safeguards enshrined into domestic law – both to provide a sharper focus to the unwieldy and often ineffective surveillance schemes deployed, and to demarcate clearer limits on the disproportionate intrusion by the state into our daily lives.

PART III

THE WRONG KIND
OF RIGHT

5

Rights Contagion

> 'Government big enough to supply everything you
> need is big enough to take everything you have ... The
> course of history shows that as a government grows,
> liberty decreases.'
>
> First attributed to THOMAS JEFFERSON

While the British idea of liberty has been subject to sustained assault, we have witnessed a surreptitious parallel development – the steady expansion of novel claims, now characterized as 'human rights'.

In an effort to anchor Britain to Europe, and its stronger socialist tradition, Labour governments signed Britain up to the European Convention on Human Rights in 1950 (the Convention), and then accepted the jurisdiction of the Strasbourg Court in 1966. Since 1975, the Strasbourg Court has taken on a life of its own, creating numerous novel claims under the Convention. Since 1997, the government has incorporated the Strasbourg case law directly into UK law, under the Human Rights Act, and touted a wider strategy that seeks to promote its vision of social justice through the spread of human rights. As a result, claimants can now select from an arsenal of new rights to command receipt of a range of diverse public services – including protective police services, NHS healthcare, social services and even environmental protection.

Britain has proved more susceptible than many other countries to the proliferation of rights because of the strength and breadth of its civil society. Human rights NGOs, campaign groups and lawyers have latched on to, and pressed the boundaries of, the expanding realm of human rights law, creating a powerful lobby for specific interest groups and particular categories of claimants. Legal aid, no-win-no-fee arrangements and the availability of *pro bono* legal representation – important bridges between the public and an expensive justice system – have also paved the way for greater access to the courts, and a corresponding increase in litigation.

The spread of rights has become contagious and, since the Human Rights Act, opened the door to vast new categories of claims, which can be judicially enforced against the government through the courts. Since a successful claim of human rights has trump card status, it is a way of forcing the state to prioritize the interest of the individual claimant over the claims of other individuals and the rest of society. For those subject to these new claims, the rapid growth of rights has created widespread uncertainty, as judges, civil servants and public service providers have struggled to keep up with, and make sense of, rapid changes in the law. Legal uncertainty has fuelled a compensation culture, with government departments being forced to settle swathes of new claims out of court. Confusion amongst the police, probation and prison services and local authorities has led them to place the rights of criminal prisoners and fugitives ahead of public safety, for fear of being sued.

More generally, police officers, doctors, social workers and other public servants now regularly find their professional judgement being trumped. Their ability to assess, weigh up and balance the wider public interest in prioritizing police investigations, dispensing NHS drugs or enforcing border controls is fettered by the diverse and onerous new burdens dictated by human rights. Resources dedicated to policing, healthcare, the armed forces and the prison service have been displaced to pay for all of these new rights successfully asserted.

The proliferation of rights is part of a broader shift in popular attitudes, with increasing dependency on the state and an unhealthy fixation on compensating individuals, undermining personal and civic responsibility and eclipsing a balanced consideration of the wider public interest in our society. However, the expansion of new human rights also begs questions about the moral compass of that society – when the armed forces pay the same level of compensation to a transsexual soldier for hurting his feelings, as to another soldier who lost his legs and suffered brain damage after tripping a landmine in Afghanistan. The risk of ever expanding rights is that they can lead to absurd results, which are promptly ridiculed in the media. This devalues the currency of our core – fundamental – rights, and threatens to discredit the very idea of human rights in the public mind.

Yet the most striking development has been the sheer number and range of legal claims that are now formulated as human rights. Once expanded beyond the traditional core of fundamental liberties, there is no obvious reason or basis for limiting the number and range of interests, claims and entitlements that can be dressed up as human rights. As more and more rights are created, the less 'fundamental' they have become – with the term coming to be regarded as a panacea.

Whereas fundamental liberties were developed in Britain to stop the government interfering with the freedom of the individual, many of these novel rights have had the reverse effect – increasing both the state's responsibility for what happens to the citizen and the citizen's dependence on the state. The consequence has been to inflate, rather than restrain, the role of the state in our lives. Where rights once stood for limiting government, they are increasingly the clarion call for big government.

This inflation of the role of the state is at odds with that original – and increasingly eroded – conception of British liberty. But if British fundamental rights have been cast adrift from their original moorings, they are slowly congealing around a very different set of ideas, whether classified as social democracy, socialism, dirigisme or some other communitarian philosophy. The approach of the judges in Strasbourg, and policy-makers in Whitehall, has arguably been influenced as much by these ideals as by classic liberalism, giving expression to the inherent philosophical tensions between the two schools of thought. Equally, some of the most ardent supporters of the Human Rights Act in the UK openly favour such a communitarian approach to rights, despite the very different British tradition.

What is perhaps most worrying about the situation Britain finds itself in today is that the proliferation of rights has taken place in a way that is impossible to reconcile with basic principles of democracy. The surreptitious proliferation of rights through the courts, at home and abroad, has subtly and steadily effected a dramatic change in the legal landscape, and placed a heavy burden on the public purse, with far-reaching consequences. Yet, it has taken place with minimal, meaningful democratic oversight, through the scrutiny and approval of our directly elected law-makers in Parliament.

Britain played a leading role in drafting the Convention in 1950, in the aftermath of the Second World War. The idea of international legal commitments, binding together the fragile but historically aggressive nation states of Europe, was a product of the internationalism that influenced the post-war era, with the establishment of the United Nations, the Marshall Plan for economic recovery in Europe, the Bretton Woods system of international financial regulation and, in Europe, the emergence of a European Coal and Steel Community designed to knit the economies of France and Germany more closely together. The Convention was born out of a similar post-war reflex, although its parent institution, the Council of Europe, pre-dated and remains separate from those that developed into the EU. It reflected the desire of European countries, and the wider North Atlantic Alliance, to prevent the repetition of the grotesque and widespread atrocities committed by Nazi Germany and its allies during the war.

In conducting this ground-breaking diplomacy on behalf of Britain, the Labour government led by Clement Attlee was acutely conscious that it was entering uncharted waters in international law. The UK's negotiating position was informed by domestic constitutional principles of legal certainty, separation of powers and democratic accountability, but also a palpable nervousness about the future implications of binding human rights obligations. British representatives continually stressed the importance of signing up to clear and precise obligations under the Convention. As one senior British delegate noted for the record during the negotiations: '[T]he treaty it was desired to draw up would create obligations which States would be bound to perform, and they therefore had to know the precise extent of their undertakings ... exact knowledge of the extent of their undertakings would make it easier for States to accept them.'

The diplomatic outcome was regarded as successful in that Foreign and Commonwealth Office ministers could confidently report that the new human rights treaty 'contains a definition of the rights and limitations thereto which follows almost word for word the actual texts proposed by the United Kingdom'.

Nevertheless, the government's most senior lawyers harboured deep reservations about the whole enterprise. Sir Eric Beckett, the FCO Legal Adviser, warned that a supranational European court would be a 'small paradise' for claims by NGOs and lawyers. Further FCO advice to ministers warned against signing the 'blank cheque' represented by acceptance of the jurisdiction of a European court, predicting the subversion of the Convention in support of spurious claims: 'To allow Governments to become the object of such potentially vague charges by individuals is to invite Communists, crooks and cranks of every type to bring actions.'

Yet the gravest doubts emanated from the Lord Chancellor, Lord Jowitt, who briefed the Cabinet on the draft Convention, in October 1950, in particularly disparaging – but prescient – terms:

> The real vice of the document, therefore consists in its lack of precision … It completely passes the wit of man to guess what results would be arrived at by a tribunal composed of elected persons who need not even be lawyers, drawn from various European states possessing completely different systems of law, and whose deliberations take place behind closed doors … the whole document reeks of compromise.

The international diplomatic compromise was reflected in domestic political compromise. In a show of political leadership, Britain was the first country to ratify the Convention in 1951, but opted out of the jurisdiction of the Strasbourg Court for a further fifteen years. It was not until 1966 that the Labour government led by Harold Wilson signed Britain up to the compulsory jurisdiction of the Strasbourg Court over individual claims.

Of course, every government accepting the jurisdiction of the Strasbourg Court to rule on individual human rights claims was well aware that it would be applied in unforeseen situations. All new law is subject to a degree of risk that judicial interpretation may lead to some unpredictable – and unpalatable – consequences. This was one reason why the British argued so vehemently for a defined and circumscribed list of rights, rather than an enumeration of general principles as some other states, such as France, had proposed.

Yet the text of the Convention agreed in 1950 is a pale reflection of the body of human rights law now in place. Notwithstanding the advice and warnings of those in 1950, the proliferation of new rights by the Strasbourg Court has occurred on a scale unimaginable to the governments negotiating at the time, well beyond any development that can be attributed to the realm of reasonable judicial interpretation.

In fact, the tide began to turn shortly after Britain agreed to be bound by judgments of the Strasbourg Court. During the 1970s, a series of cases marked a critical point of departure in Strasbourg. In *Golder v UK*, the Strasbourg Court read a right of access to the courts into the fair trial guarantees set out in Article 6 of the Convention. This innovation, unsupported by the Convention text, drew sharp criticism from the British judge on the court, Sir Gerald Fitzmaurice:

> Finally, it must be said that the above quoted passages from the Judgment of the Court are typical of the cry of the judicial legislator … It may, or it may not be true that a failure to see the Human Rights Convention as comprising a right of access to the courts would have untoward consequences – just as one can imagine such consequences possibly resulting from various other defects or lacunae in this Convention. But this is not the point. The point is that it is for the States upon whose consent the Convention rests, and from which consent alone it derives its obligatory force, to close the gap or put the defect right by an amendment – not for a judicial

tribunal to substitute itself for the convention-makers, to do their work for them.

This was followed, in 1978, by the exposition of a more general approach with far-reaching consequences. In *Tyrer v UK*, the Strasbourg Court held that judicial corporal punishment on the Isle of Man was sufficiently degrading that it breached the prohibition on torture and inhuman treatment, without any basis in the text of the Convention or the negotiating records, for such a novel conclusion. In so deciding, the judges shrouded their reasoning in legal jargon, which betrayed a blatant shift of approach – from a more disciplined judicial interpretation and application of Convention rights to an overtly political renovation and rewriting of the law:

> The Court must also recall that the Convention is a living instrument which, as the Commission rightly stressed, must be interpreted in the light of present-day conditions. In the case now before it the Court cannot but be influenced by the developments and commonly accepted standards in the penal policy of the member States of the Council of Europe in this field.

This seemingly innocuous paragraph marked a watershed. Far from establishing a core set of defined and circumscribed rights, the Convention was now a 'living instrument', evolving, growing and expanding into new territory. In another case, shortly after, the Strasbourg Court suggested:

> To the extent that the number of member States [party to the Convention] increases ... in such a larger, diversified community the development of common standards may well prove the best, if not the only way of achieving the Court's professed aim of ensuring

that the Convention remains a living instrument to be interpreted so
as to reflect societal changes and to remain in line with present-day
conditions.

In these cases, the Strasbourg Court declared that it would not
remain confined to interpreting and applying the text of the
Convention rights. The judges came up with the ominous phrase
'living instrument' to try to justify the idea that their proper role
was to legislate and update Convention rights. The Strasbourg
Court was no longer confined to applying existing law. It was now
explicitly in the business of making new law. Contrary to the will of
the state parties – and the fundamental principle of a separation of
powers between judges and law-makers – the Strasbourg Court had
invented, and appropriated for itself, a power of judicial legislation.
The court then set about using that power to create numerous new
human rights reflecting its diverse political views.

Where did the judges get such formidable law-making power
from? Unsurprisingly, given the negotiating history, the Convention does not mention any judicial power to create new law. On the
contrary, the very first article of the Convention makes it crystal
clear that the court should apply the list of rights as '*defined* in
Section I of this Convention' (my emphasis), rather than tacking on
new meaning. The assumption by the judges of a power to 'develop'
the Convention has evidently come from the judges themselves, a
judicial feat of breathtaking ingenuity.

The judges bestowed upon themselves a legislative function, fully
aware that there are limited means for elected governments subject
to their rulings, to exercise any meaningful democratic oversight
over them. This judicial coup represents a naked usurpation by
a judicial body of the legislative power that properly belongs to
democratically elected law-makers. To put it into context, the
legislative powers assumed by the Strasbourg Court are unique.

There is no equivalent in the UK – where creative developments under the common law can always be reversed by Parliament. Nor are they comparable to the judicial activism in constitutional courts like the US Supreme Court, where judges are held democratically accountable for their political views through Congressional scrutiny during the process of their appointment. In contrast, the Strasbourg Court is not subject to any meaningful democratic oversight or accountability.

The Strasbourg Court has not tried to hide its intention to increase the obligations imposed on governments over time. On the contrary, it basks in its judicial creativity. As one Strasbourg judge rather lackadaisically confessed:

> I also concede that the Convention organs have in this way, on occasion, reached the limits of what can be regarded as treaty interpretation in the legal sense. At times they have perhaps even crossed the boundary and entered territory which is no longer that of treaty interpretation but is actually legal policy-making. But this, as I understand it, is not for a court to do; on the contrary, policy-making is a task for the legislature or the Contracting States themselves, as the case may be.

More often than not, the Strasbourg Court has sought to justify its creativity on the basis that it must make Convention rights 'effective', or that it is duty bound to ensure human rights are adapted to prevailing modern-day social mores in Europe – although it is neither mandated nor well placed to determine what the moral, political and social standards of the day should be in modern Britain.

There are three common explanations for why the judges have shown such lack of respect for the limits of the judicial responsibilities entrusted to them. The first derives from the composition of the Strasbourg Court. In 2007, only twenty of the forty-five European judges had any prior judicial experience before joining the Strasbourg bench. The court is a mix of judges, lawyers, civil servants (mainly diplomats) and academics. The basic risk, predicted by the Lord Chancellor in 1950 and now born out in practice, is that a non-judicial court will take a non-judicial approach. Diplomats deploy their diplomatic experience, with its emphasis on compromise and negotiation over legal rules. Lawyers are used to defending and representing their clients, which involves a more partisan approach than the impartiality and independence expected of judges. Perhaps most telling, legal academics – particularly those in the human rights field – apply their academic expertise, which is to explore and expand the philosophical underpinnings of the law and legal policy in a far more creative way than strict judicial discipline should ever allow. Academic lawyers are disposed to expound on what they believe the law should be, rather than confine themselves to what it is. These risks have increased with the expansion of the Council of Europe to take in the countries of central and eastern Europe, some of which have relatively weak judicial systems. The proliferation of new human rights is a direct result of a court comprised of judges with greater political, diplomatic, academic and other legal – rather than judicial – experience.

There is a certain irony in Harold Wilson being the Prime Minister who signed Britain up to a court composed of politically active lawyers, civil servants and academics since he was all too aware of their scope for political collusion. As he told one bemused Private Secretary: 'I was a don in Oxford before the war … But I couldn't stand the intrigue of academic life so I joined the Civil Service. The intrigue of the Civil Service was even worse than at Oxford so I became a politician.'

While Wilson overlooked these risks, the flaws in the judicial

133

appointment process in Strasbourg are now widely recognized in the diplomatic community and the legal profession. In May 2003 a panel of eminent European judges and jurists, drawn from different domestic judicial systems, published a damning report on the Strasbourg bench. The panel, which included Lord Lester and Lord Justice Sedley, criticized the 'politicised processes currently adopted in the appointment of [Strasbourg] judges', noting that 'judges selected will lack the requisite skills and abilities to discharge their duties' and warning of the 'adverse effect' on the Strasbourg Court's credibility. Amongst the problems highlighted, the panel explained that nominations were frequently made on the basis of political loyalty rather than judicial merit, scrutiny was influenced by party politics and diplomatic lobbying for – and by – judicial candidates undermined the independence of those judges appointed. The net effect is 'a Court less qualified and less able to discharge its crucial mandate than it might otherwise be'. This is particularly galling for the UK, which has a reputation for nominating the very highest calibre of judges to the Strasbourg Court and other international tribunals.

A further explanation for the court's legislative approach is that international courts were originally designed as dispute settlement bodies, their main role being to decide on the specific facts of disputes submitted to them for adjudication – rather than interpret, clarify and apply general law in the way that our domestic courts do. Strasbourg judgments only bind the parties to the particular dispute before the court. They do not have the status of precedent and do not – formally at least – create general law of wider application. The Strasbourg Court is not legally required to follow its own rulings, and often chooses not to. This explains why the Strasbourg case law is often inconsistent and haphazard. While the Strasbourg Court serves a purpose as a tribunal of last resort in cases of serious human rights abuses, its case law is erratic and difficult to follow for domestic courts and officials looking for guidance in clear and certain rules.

A third explanation for the judicial creativity in Strasbourg arises from its deficiencies as a fact-finding institution, coupled with a burgeoning caseload. The Strasbourg Court has created additional human rights obligations on states as a short cut. For example, the court extended the right to life in a series of cases alleging Turkish violation of Kurdish rights, adding various requirements to the conduct of investigations into suspicious deaths or disappearances. This was motivated by the court's desire to avoid having to delve into complicated and murky factual assessments without enough evidence to decide whether the state was itself directly implicated in the deaths in question. Extending human rights to create additional procedural obligations on states served as a cost-efficient substitute for a lack of evidence to deal with a growing docket of cases. The court has legislated its way out of its own internal problems.

If the fears of those lawyers who warned against the Strasbourg Court appear to have been realized, governments have a range of measures open to them to try to mitigate the impact of over-zealous rulings from Strasbourg. The German and French legal systems have remained relatively insulated from the excesses of judicial activism, mainly because their highest courts apply their domestic constitutions ahead of the Convention and related Strasbourg case law. In contrast, the recent approach of the British government has courted confusion.

In one case, the government actually invited the Strasbourg Court to find Britain in violation of the ban on torture and inhuman treatment. The case concerned a nine-year-old boy who had been caned by his stepfather for disciplinary reasons, leaving him with bruises on his legs and backside. The stepfather was prosecuted in the UK for assault occasioning actual bodily harm, but the jury acquitted him on the basis of the defence of 'reasonable chastisement' under UK law. The stepson took a claim to the Strasbourg Court, alleging that the British government had, by failing to punish his stepfather for this degrading treatment, violated his human rights.

Initially, the British government stoutly defended the claim. After all, Parliament had carefully considered its approach to corporal punishment in the home – a subjective and politically controversial issue that elected law-makers should decide. They had adopted a law that struck a balance reflecting domestic moral and social values at that time. In the case at hand, the police had tried to bring a prosecution, and a jury of twelve members of the public had looked at the facts of the case and taken the view – rightly or wrongly – that the punishment administered was not excessive. It was no business of the Strasbourg Court to stretch the ban on torture to cover this kind of scenario.

The human rights claim was originally brought by the stepson in 1994, and the Strasbourg hearing took place shortly after the 1997 general election. The new, incoming Labour government indicated that it was minded to change the law, to tighten up the restrictions on physical punishment in the home. It had a clear democratic mandate to introduce legislation to effect a change in the law. So there was no need for it to abandon – and every reason for it to guard – its authority to decide British law in such a politically sensitive area, by changing its plea before the Strasbourg Court and accepting its competence to find the UK in violation of the ban on torture and inhuman treatment in relation to the stepson. The decision of ministers appears motivated by a desire to contrast Labour's enlightened approach to parental discipline with that of the previous government, and its broader determination to embed Britain more closely within the architecture of European integration. The Strasbourg judges readily accepted the invitation to extend their jurisdiction, ruling that the existing UK law on domestic punishment – and the decision of the jury to acquit the stepfather – violated the human rights of the child in question.

The British government deliberately lost the case and, by falling on its sword in this way, actively encouraged the expansion of the Convention by the Strasbourg Court, thereby limiting future Parliaments' right to determine the law in this area. This unnecessary handover of authority from Britain to Strasbourg was a harbinger of the confused approach to follow, culminating in the new government's enactment of the Human Rights Act, which entered into force in 2000 and incorporated the Convention – but also the Strasbourg case law – directly into UK law.

The Human Rights Act has compounded the worst effects of judicial activism in Strasbourg, contrary to predictions before it entered into force. Writing in August 2000, *The Economist* assessed the prospective impact of the new Act, noting that: 'In theory, incorporation does not confer any new rights. It merely allows British citizens to use the domestic courts to enforce the [Convention], a code of rights which Britain ratified half a century ago. Even so, the Lord Chief Justice, Lord Woolf, has said it will "revolutionise our legal world".'

Critically, *The Economist*, followed by many others, predicted that the Strasbourg case law was likely to have minimum impact as a result of the Act: 'As British courts are not bound to follow the body of case law established by the European Court in Strasbourg, but free to interpret the convention to fit local circumstances, a distinctly British Bill of Rights is likely to evolve, which would be only loosely modelled on the European Convention.'

This turned out to be wishful thinking. Others foresaw the subtle, but significant, risks involved. Lord Hoffman (one of the most senior judges in the country), writing shortly before its entry into law, warned against use of the Human Rights Act to promote judicial activism and eschewed the role of 'Platonic guardian', whereby the courts intervene to create new human rights law, because 'in the United Kingdom ... people expect such issues to be decided by Parliament'. He contrasted Britain with the US, where the Supreme Court is expected to decide controversial political issues such as abortion, and judicial appointments are subject to democratic scrutiny of their political views. In this country, he argued, people expect such moral and political issues to be decided by Parliament – as demonstrated again more recently, in 2008, by the vote on the time limit for abortion. It reflects the apolitical British judicial tradition, and the importance placed on a democratically elected Parliament resolving the major ethical and political controversies of the day. Lord Hoffman expressed the hope that: '... the passing of the [Human Rights] Act will not in any way diminish the sense of responsibility which Parliament has always shown in passing legislation affecting human rights'.

In practice, the Human Rights Act has accentuated the proliferation of rights and diminished the corresponding responsibilities of Parliament. At a general level, the very enactment of the Human Rights Act has served as a trigger for the formulation of claims by lawyers and judicial reasoning by courts, using human rights arguments that would never have been dared before. Even where courts would have ruled the same way before the Human Rights Act, it is increasingly used to explain their decision-making. The particular provisions of the Act have exacerbated this tendency, giving far greater legal effect to the Strasbourg case law than is necessary or desirable, and encouraging the UK courts to treat Strasbourg as an international court of appeal – resulting in greater deference than was expected or required. The Act also expressly licenses UK courts to rewrite the laws passed by Parliament in order to achieve these aims.

Take the impact of Strasbourg's case law. The judges in the UK and Strasbourg are playing by a very different set of judicial rules. The Strasbourg Court has inflated the rights in the Convention through the expansion of its case law. The Strasbourg judges are not bound to stick to their previous rulings, because there is no doctrine of precedent in Strasbourg, and they have often – whether consciously or otherwise – prioritized the achievement of what they view to be a just outcome in the particular cases before them, over and above judicial rigour in the general legal principles they are laying down. Given the number of judges at the court with no prior judicial experience, judgments from Strasbourg are often inconsistent and the reasoning of the judges often departs from the text of the Convention itself. As a result, the Strasbourg case law has developed rapidly, inconsistently and unpredictably.

This approach is totally alien to UK judges, who, by constitutional convention, judicial training, custom and professional practice, view their role in stricter and more disciplined terms. The House of Lords has bemoaned the haphazard nature of the Strasbourg case law:

> The problem which the House has to face, quite squarely, is that the judgments and decisions of the European Court do not speak with one voice. If the differences were merely in emphasis, they could be shrugged off as being of no great significance. In reality, however, some of them appear much more serious and so present considerable difficulties for national courts which have to try to follow the jurisprudence of the European Court.

The courts in this country apply the doctrine of precedent, the hallmark of the common law system, which demands a much higher level of respect for and adherence to previous judicial decisions. So, UK courts are presented with a dilemma. Faced with a wide body of jurisprudence from Strasbourg that is inconsistent, unclear and unpredictable, should they apply it as precedent in the UK? The UK courts are inclined by instinct to show a high degree of respect for previous judicial rulings. But in doing so, they risk unnecessarily applying a wholly different – altogether more disciplined – judicial deference than that applied by the Strasbourg Court itself to its own case law.

Given the Strasbourg Court's overtly legislative approach, extending its jurisdiction and expanding rights beyond the Convention and any democratic control, the government should try to limit the impact of the Strasbourg case law in Britain. Yet, while the Convention does not require British courts to apply the Strasbourg case law, the Human Rights Act forces UK judges to take it into account when ruling.

In practice, the Human Rights Act has been interpreted to mean that 'it is ordinarily the clear duty of our domestic courts … to give practical recognition to the principles laid down by the Strasbourg court … That court is the highest judicial authority on the interpretation of those rights.' This is not required by the Convention itself and other European countries have chosen not to import the Strasbourg case law wholesale in this way.

UK judges have reacted to this in different ways. Some have complained about the legal uncertainty created by the confused relationship with Strasbourg, or expressed reservations about the importation of unpredictable case law and its increasing tendency to override decisions that ought to lie with a democratically elected Parliament. In 1999, Lord Hoffman urged the courts that it was 'no longer necessary to rely on Strasbourg' to guide their interpretation of the Convention. Other judges have relished the opportunity to use the Human Rights Act to pioneer the creation of new human rights under UK law. According to Arden LJ in the Court of Appeal: '… following the 1998 Act, courts have now to consider questions of social policy with which they were not previously concerned.

From this, in my judgment, it is possible to conclude that courts will hold that fewer matters are now non-justiciable on the grounds that they involve policy issues.'

Of the divergent judicial approaches, the most common is to try to match the Strasbourg case law in UK law. As the most senior judge in the country, Lord Bingham, summed up: 'The duty of national courts is to keep pace with the Strasbourg jurisprudence as it evolves over time: no more, but certainly no less.'

The consequence of this unnecessary deference to Strasbourg, foisted on the courts by the Human Rights Act, is to import new and extended rights into UK law, when it is not required by the UK's international obligations as a party to the Convention.

If the Human Rights Act promotes unnecessary deference to the Strasbourg case law, this is compounded by its approach to the Strasbourg Court itself. The Convention does not require the UK courts to treat the Strasbourg Court as a further court of appeal. In fact, the Strasbourg Court does not even regard itself as such. On the contrary, it accepts that the UK authorities bear the primary responsibility for securing respect for the Convention rights. As the newly appointed Director of Public Prosecutions (DPP) – the country's most senior prosecutor, and previously a top human rights lawyer – explains in one of the leading textbooks on the subject, far from being a further extension of the UK appellate courts, 'The role of the [Strasbourg] Court is different. It is primarily concerned with supervision and its role is therefore subsidiary to that of domestic authorities: it has no role unless the domestic system for protecting human rights breaks down. This is often referred to as the principle of subsidiarity.'

So the Strasbourg Court is subsidiary – not superior – to UK courts. It is a fundamental principle, derived from the structure of the Strasbourg Court and the design of the Convention, that states are permitted some 'margin of appreciation' in applying the human rights defined in the Convention. This means that the Strasbourg Court 'is prepared to extend some leeway to the domestic authorities because it considers that they are, generally, in a better position to make the assessments in question'. The Strasbourg Court treats this margin of appreciation as applying to all domestic authorities, including our national courts. Many countries take full advantage of the margin of appreciation, and the UK has historically followed that approach. However, in the UK the Human Rights Act does not give effect to the margin of appreciation, but rather encourages the House of Lords to treat the Strasbourg Court as the 'highest judicial authority'. As a result of the government's enthusiasm for embedding Britain in Europe, and importing wholesale the Strasbourg case law, the UK courts are required to be unnecessarily deferential – forfeiting valuable leeway that would help insulate the UK against creeping judicial legislation from Strasbourg.

Finally, the Human Rights Act does not merely encourage the importation of judicial legislation. It requires British judges to interpret UK law, '[s]o far as it is possible to do so', to give effect to legislation 'in a way which is compatible with the Convention rights'. Judges must strive to apply legislation in a way that adheres to the Convention and the Strasbourg case law, even if that amounts to bending the will of Parliament. As one former Parliamentary Counsel described the practical effect, the Human Rights Act 'instructs the courts to falsify the linguistic meaning of other Acts of Parliament, which hitherto has depended on legislative intention at the time of enactment' – giving domestic judges a broad licence to rewrite British law to give effect to new rights made in Strasbourg.

This risks a ratchet effect between Strasbourg and Britain, with the widest possible interpretations of the Convention given the full force of precedent under UK law. In some cases, this judicial creativity has rubbed off in the UK courts, with judges making full use of the Human Rights Act to expand human rights law. In others, the UK courts are often just trying to apply Strasbourg case law as precedent. The UK case law suggests that this can lead to an unnecessarily defensive approach. Rather than risk being 'overruled' by the Strasbourg Court, the UK courts are encouraged to play safe and apply the Strasbourg jurisprudence strictly. In those cases, their judgments give wide scope to new rights, in order to pre-empt interference from Strasbourg. Where this happens, it means that expansive interpretations of Convention rights by the Strasbourg Court are given their widest effect in the UK, in order to avoid risking the subsequent embarrassment of an adverse ruling from Strasbourg.

Britain is the only large common law country that is a party to the Convention, so its relationship with Strasbourg is unique. Whereas the constitutional courts in Germany and France use the Strasbourg case law as a reference point only, British courts are now required to follow it more respectfully. France, Italy and Germany have interpreted the definition of torture more narrowly than Britain in deportation and asylum cases. The French courts, in particular, have regularly ignored Strasbourg case law on non-discrimination, fair trial guarantees and the deportation of individuals who face a risk of torture – and continued to avoid full adherence to Strasbourg rulings, even after the Strasbourg Court ruled against French deportation procedures in 2007. The result of the UK approach has been unnecessarily to import a raft of new human rights – invented in Strasbourg – thereby circumventing the proper role of our democratically elected Parliament in making new law.

So what new human rights have been created by the courts? When the negotiators drafted the Convention after the Second World War, the countries of Europe agreed to guarantee a core list of rights to 'everyone within their jurisdiction'. They intended to include non-citizens and even non-residents living in their country. But it is clear from the negotiating record that they only agreed to give effect to the Convention within their own territories. Yet the Strasbourg Court – now closely followed by the UK courts – has effectively rewritten this part of the Convention to allow human rights claims against a state where it exercises 'authority and/or effective control' abroad. According to the Strasbourg Court: '[T]he Convention cannot be interpreted so as to allow a state party to perpetrate violations of the Convention on the territory of another state, which it could not perpetrate on its own territory.'

So far this potentially wide principle has been applied to a limited range of scenarios, including human rights claims against military forces detaining prisoners abroad. In Britain, it was applied by a (divided) House of Lords to allow Iraqi civilians to bring human rights cases against the UK government for the actions of British troops operating in Basra. In this case, legitimate concerns about protecting civilians in war were already comprehensively regulated under the Geneva Conventions and the other provisions of international humanitarian law – with war crimes committed by UK troops punishable under specific UK criminal law tailored to ensure proper accountability. The extension of human rights claims into this area duplicates the laws of war, creating additional uncertainty for soldiers operating on the ground in testing conditions. It is an extraordinary and expansive exercise in law-making by the courts, with far-reaching and unpredictable consequences. While the scope for such extra-territorial human rights claims has been defined in relatively narrow terms to date, there is little to prevent the Strasbourg Court expanding it still further, because it views the Convention as a 'living instrument'. Few (if any) other countries outside Europe have allowed themselves to be targeted for human rights claims in this way.

The first right protected, under the Convention, is the right to life. The intention, heavily influenced by the experience of Nazi atrocities, was to ban extra-judicial executions and similar killings, committed or sanctioned by the hand of the state. But the Strasbourg Court has gradually expanded this right well beyond the original Convention text. More than fifty years on, the state can now be blamed – and sued – even when it has had no direct responsibility for someone's death. The consequences of these legal and moral acrobatics have proved far-reaching, making the government increasingly liable for the criminal actions of others.

Take policing. There is now a human right to police protection from violence and threats in our society. In *Osman v UK*, a mentally ill teacher became obsessed with one of his pupils. He shot the boy, injuring him, and killed his father. The family claimed that the police had violated the father's right to life by failing to prevent his death. The claim of police negligence failed in the UK courts. The claim was then taken to the Strasbourg Court in 1998. The family's claim was rejected on the facts of the case, but the court nonetheless held that the right to life placed a general duty on the police to do everything 'that can be reasonably expected of them to avoid a real and immediate risk to life of which they have or ought to have knowledge'. It ruled that limits on negligence claims against the police under UK law were unduly restrictive and amounted to a violation of the claimants' right to access to court.

Since the Human Rights Act, attempts to stretch this principle still further in the UK have got as far as the Court of Appeal, which found a police force in breach of the right to life for failing to prevent the murder of a witness in a theft trial, having been made aware of threats against the victim. While that decision was overturned on the facts in the House of Lords, the Law Lords were divided on how to apply the Strasbourg case law to police liability for failing to prevent crimes.

These cases illustrate a worrying trend. It is one thing to regulate the police in the exercise of lethal force in the pursuit of criminal fugitives or to prevent a terrorist attack, in order to protect the innocent and maintain public confidence. The state should be held accountable for the mistakes it makes in such circumstances. Yet by creating judicially enforceable claims to preventative police protection against general violence – carried out by other people – human rights now place an extraordinary burden on officers. Police forces function with a limited budget, and discharge their duties under acute operational pressures. They are forced to balance a large number – and wide range – of threats to public safety, well beyond the facts of any individual claim considered by a court, looking back with the convenient benefit of hindsight.

This kind of expansion of rights has had unintended consequences. Since human rights apply, by definition, to everyone, the – much extended – right to life forces the police to offer the same level of police protection to innocent members of the public as to the worst criminals. Yet violent criminals and gangsters are more likely to attract revenge and retribution than other citizens, so they are more likely to need such protective services. Their choice of business dealings and lifestyle puts them at risk. Despite that choice, they can now claim police protection, not just as a matter of policy or moral imperative but as a judicially enforceable human right. As a result, an increasing amount of police time is being diverted to provide witness protection to gangsters giving evidence in mafia trials. This inevitably displaces the police resources allocated to protect law-abiding members of society. It has been estimated that the British police now spend £20 million a year protecting gangsters from each other – at a time of rising violent crime and an unprecedented terrorist threat – a direct consequence of the extension of the right to life. There are strong reasons for the police to try to prosecute organized crime, and this may well require offering witness protection to undesirable characters. That is a judgement call for the police and governments to make. But those who blight our society with drugs, human trafficking and murder – and choose the dangerous lifestyle that comes with it – should not be given a human rights guarantee that trumps the rest of society by forcing the police to prioritize protective services in their favour.

Far from helping the police to fight crime or prevent the violence which afflicts everyone in our society, such extensions of the right to life hamper public protection. They create a regulatory strait-jacket for officers, forcing them to look over their shoulder at the possibility of litigation and requiring them to allocate scarce resources to minimize and contest legal liability when that money would be better spent putting more officers on the street.

While the police should be held accountable, there exists a range of mechanisms better placed to achieve oversight and accountability, without resort to human rights litigation. Before the Strasburg ruling in 1998, the police could be sued for negligence in certain strictly defined circumstances, prosecuted under criminal law and were subject to a general public duty to enforce the law. Since 2004, the Independent Police Complaints Commission has provided a further tier of accountability, reviewing complaints against the police. It is far from clear why the police need to be exposed to additional human rights claims, particularly those that hold them liable for crimes committed by other people.

The risks of subjecting the police to such claims were highlighted by the House of Lords in 1988, in the wake of a claim by the family of the last victim of Peter Sutcliffe, the notorious 'Yorkshire Ripper'. The claim was brought on behalf of Jacqueline Hill, a twenty-year-old student, against West Yorkshire Police. The police force was accused of negligently conducting the investigation, failing to collate information properly and ignoring leads that would have led to the apprehension of Sutcliffe before he killed Ms Hill. The House of

Lords accepted that the police had committed serious failings. It took the view that officers would have caught Sutcliffe, before he killed Ms Hill, if they had exercised a reasonable level of care and skill. But the judges still rejected the claim, on the basis that liability would not improve the police's capacity to fight crime, and warned that 'liability may lead to the exercise of a function being carried on in a detrimentally defensive frame of mind'. The court drew attention to the existing procedures for holding the police to account, warned against any further judicial second-guessing of the conduct of police investigations and referred to the diversion of precious police resources that would inevitably follow any extension of liability.

These notes of caution were brushed aside by the Strasbourg Court. Responding to the *Osman* case in the UK – before the Human Rights Act entered into force – Lord Hoffman characterized the ruling as 'essentially ... about the obligations of the welfare state', warning, 'I am bound to say that this decision fills me with apprehension', because it involved the Strasbourg Court 'challenging the autonomy of the courts and indeed the Parliament of the United Kingdom to deal with what are essentially social welfare questions involving budgetary limits and efficient public administration'. He went on to say that this kind of case 'serves to reinforce the doubts I have had for a long time about the suitability, at least for this country, of having questions of human rights determined by an international tribunal made up of judges from many countries', adding:

> I accept that there is an irreducible minimum of human rights which must be universally true. But most of the jurisprudence which comes out of Strasbourg is not about the irreducible minimum ... It is often said that the tendency of every court is to increase its jurisdiction and the Strasbourg court is no exception. So far as the

margin of appreciation accommodates national choices, the jurisdiction of the European court is unnecessary; so far as it does not,
it is undesirable.

He concluded:

> … the jurisprudence of the Strasbourg court does create a dilemma
> because it seems to me to have passed far beyond its original modest
> ambitions and is seeking to impose a Voltairean uniformity of values
> upon all member States. This I hope we shall resist.

In practice, the courts in this country have not resisted the Strasbourg case law, but sought to match it – and sometimes extend it –
under UK law. Relying on the *Osman* ruling, the Strasbourg Court
– followed by UK judges acting under the Human Rights Act – has
deployed the right to life to sidestep the carefully calibrated rules
on police liability, overruling the UK law of negligence. By allowing
these claims against the police to succeed on human rights grounds,
the courts have prevented Britain's democratically elected law-
makers from determining the proper balance in this delicate – and
inherently political – area of public policy.

A broad interpretation of the right to life has been applied in other
contexts. In another ground-breaking case, the UK courts used
the Human Rights Act to stretch the right to life to include claims
against the government for the deaths of soldiers in combat,
including where they have been killed by enemy troops or die
from sickness, and their equipment is defective or medical care is
inadequate. The claim was brought by the mother of a soldier
deployed in Iraq who died of hyperthermia in the heat of Basra in
2003.

The government is expected to equip properly the troops it

sends abroad to fight, under what is known as the military covenant. It should be held accountable if it puts soldiers at unnecessary risk, under the procedure for coroners' inquests and, if necessary, judicial enquiry. The government also has a moral obligation to ensure due care and provision for the families of those who die fighting for their country. Equally, people sign up to join the armed services, conscious of – and often attracted by – the risks inherent in military service. For its part, the government is faced with a steady stream of difficult decisions, from the choice of equipment and hardware to invest in and the formulation of military strategy, through to operational decisions taken during the heat of combat. Extended human rights duties offer a narrow lens through which to assess a wide range of competing considerations.

The novel expansion of the right to life inevitably involves the courts in retrospectively second-guessing the decisions of military commanders and the Ministry of Defence. In the case of the soldier who died from hyperthermia, the British judge strived to extend the scope of the right to life – ignoring the negotiating history of the Convention, brushing aside the absence of any previous legal authority for the claim and supporting his decision with passing references to the Crimean War and the Charge of the Light Brigade. The full extent of the ruling was left unclear, paving the way for further litigation in this area, with the risk that British forces may in the future have to fight with one eye on the risk of legal liability across a whole new range of decisions taken under extreme pressure. Equally, finely balanced investment and procurement decisions taken by the Ministry of Defence – which weigh up a wide range of competing priorities – can now lead to human rights claims. Subjecting the armed forces to such claims is unlikely to improve the safety of British troops in battle. On the contrary, the countervailing risk is that the UK courts' encouragement of human rights claims – by both soldiers and foreign nationals – will distract from the effective conduct of military operations, which may put troops at greater risk.

It is far from clear where the full implications of this logic will end. What happens, for example, if British troops or supplies are stretched thin under the pressure of military attack? Throughout its history, Britain has been attacked from abroad and, occasionally, caught by surprise. Take the Falklands War. The UK was not fully prepared to defend the islands from surprise Argentine attack. British armed forces responded as best they could, given the conditions and timeframe in which they were compelled to operate. Yet under expanded human rights rulings, if ill-prepared troops die in battle the courts may be required to decide whether the military commanders and civil servants acted reasonably in sending them to fight under such challenging circumstances in the first place. Judges are not well placed to make, nor can they be held accountable for, such finely balanced military, political – and ultimately moral – assessments. If the Argentine attack occurred today, the courts would be the wrong place to decide whether or not the British government should try to save the Falkland islanders, bearing in mind the unavoidably high risk of British casualties. Remarkably, the recent extension of human rights has made this a real possibility in the future.

There is ample scope for additional extensions of the right to life, imposing yet more positive duties on the state to protect its citizens from harm. The Strasbourg Court has already held that the right to life can be used to sue the state for failing to prevent toxic factory emissions, the ineffective regulation of waste disposal sites and even the failure to make generally available a certain standard of healthcare. Many of these rulings have been confined to specific situations, but they inevitably pave the way for further judicial innovations. The public expect the government to consider, and try to cater for, all of these different risks. Yet in each area decisions on budgeting and priorities require a delicate balance to be struck by civil servants, law-makers and the elected government of the day, ultimately held accountable at the ballot box. Priorities change over time. Decisions are taken under pressure and the government has to allocate finite resources to an insatiable range of demands for public services. The courts are not well placed to second-guess these inherently financial and political assessments. They hear only a limited number of cases, based on the ability of an individual claimant to fund litigation or get the backing of *pro bono* representation from a human rights barrister or NGO. Human rights campaign groups have a valuable role to play in highlighting government failures and injustices, and making the case for reform. However, they also represent a limited number of narrowly defined claims, and often select 'test cases' with the specific objective of testing – i.e. seeking to extend – the scope of human rights law in contentious areas. Successful claims in sensitive areas, particularly those that impose positive obligations on the state, involve the courts in trumping complex and diverse assessments of the public interest. In such cases, upgrading a particular claim or interest to the status of a 'fundamental' human right – with trump card status over the other interests, individuals and groups in our society – risks displacing and distorting a balanced, overarching assessment of the wider public interest.

Judicial innovation has not been limited to the right to life. The ban on torture – and the related prohibition on inhuman or degrading treatment or punishment – has rapidly expanded well beyond the horrors of the Nazi camps that inspired the drafters of the Convention. The original intention was to prevent the state from torturing, experimenting on or otherwise persecuting its citizens, particularly vulnerable minorities, but the Strasbourg Court has effectively rewritten the relevant article of the treaty.

The definition of torture and inhuman treatment is now so broad that it can include 'grossly defamatory remarks and extreme and continuous police surveillance'. It has also been exponentially expanded to allow human rights claims for accommodation and healthcare in circumstances where, if the state did not provide it, the claimant would be homeless and without any other means of support.

In 2005, the House of Lords applied this expanded definition, under the Human Rights Act, to overrule legislation denying social services support to asylum seekers who fail to submit their claim 'as soon as is reasonably practicable'. The denial of state support was ruled a violation of the ban on torture and inhuman treatment, where 'a late applicant with no means and no alternative sources of support, unable to support himself, is ... denied shelter, food or the most basic necessities of life'. In many cases, the condition of those denied such state support would be extremely harsh. As a matter of compassion, it may be that the state should extend social services in these cases. But the reality is that there are many diverse individual and social demands on the state, and only finite resources available. What is extraordinary in these cases is that a new 'human right' to accommodation and other support from social services has been created out of the elastic language of the ban on torture, which was designed to deal with an entirely different type of state-inflicted suffering. Equally, the courts – in Strasbourg and at home – have trumped legislation enacted by our directly elected representatives, who have a democratic mandate to weigh up these and all the other competing claims to a sympathetic response from the state.

Similar logic has given rise to rights to other social benefits provided by the state. A drug trafficker with AIDS wielded this novel right to block his deportation and force the government to let him remain in the UK in order to receive medical treatment on the NHS. The Strasbourg Court was moved by the plight of the individual claimant before it, but oblivious to and poorly placed to weigh up the multitude of other compelling demands on NHS resources. The UK courts have struggled with the uncertainty and potentially far-reaching implications of this ruling and the opaque reasoning from Strasbourg, which they are required to follow as a result of the Human Rights Act.

In another remarkable case in 2006, the British government settled claims out of court from drug-addicted prisoners, estimated to cost the public purse over a million pounds. The prisoners claimed that their human right to methadone should trump the Prison Service's professional judgement on the appropriate approach to drug rehabilitation. The government capitulated, having apparently been advised that it would lose the claims if they went to court.

As the Strasbourg Court has expanded the definition of torture, the range of the duties on the state to prevent it has mounted. Judges have invented swathes of new responsibilities for the state to discharge, trumping its policy assessment of the public interest. It is now well established under human rights law that not only must the state prevent and punish torture by its agents and officials, but it must also act to prevent torture – and the other extended categories of mistreatment – by anyone else. For example, claims citing the prohibition of torture and inhuman treatment have been deployed to force the British government to ban parents from smacking their children, despite domestic laws passed by Parliament – and enforced by the UK authorities – regulating the use of 'reasonable chastisement' in the home.

The ban on torture and inhuman treatment has also enabled successful human rights claims to be brought against the government for not acting quickly enough to remove children from abusive parents and into protective custody, overruling the balance struck by existing rules under the law of negligence. This intrusive ruling paved the way for judges to second-guess the difficult judgement calls made by social services, who must weigh up the countervailing risks of prematurely or unnecessarily removing children from their parents. On the one hand, the British state's record as a substitute for parental care – in terms of educational attainment, subsequent involvement in criminal activity and a range of other indicators – suggests that removing children from their natural parents should be a last resort. On the other hand, where children are removed into care, the parents can also now sue social services under expanded interpretations of the right to family life. This legal minefield leaves local authorities to carry out an already difficult job with looming threats of litigation on all sides. Nor is the government's extended responsibility limited to family custody arrangements in the UK. It can now also be sued on human rights grounds, when families from abroad are living in the UK, for failing to take 'adequate and effective' measures to enforce custodial arrangements set in their home countries.

If the extended ban on torture and inhuman treatment has left social services to walk a legal tightrope, it has also severely narrowed the scope of the government's discretion in enforcing immigration controls, even though this was not what the Convention was originally intended for. The Strasbourg Court has legislated to extend the ban on torture and inhuman treatment, making it much more difficult for governments to deport people who pose a threat to national security or public safety. This goes well beyond the list of rights set out in either the United Nations Refugee Convention or the United Nations Convention against Torture, both of which were specifically designed to address the difficult and delicate issue of deporting undesirable characters who might be mistreated if returned home.

In *Chahal v UK* (1996), the government sought to deport Mr Chahal, a Sikh separatist, to India on the basis of his conduct in the

UK which gave rise to a suspicion of involvement in terrorism and other criminal conduct. Mr Chahal had previously been arrested, but not charged, with conspiracy to assassinate the Indian Prime Minister on a visit to Britain. The Strasbourg Court barred Mr Chahal's deportation, concluding he would face a real risk of torture at the hands of rogue elements in the Punjab police.

Yet deportation is not just blocked when there is a specific risk of torture or inhuman treatment by the state or its officials. In another Strasbourg case, a convicted armed robber managed to prevent his deportation to Somalia because of the risk that he would be caught up in the civil war raging there, rather than any fear of persecution by the government. In Britain, the Home Office has stretched asylum rules to reflect the widest interpretations offered by the Strasbourg Court, and now bars deportation even where there is a general risk of 'indiscriminate violence' arising from a civil war, rather than any specific threat of persecution from the state or other non-state groups. In one recent UK case a woman was able to block her return to Uganda because the risk that she would not be able to find decent housing or employment rendered her vulnerable to being drawn into a life of prostitution.

As already considered above, the absence of adequate medical care abroad – as opposed to any specific risk – has also been used to block deportation on human rights grounds. These types of cases have been brought citing the ban on torture and inhuman treatment, but this has become a fig leaf for broader claims to medical treatment. In 2008, the Strasbourg Court confirmed that the scope of the bar on deportation extends to '... the expulsion of any person afflicted with any serious, naturally occurring physical or mental illness which may cause suffering, pain and reduced life expectancy and require specialised medical treatment which may not be so readily available in the applicant's country of origin or which may be available only at substantial cost'.

In this way the Strasbourg Court has extended the ban on torture to create rights to healthcare, albeit in exceptional circumstances. As Lord Nicholls, a senior British judge, commented in a recent deportation case: 'I express the obligation in terms of provision of medical care because that is what cases of this type are all about.'

The potential scope of such new medical rights, created by the Strasbourg Court, has created confusion and uncertainty for the UK courts, which have on occasion tried to contain the implications but are required to follow its lead under the Human Rights Act. As Lord Hope has complained: 'It may be said that the [Strasbourg] court has not really faced up to the consequences of the developments in medical techniques ...'

As a result of advances in AIDS treatments, Lord Hope observed, deportation will often mean disconnecting patients from life-saving treatment. As tragic as that may be, allowing such claims to succeed 'would risk drawing into the United Kingdom large numbers of people already suffering from HIV in the hope that they too could remain here indefinitely so that they could take the benefit of the medical resources that are available in this country'. That, he noted, 'would result in a very great and no doubt unquantifiable commitment of resources'.

These judicial innovations have had four consequences. First, a whole range of comparatively minor mistreatment is now covered by the wide ban on torture and inhuman treatment, well beyond the original intention of the Convention. In addition, the fundamental right of the individual not to be subjected to torture by the state has been stretched – beyond recognition – to create new burdens on government to prevent a range of social ills. Second, when it comes to deportation decisions, the government is not even allowed to consider the threat posed by a claimant to UK public safety, where there is a possibility that he might suffer mistreatment if returned home. The government is prevented from balancing the rights of the claimant with the right to safety of the rest of the public. That rule is stricter than the requirements of the UN Refugee Convention, which expressly allow governments to weigh both the rights of the individual and the public interest in deporting suspected criminals or terrorist suspects. Third, the burden of proof has been stacked against the government. A claimant seeking to avoid deportation merely has to establish a 'real risk' of mistreatment – by anyone, not just his own government – to avoid being removed. He does not have to prove that he would be tortured or mistreated if deported home, nor even demonstrate that it is probable. Nor does it matter whether the risk comes from the state security services, a paramilitary group or even just the general risk of violence that everyone is exposed to in a country facing civil war. This is a lower burden of proof than the UN Convention against Torture and places immense responsibility on the government to prove a negative – that the claimant will not be mistreated on return – in order to prevent the human rights claim from trumping a deportation order. Finally, these developments cannot be explained solely by reference to the Convention, because Britain has interpreted the restrictions on deportation more widely than other parties, most notably France. The UK government has given this inflated list of novel rights a wider scope than other countries, by treating the case law of the Strasbourg Court as binding precedent.

The expansion of new rights has gone too far, and looks set to continue still further in the years ahead. Many countries outside Europe – for example, Canada – remain committed to the absolute prohibition on torture under international law, without placing such excessive and disproportionate restrictions on the right of a government to deport those who threaten public safety. However, it is perhaps even more concerning that judges in Strasbourg and the UK have deliberately expanded the law in such a delicate, controversial and political area, ignoring the clear intentions of those who drafted the Convention and the democratic will of Parliament. The result has been to make it easier for claimants to block deportation on extended human rights grounds, irrespective of their behaviour or the future risk to those living in the UK. Britain has a proud tradition of offering safe haven to those persecuted abroad. It receives the third highest number of applications for asylum in the world. But the government also has a right – and a duty – to protect its citizens, which is increasingly being trumped on human rights grounds.

Beyond the ban on torture a steady stream of new human rights has been created by the courts, reducing the government's discretion over the release and recall of serious criminals sentenced to prison. In April 2008, the Court of Appeal delivered a further unprecedented judgment, ending the forty-year-old power of the Justice Secretary to veto the release of dangerous – convicted – criminals on the grounds of public safety. The court extended the right to liberty of a vicious armed robber, despite the government's objections on grounds of public protection.

Prisoners have benefited more than most from the numerous new categories of human rights, many foisted on Britain contrary to the wishes of Parliament. Unlikely libertarians, pioneering prisoners have successfully claimed novel rights to vote, access to fertility treatment (while still in prison) and – in one of the most bizarre policies articulated by any government department – the right to keep twigs, to wave as wands, in order to exercise the right to practise paganism in their prison cells.

Outside the prison gates, the right to private and family life has provided fertile ground for the judicial imagination. In the UK courts, human rights claims have been used to support successful claims for previously unavailable drugs. At the Strasbourg Court, the judges interpreted the right to a private life to include the possibility of claims to medical treatment for mental health problems and, in another case, blocked the deportation of a gang rapist because it would interfere with his family life.

Somewhat counter-intuitively, extensions to the right to family life have become so contorted that they now also give rise to a right to divorce. In a further string of cases dealing with transsexuals, the right to a private life has generated a right to hormone treatment, from public funds, to facilitate sex changes. This new right comes with a range of positive duties on government to recognize sex changes – including a duty on social services to alter past personal records in order to hide the fact that such treatment has taken place. Legal recognition of transsexuals is only fair in a tolerant society, but by labelling this kind of claim a human right it becomes more highly valued than other equally – or even more – compelling claims. Compare the paratrooper who won £250,000 from the Ministry of Defence for injured feelings, when he (later she) was required to continue wearing a male army uniform after a sex change, with the Afghanistan veteran who had to haggle for the same level of compensation after a Taliban landmine blew off his legs and left him with brain damage. The former discrimination claim was supported by new human rights rulings. The latter claim had no such trump card status. To many, their legal equivalence reflects a moral compass in our society that has become warped; and a human rights culture, grown out of control, which produces arbitrary and unfair results.

Admittedly, the contrast does not compare like for like. The discrimination claim was made against the government for its own actions, whereas the injured soldier's claim was not based on any wrongdoing by the government. He was just one of the many brave servicemen and women injured in battle for whom the Ministry of Defence makes provision. Nevertheless, the outcomes in these two cases, compared as competing claims on the finite resources of the Ministry of Defence, suggest a distorted order of priorities. One answer is to pay the disabled veteran soldier more, or hand out even more human rights – to soldiers injured in battle – to balance the moral equation. But that would mean identifying cuts in the already stretched defence budget – or from the resources devoted to health-care, schools, policing or housing – to pay for the extra rights. Another option is to increase taxation to bridge the moral discrep-ancies generated by the haphazard proliferation of novel rights. But even then, at some point we have to draw a line. However we choose to answer these difficult and delicate questions, such subjective assessments of the public interest should not be made surrepti-tiously, by unaccountable judges, but openly, after public debate, by elected and accountable law-makers.

Similarly, under the Human Rights Act, the UK courts have been forced to apply the interpretation of the Strasbourg Court as to the proper balance between the competing rights to privacy and free-dom of expression. In 2008 Max Mosley, the head of Formula One racing, successfully sued the *News of the World* under the extended right to privacy for publishing sensational details about his sex life. The UK courts, following the Strasbourg case law, held that there was no public interest that could justify the disclosures. Since dif-ferent countries and cultures will, quite reasonably, take different views on the respective weight that should be accorded to the rights to privacy and freedom of expression, this is the kind of political balancing that should be determined by elected law-makers at home rather than by unaccountable judges abroad. While the British tradition of liberty prizes free speech highly, the Strasbourg Court has a track record of placing relatively less weight on it compared to other rights. In one German case, the Strasbourg judges ruled that freedom of thought, conscience and religion actually required the censorship, rather than protection, of a theatre's right to show an offensive play, highly critical of Christianity, based on the state's duty to prevent inhibitions against those practising religious beliefs.

There is boundless further scope for new rights – which need not even be limited to claims on behalf of individuals, as civil liberties were traditionally designed for. Human rights now compel affirmative action by the state to protect ethnic minorities and other groups – including, for example, 'a positive obligation … to facilitate the gypsy way of life'. The UK courts have accepted the possibility of successful claims to a human right to drain repairs under the Human Rights Act. Protection from pollution, far from being a social and, indeed, international problem, can now also be enforced by individuals as a human right, under an expanded interpretation of the right to private life, even if an individual claimant's health is not seriously affected. In one UK case, this gave rise to a right to compel the government to prevent or limit noise from an airport – effectively creating a right to regulation.

The innovations of the Strasbourg Court also form part of the government's drive towards European integration. They have been compounded by developments in the EU, under the Social Chapter, a stream of Directives and Regulations on specific matters – particularly within the field of Justice and Home Affairs – and most recently the new Lisbon Treaty, designed to provide an overarching EU constitutional framework. Some of the new EU law restrictions on deportation now surpass even the strict tests laid down in the *Chahal* judgment. In one controversial UK case, an EU Directive blocked the Home Office's attempt to deport Learco Chindamo, an Italian national jailed for murdering a school headmaster, Chindamo's right to family life, as articulated in the Directive, trumping the high level of risk and ongoing threat he posed to the British public. If the Lisbon Treaty enters into force, it risks enmeshing the UK in a further, additional body of EU human rights law subject to the jurisdiction of the European Court of Justice in Luxembourg.

These are just a selection of the cases of human rights being upheld by the courts in the UK and Strasbourg. In turn, those cases decided in court are only a fraction of the overall number of human rights claims. By creating wide new categories of claims, the proliferation of rights has made the law much less predictable, with further knock-on effects resulting from the confusion that this has created. There is growing evidence that the fear of falling foul of expanded human rights interpretations is leading to a large number of human rights cases being settled out of court. In 2006, the Prison Service settled a series of claims by drug-addicted prisoners claiming a right to methadone. This is not an isolated example. Between 2002 and 2007, the police were subject to more than 31,000 claims costing £44 million – three-quarters of which were settled out of court. Many of the claims, mainly for police misconduct, included a Human Rights Act element. Of course, some of the claims settled will be deserving cases from which the police, prison service and other authorities must learn. However, it also suggests a growing fear of adverse court rulings, on the part of government officials and other civil servants, and increasing uncertainty about the current state of human rights law.

Settling out of court has two downsides, which perpetuate the problems created by the proliferation of rights. First, it prevents the courts clarifying the law, where there is confusion. Second, it encourages others to sue, contributing to increasing litigation in the UK and the growth of a compensation culture. It is difficult to gauge the full extent of the problem, because the government does not know how many human rights cases have been brought against it or how many have been settled out of court. Government departments have refused to answer parliamentary questions requesting information on the amount of taxpayers' money used to settle human rights claims out of court, claiming, with more than a hint of irony, that providing such information could only be done at disproportionate cost.

In numerous other cases, the uncertainty created by the expansive and unpredictable application of human rights has led to confusion. Government officials, local authorities and other public servants have struggled to keep up with the rapidly changing law. As a result, they are increasingly cautious in the discharge of their duties, as they struggle to take into account the never-ending list of rights they have to consider and prioritize in order to ward off the risk of legal challenge. Police have withheld the identity of suspected killers on the run, and a paedophile was allowed to use the same gym facilities as schoolchildren, in both cases for fear of violating their right to a private life. The police and local council stated that the decisions were at least partly based on human rights considerations, despite the countervailing risk to the public, leading the *Sun* to blast with indignation 'What about OUR rights?'

In response to widespread media reporting of such abusive reliance on human rights by unsavoury characters, in 2006 the Lord Chancellor published a government review of the implementation of the Human Rights Act. In a section on 'myths and misperceptions', the report points out that many of the absurd cases reported in the media are not cases where the Human Rights Act has legally conferred any rights at all. A number of cases have been seized upon by the press. In one notorious example, the police publicly relied on human rights grounds to explain their decision to pass up Kentucky Fried Chicken to a fugitive thief, Barry Chambers, holding out on top of a roof. Gloucestershire police were widely reported as defending the move on human rights grounds, a police spokesperson quoted as saying, 'although he's a nuisance, we still have to look after his wellbeing and human rights'. This led to wide-spread derision in the media, with the *Daily Mail* asking, 'Why have our police lost all common sense?' The Lord Chancellor's review explains that this case and many others reported in the media are not genuine examples of human rights being upheld by the courts. That is certainly true, but it also misses the point. They may not be examples of the courts upholding human rights, but they are examples of situations in which the government or officials have explained their actions by reference to the human rights obligations. If officials got it wrong, it only serves to demonstrate the pervasive confusion – and lack of legal certainty – sowed by the Human Rights Act and the wider approach to the ever expanding list of new rights. The Lord Chancellor complained about a lack of common sense in the interpretation of human rights, and pledged to redouble the training of police and other public servants so that they better appreciate the real scope of human rights. But ministers steadfastly refused to accept that the proliferation of rights, and the ensuing confusion, goes some way to explaining the problems of interpretation and misunderstandings by those charged to deliver public services on the front line.

While the Human Rights Act may have made matters worse, it is merely the most obvious product of a wider strategic approach – which actively promotes the proliferation of rights as part of the government's social policy, ignoring the confusion created in public services, periodic bouts of media outrage sparked by absurd claims to rights and wider expressions of public concern. Far from limiting the negative impact of the Human Rights Act, the government is widening its scope even further.

In 2008 a report commissioned by the Ministry of Justice recommended expanding human rights as a 'customer care' tool for delivering public services. This involves 'mainstreaming' human rights as the focus of public services, in order to 'respect the spirit – the underlying principles and core values – of the Human Rights Act', as well as the already inflated requirements of human rights laid down by the courts.

In practice, the government is driving ahead with a policy to expand human rights to the delivery of various public services. Despite the disruptive impact the proliferation of rights has had on police forces, in July 2008 the Home Secretary announced a Green Paper that pledged to roll out 'nationally agreed rights' to policing. In a futile attempt to improve police responsiveness through increased Whitehall control, the Green Paper commits the police to a range of minimum standards, including rights of individual members of the public to have telephone calls and emails answered within twenty-four hours, further binding the hands of officers on the front line in a straitjacket of central government targets, and fettering the exercise of their professional discretion in judging policing priorities.

The government is adopting a similar approach to health policy, with the Department of Health publishing a draft NHS Constitution in June 2008, setting out a wide range of 'patient rights', including access to NHS treatments, maximum waiting times and the right to NHS drugs and vaccines. Confusingly, the Constitution claims that any new rights will not have legal effect, thereby avoiding any 'spur to litigation', but goes on to say that '[t]he courts may of course still take account of the Constitution in some instances' – a sure-fire recipe for legal uncertainty, confusion amongst medical practitioners and distorted public expectations. This exercise in legal and policy ambiguity was savaged by Danny Finkelstein of *The Times* who accused the government of ducking the hard financial and political choices of deciding which NHS treatments and drugs are affordable, as of right, to everyone in Britain:

A technological revolution in medical services is under way. It means that we are going to reach the point, are already reaching the point, when the range of services we could, in theory, obtain is so great that it tests our willingness to pay for it all for everyone. We are going to have to decide where the limits of social provision lie.

Finkelstein points out that the pretence of cloaking healthcare in the language of human rights – offering everything to everyone – dodges the tough decisions that any government, of whatever political persuasion, must make: 'On its first page [the NHS Constitution] boldly, but extraordinarily, announces that the NHS "has a wider social duty to promote equality through its services". It cannot therefore acknowledge a reality that makes complete equality impossible. Yet refusing to acknowledge a reality does not make it go away.'

He concludes that what we really need is a list of 'all the things you don't have a right to and the NHS refuses to promise you'. This basic dilemma, ducked by the government, has been thrown into sharp relief by recent cases of drugs being refused on the NHS. In 2008, a number of drugs to treat advanced kidney cancer were refused NHS funding, leading twenty-six cancer specialists to write a public letter of complaint about the way the government sanctions cancer drugs. In response, the heads of the National Institute of Health and Clinical Excellence, the body that decides on NHS funding for treatments, said: 'There is a finite pot of money for the NHS, which is determined annually by parliament. If one group of patients is provided with cost-ineffective care, other groups – lacking powerful lobbyists – will be denied cost-effective care for miserable conditions like schizophrenia, Crohn's disease or cystic fibrosis.'

The inherently difficult choices involved in 'drug rationing' on the NHS are not made easier by glib statements by the government about equality in healthcare. They are tough decisions, with strong moral, social and political dimensions, for which, ultimately, elected politicians need to be held democratically accountable. It is one thing to provide the NHS with a governing document, setting out statutory responsibilities and giving patients a consultative voice through local and national bodies. But it is another thing to deploy the language of human rights as an answer to tough questions about priorities in healthcare. If anything, dressing up those choices as constitutionally guaranteed rights – and passing them off for the courts to decide – prevents policy-makers from responding to constant changes in technology and patient demand, which must be weighed against the public resources available under the economic conditions prevailing.

6

The Risks of Rights

*'Nor is there liberty if the power of judging is not
separate from legislative power ... If it were joined to
legislative power, the power over the life and liberty of
the citizens would be arbitrary, for the judge would be
legislator.'*

MONTESQUIEU

The rising rights culture has changed the climate in Britain, and
brought with it a range of new risks – for our society and democracy – many of which derive from the wholesale metamorphosis in
the basic idea of rights. Locke, Mill and Berlin represented a liberal
tradition that had focused on the idea that, whatever else his lot
in life, the individual should be left free, unmolested by the state,
within certain legally defined bounds. They stood for a pluralistic
society that gave voice to a diverse range of views, and left its citizens
to decide their own affairs and lead their own idea of the good life.
This simple idea informed heroic struggles for freedom in the
twentieth century. The idea of fundamental rights has travelled
a long way since then. It is difficult to characterize many of the
new rights as 'fundamental', compared to the epic campaigns for

freedom led by Andrei Sakharov, Martin Luther King and Nelson Mandela. Nor do they fit the traditional mould of rights – at least in the sense of the struggle for civil and political liberties pioneered in this country by the likes of William Wilberforce and Emmeline Pankhurst.

In Britain today, human rights are not restricted to protecting the individual from abuse by the state, or even other individuals. Nor are they limited to restraining the state, but increasingly place cumbersome and costly new obligations on it. Where rights once stood as protectors, they have now become providers. Human rights claims and campaigns are just as likely to press the government for some new category of social support as seek to limit the reach of its power.

From that point, having moved beyond the limited category of minimum core rights comprised of fundamental liberties, it is in theory possible to keep extending the list of rights almost indefinitely. Housing, education, employment, policing, travel, healthcare and a multitude of other areas provide fertile ground for the future development of human rights law. In effect, any human interest, need, desire, claim or want can be formulated as a human right.

Yet there is a law of diminishing returns. If rights exercise trump card status, in that other collective interests – whether economic, social or security – cannot override them, then their value is relative to those interests. But not every claim can have trump card status, without reducing all claims back to the ordinary level. Inflation risks debasing the very currency of rights, including our most fundamental liberties.

The promotion of a wider human rights agenda reflects the Marxist critique of liberal democracy, which views liberty and democracy as empty shells that do nothing to guarantee that actual equal treatment of all members of society. Commentators on the left, like Polly Toynbee of the *Guardian*, criticize the 'middle-class' obsession with civil liberties, claiming that they ignore far more pressing social injustices. Human rights academics, like Professor Francesca Klug, seek to meet this critique by promoting interpretations of the Human Rights Act that address social inequality – in a manner which 'extends far beyond equal treatment' and reflects a 'communitarian approach to human rights', in order to 'promote social change'. And lawyers, like David Pannick QC, regard such an approach to rights – through the Human Rights Act, the Convention and the Strasbourg Court – as umbilically linked to British membership of the EU.

Hidden beneath technical legal arguments are fundamental questions about the direction in which Britain is heading. Those promoting new economic, social and other rights by anchoring Britain to Europe are trying to edge Britain towards a vision of social – even socialist – democracy, whereas Britain has historically been a liberal democracy.

Socialists and social democrats take a fundamentally different approach to the liberal conception of rights. For the liberal, individual liberty and choice must be respected, with the quid pro quo that the same individual has – and must take – personal responsibility for his actions. Respect for individual choice includes the freedom to take risks and make mistakes. In fact, a healthy society requires the creative risk-taking that liberty preserves. In contrast, socialists and social democrats to varying degrees are more likely to view the individual – his freedom, opportunity and all the risks that go with it – as products of society, conditioned by background and limited by personal circumstances. Anti-social actions are more likely to be excused, as a reflection of social conditioning or a deprived background. The state is more likely to be viewed, not as a necessary evil, but rather as a positive force for correcting social inequality.

In this way, the proliferation of novel rights is bound up in a much deeper shift in political fault lines in Britain since 1997. The shift in emphasis, from protecting individual liberty to providing public services, is part of that change. But there are other related symptoms. The growing compensation culture, and the exponential expansion of health and safety law to novel – often trivial – scenarios, reflects this broader change in approach to the burden of risk and responsibility in society – away from the individual, and onto the state. Equally as the responsibility of, and dependence on, the state has increased, so too personal responsibility and an ethos of civic duty have been undermined.

Paradoxically for those on the left, the extension of human rights and other legal protections to address social problems – for the most disadvantaged, deprived and vulnerable – has led to a distorted focus on the individual, at the expense of the rest of society. Bit by bit, the state has intervened in a vain effort to choreograph and control the balance of risk and responsibility in our society, wrapping the individual up in legislative cotton wool, relieving him of personal responsibility for his own actions and warping a common sense balance of risk in our daily lives.

However, at least the distorted approach to health and safety has readily identifiable – and democratically accountable – sources, in health and safety legislation, the Health and Safety Executive, the common law rules on negligence and the skewed interpretation of officials. In marked contrast, the judicial expansion of human rights has dislocated law-making authority from Parliament, the only legislative authority directly accountable to the British electorate.

The rights contagion stems from a basic distortion of language. While human rights were originally based on the idea of liberty or freedom, to describe claims to social services, healthcare or policing as liberties is artificial. Nor can the availability of a specific drug on the NHS or housing support be meaningfully characterized as freedom. Because liberty is different from our other needs and wants in life, it does not help to confuse them.

But why can't we have our cake and eat it? Even if liberty is to be distinguished from other economic and social interests, why can't human rights envelop both? The practical answer is that a society can guarantee liberty, but it can only aspire towards the full realization of every member's economic and social interests through state support and the provision of public services.

Temporary security emergencies aside, there is no reason – moral, financial or legal – not to guarantee, in law and to everyone in Britain, certain core, fundamental, civil and political liberties. In contrast, in a relatively free and prosperous society like Britain, most people have the opportunity to provide most of their economic and social needs for themselves – including earning a living, buying or renting a home and raising a family. Equally, financial realities – especially during an economic downturn – mean that the state cannot fully make up the difference, by guaranteeing full employment, public healthcare and universal schooling at the highest private standards and setting a minimum wage pegged to executive rates. We have to choose and prioritize. The state can provide for some public goods at a reasonable level, for the most disadvantaged, and strive to improve the level of support. But that level – and any society's priorities – will change over time. Our economic and social aspirations reflect fluid priorities. So, the level and type of public service provision by the state will also change over time. They may be promoted as policy or even, to some degree, protected by ordinary law. But they are not the kinds of things that we can – or should – cast in stone in the form of constitutionally guaranteed rights, enforceable in court. While liberty can be readily defined, relatively fixed and reasonably balanced against other competing claims to liberty and the wider public interest, wider economic and social interests are not amenable to adjudication or strict legal enforcement. As such, they do not easily fit the philosophical or legal model of human rights.

These are not arguments against prioritizing healthcare, education or housing above civil liberties. They are arguments about the philosophical and practical viability of shoe-horning every want or need into the legal language of human rights. Given Marx's natural antipathy towards individualistic rights that protect liberty, this ought to be an area of broad agreement for both the left and the right. Yet there remains a natural suspicion on the left that arguments against the new generation of human rights amount to advocacy of a form of legal apartheid, relegating economic and social interests to a lower level of priority. Polly Toynbee expresses this concern when she attacks 'the right-wing wolf in civil liberties sheep's clothing that pursues individual freedoms for the powerful at the expense of collective freedoms for all'. She argues that the obsession with fundamental liberties obscures attention from 'real injustices', like human trafficking, squalid prison conditions, inadequate support for parents with disabled children, social immobility and neglect of the elderly. However, Toynbee cannot – and does not even try to – explain how protecting habeas corpus, free speech or the right to a fair trial could come 'at the expense of' others suffering in our society. Because they don't – it is scarcely credible to blame the forced prostitution of young girls, slopping out in prisons or mistreatment in care homes on civil liberties. There is no trade-off between the two, either in theory or practice.

The protection of liberty in Britain has developed under legal guarantees that each individual has, as of right. While some require a minimum of positive government action – fair trial guarantees need state-funded courts and legal aid – fundamental liberties free the individual from interference by the state, rather than rendering him dependent on it. It is because civil liberties check the state, carve out a limited, minimum, area of autonomy for the individual, and do not come 'at the expense of' other economic and social interests, that they can be formulated as rights that – subject to limited exceptions – trump the zeal of an overbearing government or repressive laws passed by Parliament. Equally, it is because the balance, between the liberties of one person and another or the wider public interest, requires the weighing up of a relatively confined range of considerations, that these rights are amenable to judicial determination in the bipolar, adversarial setting of a court-room.

In contrast, the 'collective freedoms for all' that Toynbee defends are not really freedoms within the ordinary meaning of that word. The examples she gives represent either social and economic hardships or aspirations. They may well be more important preoccupations for some, particularly the most deprived in our society. But irrespective – or even because – of this, they are not the same thing as liberty. As Berlin recognized: '… it is a confusion of values to say that although my "liberal", individual freedom may go by the board, some other kind of freedom – "social or economic" – is increased'.

If liberty and equality are not the same, it is questionable whether it is appropriate to use the same means to protect liberty as to promote equality and social justice. Given Toynbee's warning against 'the individualistic my-rights culture' – and Marx's acerbic contempt for freedoms formulated as legal rights – the provision of public services through the development of human rights presents something of an anomaly for the left.

Far from civil liberties coming at the 'expense of collective freedoms for all', as Toynbee suggests, in practice the proliferation of novel human rights has had the reverse effect. For example, expanded human rights obligations have added to the operational burdens on police forces. It is precisely because the police are struggling to cope with a growing terrorist threat – with finite resources and increasing legal responsibilities – that the government has sought to take short cuts with our fundamental liberties, like extending the maximum period of detention without charge. The inflation of the size, role and reach of the state – accompanying the proliferation of rights – correlates with the government's sustained assault on liberty.

If the rights contagion has weighed down public services, it is also part of a wider claims culture, encouraging a narrow fixation on the claims of the individual which tends to displace the interests of the rest of society. Both are hampering the decision-making of those charged with public protection.

Public servants have struggled to keep up with the rapidly expanding lists of new rights, leading them to err on the side of caution – thereby avoiding interference with individual rights and the risk of legal liability – at the expense of taking a robust approach to protecting the wider public. This has led to confusion and mistakes. The government's rebuke that local authorities – and the press – misunderstand the true limits on human rights obligations is a deft attempt to pass the buck and avoid taking responsibility for the consequences of its own flawed approach. It ignores strong evidence of a much deeper problem, whereby uncertainty in the law has sown confusion amongst officials. On 17 August 2005, Naomi Bryant was strangled and stabbed to death by Anthony Rice, a serial criminal with a long list of prior convictions for violent and sexual offences. In 1989, Rice had been given a discretionary life sentence of imprisonment for attempted rape, indecent assault and assault occasioning actual bodily harm. Rice had attacked a woman in the street at midnight and subjected her to a harrowing ninety-minute ordeal. The trial judge had sentenced him to a minimum of ten years in prison, after which his release would be determined by the Parole Board. He was subsequently released on licence in November 2004. He then went on to kill Naomi Bryant despite a number of warning signs that should have been picked up by the authorities monitoring him. An independent review, conducted by Her Majesty's Inspectorate of Probation (HMIP), highlighted a range of practical mistakes and administrative failings that contributed to the tragic murder. However, the report also focused on the way in which human rights considerations had undermined the decision-making by the Parole Board and probation authorities. One of HMIP's key recommendations was that: '… although proper attention should be given to the human rights issues, the relevant authorities involved should maintain in practice a top priority focus on the public protection requirements of the case'.

According to HMIP, Rice's right to a private life and freedom of association had obscured the focus on public protection. The assessments that led to the decision to release him and the formulation of the conditions of Rice's licence became dominated by the debate on whether or not the restrictions on his private life were 'necessary and proportionate' as required under the Human Rights Act. The consideration of the enforcement of the conditions was flawed. The authorities had not even considered electronic tagging or police surveillance to monitor his movements. Representations were made by Rice's lawyer and the Home Office that the conditions of his licence were too restrictive, specifically bearing in mind recent court rulings under the Human Rights Act and the imminent possibility of judicial review of any decision they made. In its report, HMIP stated: 'We find it regrettable that attention to effectiveness and enforceability was undermined by the attention devoted to issues of lawfulness and proportionality.'

The effect of these preoccupations was to dilute the licence conditions, render them less precise and allow Rice to manipulate restrictions designed to protect the public. The authorities used woolly language to define the licence conditions, in order to comply with the human rights arguments continually pressed upon them. This allowed Rice to breach the conditions with minimal effect, because they were inherently unclear. In the words of HMIP, the authorities 'appear to have let their desire to encourage his resettlement to displace their priority need to focus on public protection'. HMIP found that:

> This whole process is additionally complicated by the human rights considerations in each case which have grown in importance following a series of Court judgements. Prisoners are now legally represented at Parole Board hearings, often by counsel, who also have recourse to judicial review. It is a challenging task for people who are charged with managing offenders effectively to ensure that public protection considerations are not undermined by the human rights considerations.

Tragically, these flaws in the decision-making process contributed to the savage and unnecessary death of an innocent woman. It demonstrates how expanded interpretations of the rights of a dangerous criminal can subtly displace those of potential victims and the wider public.

While some of the confusion may generate from misinterpretation by officials of the Human Rights Act, as the government claims, the fact is that the Act itself has fuelled that uncertainty. In the Rice case, HMIP indicated that the distorted decision-making process was linked to recent adverse court judgments. Nor was the Rice case a one-off example of sporadic failings by individual decision-makers. The government targets, at the relevant time, reveal an inexplicably lax institutional approach to public risk assessment – only aiming for 90 per cent of risk assessments on 'very high risk' and 'prolific offenders' to be conducted within five days *after* their release into the community. Even these complacent targets were missed. The murder of Naomi Bryant is a case study in how expanded interpretations of human rights can skew the attitudes and approach of public authorities charged with protecting the public. Ministerial attempts to blame the case on the 'misunderstanding of human rights considerations' by officials are an unacceptable abdication of government responsibility for the direct consequences of its own policies.

A similar conclusion was drawn by the authorities reviewing the escape by a serial rapist from a secure hospital, where the sensibilities of a dangerous criminal were allowed to trump the overriding duty to protect the public. Terrence O'Keefe escaped twice from a secure mental facility at Lambeth Hospital in London. A review by the NHS Trust found that the staff treating him were unaware of the level of threat he posed and failed to handcuff him. The report stated that O'Keefe had been described in opaque language as a 'medium secure patient', leading to misunderstandings as to his threat level, for fear of causing him offence. It recommended that '[c]onsideration is therefore required as to how we portray or use common language whilst remaining sensitive to the patient's treatment needs'.

In another widely reported case, the trial judge who convicted a youth who kicked to death Garry Newlove, a father of three, while on bail for another offence, criticized the application of bail criteria that left him free to murder. The judge said that the 'concentration on rights forgets duties and responsibilities'.

There is increasing evidence of a more pervasive effect on public authorities as a result of the 'claims culture' closely associated with the proliferation of rights. Official complaints against the police increased by 83 per cent between 2003 and 2007. In 2006, the Police Federation, which represents rank and file officers, published a study on 'response policing'. In addition to considerations of red tape, targets and bureaucracy, it found that a claims culture was leading to defensive policing. The report concluded that police officers: '"work the paper" to protect themselves and defend their actions through their reports'.

This means that police are busy recording excessive amounts of reporting detail when they might otherwise be on patrol. Fear of litigation is evidently contributing to this. It is not always based on the Human Rights Act, but prevailing human rights considerations often inform or influence the way that claims are brought.

The claims culture has also rubbed off on those who have born the brunt of it. Faced with an increasing number of claims from the public and a rising risk of legal liability, the police themselves have resorted to complaining more – with serious implications for force morale and discipline. A report by HMIC in 2008 found that police sergeants are shying away from enforcing standards of professionalism – as basic as dress code – for fear of junior officers submitting complaints against them. The problem was summed up by a sergeant who explained: 'PCs now get away with blue murder as people are afraid to challenge due to HR [Human Resources] legislation and are not supported by managers.'

One Chief Superintendent blamed the decline in standards on: '… the culture of counter-bullying, where constables who are challenged take a grievance out against the sergeant who challenged them, stating they have been bullied in the workplace'.

The consequences of the growing claims culture are worrying. The HMIC report highlighted a widespread belief by officers themselves that policing has suffered an 'erosion of basic levels of adherence to fundamental standards of professionalism'.

The rising claims culture bears a striking resemblance to the parallel expansion of health and safety regulation, which has had a debilitating effect on the emergency services and others charged with protecting the public. Both phenomena are part of a sea change over the last decade, reflecting and feeding a contorted consideration of the respective rights and responsibilities of – and risks to – the individual and the wider public.

In 2003, the High Court criticized the Health and Safety Executive for trying (unsuccessfully) to prosecute the Metropolitan Police for failing to secure the health and safety of an officer who fell to his death while pursuing two burglars across a roof. The decision to bring criminal charges, costing the Metropolitan Police £3 million to defend, was castigated by the two Metropolitan Police Commissioners in the dock. Sir (now Lord) John Stevens said: 'This prosecution has clearly demonstrated a fundamental lack of understanding of the unique nature of policing ... At a time of unprecedented demand on London policing, Lord Condon and I have sat as defendants for five weeks in the highest criminal court in the land.'

Previously exempted from its scope, the Health and Safety at Work Act 1974 was extended to cover the police in March 1997. The 1974 Act was originally designed to ensure that employers provide a safe place of work for employees and those around them. However, the legislation has been stretched beyond its original aims by later government regulations – often as a result of EU Directives. In this case, the Health and Safety Executive sought to attach criminal liability to the police force for its failure to ensure that the risk to the individual officer was prioritized above the public interest in catching a criminal fugitive. In the case of a fugitive burglar, the consequences will be limited – a medium-level criminal may escape arrest. However, the following year, the police delayed deploying to an emergency call near Henley, where Stuart Horgan had shot dead his estranged wife and her sister and seriously injured their mother. While neighbours rushed to give first aid, armed officers and paramedics delayed for over an hour on health and safety grounds, despite it being reasonably clear after twenty-two minutes that Horgan had left the scene. Thames Valley Police reviewed the incident, and concluded that one of the victims might not have died if the police and ambulance services had arrived sooner. The review criticized the police for focusing on trying 'to eliminate risk rather than manage it' and taking an 'overly cautious approach' on health and safety grounds. The rights of, and risks to, police officers and other emergency response workers were placed above those of the victims of a shooting and the public in the vicinity.

Then, in May 2007, ten-year-old Jordon Lyon drowned in a local park pond in Wigan, having rescued his younger sister. Two uniformed officers arrived at the scene, but radioed for assistance rather than intervene, because under health and safety rules they did not have the requisite training in 'water rescue' and would have risked exposing their force to legal liability. Again, the risk to the officers – in this case minimal – was wrongly prioritized over the risk of losing the life of a drowning boy. While the police force in question was subject to widespread criticism, it was acting according to expanded interpretations of a legal regime extended to it by the government.

Expanded health and safety rules do not merely prevent a reasonable level of risk-taking by police and other emergency services, they now also penalize it. So when the police do intervene, putting themselves in harm's way, they increasingly risk litigation or – worse still – criminal prosecution. A health and safety prosecution was successfully brought against the Metropolitan Police for the killing of Jean Charles de Menezes, in the course of counter-terrorism operations in July 2005. Just as various Convention rights have been expanded by judicial interpretation, so the stretching of the Health and Safety at Work Act 1974 to scrutinize a counter-terrorism operation defied the original intention of the legislation.

The prosecution was launched on the basis that the police operation put the public, not just Mr de Menezes, at unnecessary risk. But the case was brought using the contrived device of a law designed to prevent accidents in the workplace. The 1974 Act was used because the Crown Prosecution Service did not have sufficient evidence to charge any individual officers with a criminal offence. The precedent has generated serious concern amongst the police that cases like this will lead to defensive policing in high-pressured situations, which would put the public at greater – not less – risk. While there ought to be accountability and transparency for botched police operations, especially where the use of armed force results in the loss of innocent life, in practice the health and safety prosecution had the perverse effect of hampering both – delaying publication of the Independent Police Complaints Commission report, due to the ongoing trial, until more than two years after the shooting.

The health and safety culture mirrors the distortion of risk and responsibility wrought by the proliferation of rights. The impact is not limited to momentary lapses in common sense by individual officers. It has become institutionally embedded. One police force's guidance requires officers attending 'water-related incidents' to conduct a prior risk assessment before throwing a lifebelt to a drowning member of the public. It goes on to state that: 'Physical contact with a struggling casualty should be avoided … to prevent the rescuer becoming overwhelmed and pulled into the water and submerged.'

Like inflated human rights obligations, expanded health and safety interpretations increasingly cosset the police in situations which present ordinary operational risks that the public expect them to be able to manage. In 2008, when residents in Kent complained about an illegal rave, the police refused to shut it down on health and safety grounds, despite the night-long nuisance to hundreds of homes nearby, claiming it was too dark for them to intervene.

The police and other emergency services are expected to take some personal risks to ensure public safety, without recklessly exposing themselves or others to danger. They should receive support, training and respect – not the threat of criminal liability – for the tough operational decisions they have to make in split seconds. Sooner or later, if we keep deterring the bravery of those in whom we vest responsibility for public protection, we will eventually get what we are asking for – less effective emergency services and greater levels of avoidable risk to the public. An award-wining coastguard who sped to save a schoolgirl hanging off a crumbling cliff edge – without first putting on a harness – recently left the service disillusioned, after being investigated and censured on health and safety grounds. The Coastguard said they were 'not looking for dead heroes'.

The excessive preoccupation with health and safety has also had a disruptive effect in schools. Since the campaigns against child abuse during the 1980s pioneered by people like the journalist and presenter Esther Rantzen, there has been an increase in awareness and focus on children's rights. These campaigns shone a much-needed light on the plight of children suffering abuse in the home. However, there are increasing signs that the pendulum has swung too far the other way, with nervous teachers afraid to uphold discipline in class and truculent pupils (and parents) relying on their 'rights' to bring spurious claims against innocent teachers, with devastating consequences for those falsely accused and a paralysing impact on the classroom.

Fear of litigation brought by pupils and parents has led to a swathe of new regulations, as schools try to stave off the risks of legal liability. This has led to absurd results, with schools banning the sack and three-legged races from sports day because children might fall over and hurt themselves. Teachers have been banned from applying sun cream to pupils, in case they are accused of sexual abuse. Somewhat predictably, this decision was later followed by official advice to consider cancelling summer school trips because of the now increased risk of children getting skin cancer. In Carlisle, a head teacher introduced safety goggles for children playing conkers, pleading health and safety: 'It's just being sensible. We live in a litigious society.' The Health and Safety Executive later hit back at critics with one of its 'Great Health and Safety Myths' rebuttals:

> 'The myth: Kids must wear goggles to play conkers.
> The reality: This is one of the oldest chestnuts around, a truly classic myth. A well-meaning head teacher decided children should wear safety goggles to play conkers.'

Such is the fine line between fact and fiction at the Health and Safety Executive. In a thoughtful speech, one head teacher has warned of the: '... danger of using health and safety to replace thought, judgment and personal responsibility ... If we take drowning as an example, the best form of protection is to teach children how to swim, not putting up large numbers of notices "banning swimming".'

A generation of young children are being let down by well-meaning but counter-productive rules that prevent them from evaluating for themselves the risks around them.

It is not just the children who are being molly-coddled. In July 2008, a head teacher was escorted from a primary school in Marschapel eight days before retiring for working too hard, because she exceeded the limited hours prescribed to her on return to the school after a back injury. The school governors feared being sued on health and safety grounds if Mrs Aldridge hurt herself again in the course of her duties. The decision undermined morale at the school – leaving Mrs Aldridge devastated, and causing a number of parents to withdraw their children in protest.

Beyond the school gates, the balance between individual rights and responsibilities, and our society's approach to risk, is also – slowly but surely – being thrown out of kilter. In one case, parents who put up a bouncy castle in a park for a children's birthday party were successfully sued when a boy was badly injured after colliding with another child. The injured boy had not been invited to the party, but had joined in with his father waiting nearby. The case raised the question of who – if anyone – should bear the responsibility, and legal liability, for the injuries resulting from the accident. The basic choice was between the responsibilities of the parents of the boy and those of the organizers of the birthday party, who had not invited him nor had any previous relationship with the boy or his family. The trial judge in the case held the parents who hired the bouncy castle responsible for the accident. While the Court of Appeal eventually overruled the decision, the costs to individuals and local authorities of defending such claims, and the uncertain state of the law, is making schools and families think twice before arranging entertainment for children in the future.

Absurd extensions of health and safety regulation are also stifling a range of local and national customs that add to the entertainment and diversity of the British way of life. Police forced organizers of a pie-throwing competition in Brighton to cancel the event on health and safety grounds. A six-hundred-year-old Pancake Day race in Ripon was scrapped after local health and safety assessments deemed the cobbled streets too treacherous. The Federation of Small Businesses has warned that the law now requires such excessive precautions that shops and other small companies cannot afford to put up Christmas lights in local towns. To cap it off, an organ grinder was barred from performing in Ripley town centre during the summer holidays, pending a thorough risk assessment. Paddy Cooke has fifteen years of grinding experience and was dismayed to receive the council's ruling, complaining: 'It's not as if I have a live monkey which might jump at people. Mine is a battery-operated interactive toy and the best I have ever had.'

We are replacing harmless local customs with a culture of risk aversion, based more on the fear of litigation than a balanced assessment of safety. The priority and protection accorded to preventing any risk from materializing – weighed against the freedoms we all enjoy – has been distorted beyond all reasonable proportions. Most people accept the ordinary minor hazards that are part and parcel of leading a healthy life, comfortable with the idea that we accept a little risk for much greater social benefits. The danger is that the law – and its application – has lost sight of the big picture, defying common sense by seeking to wrap our society in cotton wool. The public is being deterred from engaging in pastimes and entertainment – hardly daredevil or dangerous stunts – because of minimal levels of risk voluntarily assumed. The real danger is that this paternalistic micromanagement of what we do on a day-to-day basis will have a suffocating impact on our lives.

The state's obsessive efforts to eliminate risk often have unintended and counter-productive consequences. In one case, an eleven-year-old boy who went to retrieve a ball on a slope in a communal area slipped and cut his leg on glass shards hidden in long grass. When his mother complained, the council refused to cut the grass, officials citing health and safety: 'The grass on the embankment is not cut on a regular basis because of the dangers of working on a steep gradient.'

Instead of cutting the grass, the council promised to look at ways to 'discourage children from playing in the area'.

Onerous new safety standards for trees now require rigorous annual inspections, although only six people die per year as a result of falling trees and branches. According to the Forestry Commission, the result has not been drastic improvements in tree safety, but rather that owners increasingly cut down their trees – at a time when the government is trying to promote environmental awareness – in order to avoid servicing the new regulatory regime and the risk of being sued.

While the right has traditionally resented the creeping attentions of the nanny state, some on the left are now equally concerned about its neurotic focus on protecting the individual at all costs. Writing in response to a ban on Kinder Surprise chocolate eggs – outlawed in Germany because children might choke on the plastic toy inside – the *Guardian*'s Charlie Brooker rages:

> How did we get to this point? Our sense of self grew too strong. We gazed up our own bums for so long, we each became the centre of the universe. We're not mere specks of flesh, jostled by the forces of chance. We're flawless deities, and goddammit we deny – deny! – the very existence of simple bad luck. If we trip on the pavement, someone else is to blame. Of course they are. And we'll sue them to prove it if necessary.
>
> In a bid to pre-empt our self-important litigiousness, armies of risk assessors scan the horizon, dreaming of every conceivable threat. You could bang your head on that branch. Crack a rib on that teaspoon. Choke to death on that chocolate egg.

We now need a comprehensive review of health and safety regulation, in order to scale back the state's interference with the daily risks in life that should be left for people to manage as they see fit. In particular, the application of the law to the emergency services needs to be recalibrated to ensure that, while avoiding reckless risks to individual officers, there is a clearer focus on the overriding importance of protecting the public from harm.

As the balance of rights, risk and responsibility in our society has skewed, those seeking to defend themselves, protect their neighbourhood or intervene to prevent crime or anti-social behaviour have increasingly found themselves on the wrong side of the law.

In 2006 Nicholas Tyers, a chip shop owner in Bridlington, faced a young tearaway who spat at a customer and smashed a shop window. Mr Tyers performed a citizen's arrest and called the police. Instead of being thanked, he was prosecuted for kidnapping the child, because the police unquestioningly accepted the boy's version of events. After a six-month ordeal, estimated to have cost the taxpayer £60,000, the judge threw the case out. In the meantime, Mr Tyers was forced to sell his shop because of persistent vandalism from local youths. Cleared at trial, Mr Tyers said:

> I have faced six months of hell waiting to prove my innocence. I have lost my faith in the judicial process. The case should never have been brought.
>
> When you are the victim of crime and you see the culprit your immediate reaction is to take him to the police. I can see why people turn a blind eye to crime and don't bother reporting it.
>
> We were going down the police station on the understanding we were going to make a statement as victims. The police turned the tables on us. I was finger printed and had my picture taken and treated like a criminal.

All too often in such cases, the innocent are punished while the real offender goes free. While this is not the direct result of the Human Rights Act – police performance targets are encouraging officers to pick on soft targets – it does reflect a broader, increasingly prevalent distortion of the proper balance between the competing rights of victims, criminals and the wider interests of our society.

A year later, Sue Pearson faced similar treatment when she intervened to remonstrate with a rowdy group of teenage girls who were swearing and hurling abuse outside her home. When the police were called, rather than deal with the unruly girls they arrested Mrs Pearson on unsubstantiated allegations of assault and held her for sixteen hours in a police cell. Her fingerprints and DNA were taken. She was then hauled before the courts. The magistrates threw out the case. Having been vindicated by the court, Mrs Pearson criticized the police, saying, '[i]t is the way this country is going. The rights of the victim are second to those of the perpetrators', adding, 'I certainly will think twice before intervening in anything again.'

Then, in 2008, Frank McCourt was charged with assault for trying to put a yob under citizen's arrest. The boy was one of a group who had hurled insults at Mr McCourt and his wife, kicked him, thrown stones at his home and threatened to kill his three dogs. Mr McCourt thanked the police when they arrived, but they arrested him for kidnapping, took his DNA and later charged him with assault. The case was dropped after two and a half months, just days before trial, because prosecutors did not have any evidence to sustain a prosecution. Sussex police eventually apologized, but after a prolonged ordeal that left Mr McCourt on antidepressants, he complained: 'It seems this country's justice system is totally back to front. They dragged me through the courts, while doing everything they could to protect those kids who terrorised my neighbourhood.'

These cases are having a wider impact. Research shows that six out of ten people in Britain would be unlikely to challenge a group of teenage boys vandalizing a bus shelter, compared to six out of ten who would challenge the group in Germany. The reluctance to intervene in the UK is also greater than in other comparable European countries, such as France, Italy and Spain. The actions of the state are deterring Britons from intervening to prevent crime and uphold the law out of a basic sense of civic duty, which risks turning Britain into a walk-on-by society.

The exercise of self-defence by homeowners to protect themselves, their families and their property against illegal intruders has raised similar concerns. While the current law recognizes a right to take proportionate measures in self-defence, this has been interpreted in favour of burglars and against their victims. Proposals introduced to the House of Commons to strengthen the position of homeowners under the law, by providing a right of self-defence except where the level of force used is 'grossly disproportionate', were rejected by the government on human rights grounds. The Justice Secretary claimed that Strasbourg case law on the right to life prevented a change in the law, thereby protecting burglars at the expense of those seeking to protect themselves and their homes.

If the proliferation of rights has had wider social repercussions, it has also undermined our democracy – eroding the rule of law, blurring the separation of powers and dislocating the accountability of law-making from our elected representatives. Since 1975, the Strasbourg Court has dramatically increased its rate of judicial legislation, without any democratic means of control. While there has always been a limited creative element to judicial decision-making under the common law, it has substantially increased as a result of the Human Rights Act which incorporates the Strasbourg case law into UK law and encourages judicial activism at home.

The rapid expansion of rights undercuts legal certainty, an essential characteristic of the rule of law. The rule of law, a pillar of any democracy, is based on the idea of reasonably predictable rules. Legal certainty is not just an abstract value – it lays the foundations that underpin our daily lives. If the law is unpredictable, it makes it more difficult for individuals, families, businesses and government to plan around. Law that is inconsistent, unpredictable or arbitrary is hugely disruptive. Governments cannot know if their policies will withstand legal challenge, public servants cannot be sure whether or not they will incur corporate or individual liability in the course of their official duties, and the public suffer as a result of the confusion.

As Lord Denning, himself one of the most creative judges in British history, remarked: 'The Convention is drafted in a style very different from the way in which we are used to in legislation. It contains wide general statements of principle. They are apt to lead to much difficulty in application: because they give rise to much uncertainty.'

Inherent opacity has been compounded by expanded judicial interpretations of Convention rights in totally unforeseen areas – our exposure to which has increased as a result of the Human Rights Act. As one former Parliamentary Counsel has observed, the Act has brought: '... confusion to our laws with little corresponding benefit – except to legal practitioners in the field'.

Judicial legislation also offends against the constitutional principle of the separation of powers – between government, elected law-makers and independent courts. The separation of powers in Britain is largely unwritten, but still provides an important system of checks and balances. The judges check the legislature and the executive. In return, in order to safeguard their independence, they restrict themselves to interpreting and applying the law of the land.

The judicial function is well suited to deciding cases that present two, more or less opposing parties or sets of interests – like a contractual dispute or a personal injury claim. The adversarial setting of a courtroom allows a two-way debate, overseen by a judge, to test opposing arguments. That setting can accommodate the adjudication of civil and political liberties that pit an individual's rights against those of another person or the state, for example the right to free speech against a government claim to censorship. But the structure of the court and its procedure are not designed to accommodate multi-dimensional economic, social and political issues that require the assessment of a whole range of different interests. Decisions on the appropriate level of taxation, public service priorities and who in our society are most deserving or needing of state support are not zero-sum matters, amenable to deductive determination through judicial reasoning – they need wider debate, involving subjective moral evaluations, and require stark political choices.

Transforming social and economic interests into rights drags them into the courtroom, and politicizes the judicial function. It involves judges determining – or, rather, skewing – a balanced assessment of competing public service priorities. If a judge determines – in one particular case, on one set of facts – that the law should guarantee a right to one or other public service, he does so without having considered all the other competing demands on the public purse. The myopic perspective of a courtroom is the wrong place to make such decisions.

In fact, the situation is even less tenable still. Judges are not just applying extended definitions of rights imposing positive duties on the state, they are also deciding to create those additional rights in the first place. The risk is that, in the narrow confines of a courtroom, only a limited set of arguments and interests is heard. The new rights being created are often a response to the particular interests pursued in human rights test cases, to the exclusion of a vast range of other compelling – and competing – interests. For the savvy litigant, with legal representation and the requisite resources to support litigation, the expansion of novel rights offers a panorama of opportunities to foist new claims on the state and secure priority access to public services – expanding human rights claims present opportunities for legal queue jumping. The danger of law-making according to special interests is that wider – but less vocal – social interests, needs and priorities are eclipsed and drowned out under the powerful but narrow advocacy put before the judge in a particular case.

If the courtroom is the wrong place to determine these kinds of matters, judges are the wrong people to be making the decisions. Economic and social questions are subjective, so they should – so far as possible – be made by directly elected law-makers. This has been subverted by judicial legislation. The creative potential of the common law proved manageable, because the incremental application of the principles of case law to new situations is largely deductive and new precedents can always be overruled by Parliament. Upholding fundamental liberties, enacted by Parliament, is also amenable to adjudication. Although balancing civil liberties against the wider public interest may involve judges in areas of political controversy, they are still justiceable issues, raising legal questions that can be resolved in a courtroom. However, the broader the positive duties being placed on the limited resources of the state, the more judges become politicized. Determining the balance of economic and social rights – to schooling, hospital treatment or police protection – involves moral and political choices. Judges have no democratic mandate to determine the public interest between competing public services, thereby narrowing the scope for elected governments and Parliament to consider these matters in the round. These issues must remain subject to democratic oversight and accountability, through our elected law-makers. The authority to debate and decide such matters should be restored to Parliament.

There ought to be broad agreement across the political spectrum on this point, particularly for those genuinely committed to strengthening our democracy.

In the 1990s it had been a long-standing grievance on the left that the courts were making politically biased decisions without proper democratic accountability. Today, those on the left and the right may reasonably disagree about *what* should be protected as human rights – whether confined to civil and political liberties, or extended to include economic and social rights. But they cannot disagree about *how* the selection should be made – at least, without ceasing to be democrats. Marxists – whether socialist or communist – need not be bound by such democratic strictures. But social democrats must. The spread of new human rights by judicial stealth – side-stepping Parliament – is slowly subverting our democracy, and should be a cause of concern across the political divides.

Defining the role of the state, the size of government and the scope of public services is part of a modern debate between liberal and social democracy in this country and beyond. These issues should be decided openly and honestly, in the debating chambers of Parliament and at the ballot box, not surreptitiously by unaccountable judges, whether in the UK or Strasbourg. Courts cannot be unaccountable legislators, just as judges are not benevolent dictators. As the American judge Learned Hand famously said, urging restraint on judicial activism in the US, '[i]t would be most irksome to be ruled by a bevy of Platonic Guardians'. The judicial invention of new rights is no substitute for democratic debate on the reach and responsibilities of the state.

So what means of democratic accountability do we have to review and revise judicial legislation in Strasbourg and the UK? Why can't the British government and Parliament just overrule the judges? In theory, the state parties can amend the Convention, to straighten out any judicial innovations of which they disapprove. There have been fourteen amending protocols to the Convention since 1950. However, in practice, these dealt with procedural matters or added extra rights. While the Convention originally entered into force with ten countries, there are now forty-seven state parties, which makes reaching agreement on any substantive amendment to the Convention difficult, although not impossible. Having not foreseen the exponential growth in rights, the designers of the Convention and the Strasbourg Court left few practical means for stemming the flow of judicial legislation. Equally, they presumed – and agreed – that the judges would have no law-making power, and that their case law would not create binding precedents.

At home, the Human Rights Act has tended to accentuate rather than mitigate the scope for judicial legislation. While under the Act the ultimate recourse for direct conflicts between primary legislation and human rights is a review by Parliament, the courts are also given wide scope to rewrite legislation, in order to avoid having to declare it in conflict with the Human Rights Act. Nevertheless, the Act itself can be amended by Parliament, an option which is considered in the final chapter.

This is a remarkable reversal of the history of human rights in this country. The campaigners for early rights, the pioneers of our liberal tradition, advocated personal freedom to strengthen a British model of liberal democracy – rights supported and reinforced the foundations of our democratic architecture. Freedom under law, the separation of powers and liberal democracy were inextricably woven together. Now, the proliferation of rights is undermining these foundations. There are several putative explanations for this. Some supporters deny that expanding human rights run against the democratic grain, by pointing to the residual formal structures of oversight. In theory, Britain could amend the Convention if it could persuade enough fellow Europeans to join it, although it would not be straightforward and the present government has shown no appetite for such an initiative. That may be put down to failure of diplomacy rather than democracy. Except, it is a curious fate for British democracy that accountability for law-making in such a fundamental area of our lives is now determined in foreign capitals – in Berlin, Bucharest, Baku and many others, rather than London. On the other hand, British law-makers could certainly repeal the Human Rights Act, so in that sense an important element of democratic accountability remains. Yet until that happens, our judges have been licensed to promote the spread of novel rights, overrule our elected law-makers and rewrite the law in order to achieve both of these ends.

A second possible explanation lies with the rising scepticism about Parliament and politics. Amidst complaints that Members of Parliament – and the politic class in general – have succumbed to an unhealthy malaise, sidelined by an increasingly presidential system of governance, corroded by allegations of financial impropriety and paralysed by a stifling consensus across the political parties, some human rights advocates are quietly content to rely on the judges to keep the torch alive, promoting human rights and incrementally working towards their ideal of a fairer society. If so, this is likely to prove short-sighted. If there are problems with our democracy – and all the main political parties have proposed measures to strengthen the role of Parliament – then the answer is to work to resolve them. Delegating backdoor law-making power to unelected judges – or anyone else for that matter – is a reckless response to political apathy and cynicism, which risks doing long-term harm to British democracy.

A third variant posits that, having secured civil and political freedoms in Britain, the modern-day champions of human rights, rather than go out of business, have turned their sights on the lost elixir of social justice, coldly abandoned by New Labour. Socialists, social democrats and others on the left believe that, by tying Britain to a rising tide of continental rules, they may slowly but surely achieve elements of a political agenda they have not been able to achieve at home. The Convention and the Strasbourg Court, like other supranational bodies – including most obviously the EU –

offer the glimmer of hope, otherwise extinguished by the rejection of socialist ideas by the British electorate.

Whatever the dubious merits of these respective explanations, one salient risk stands out above all others. Despite the recent assault on liberty, Britain has a historic tradition of protecting fundamental freedoms and a justice system renowned the world over. But there are increasing concerns – and not just in the tabloid media – that the pendulum in favour of human rights has swung too far. Allowing the further proliferation of rights – quietly and clandestinely – and acquiescing in the erosion of democratic accountability, is to court long-term and lasting damage to the credibility of the basic idea of fundamental rights in this country.

The rights contagion has had a profound affect in Britain, creating risks for our society and democracy that look set to continue, if not gather in momentum, unless checked. Debate on these issues will continue to polarize opinion. There is a widening chasm between those who regard the Convention, the Human Rights Act – and all the rights that came with them – as unimpeachable, and those who would dispense with the lot. Neither approach is necessary or desirable. While human rights in Britain have been both undermined and abused, it is possible to restore them to sounder foundations – if we recast the debate on rights in terms of Britain's proud liberal tradition, the wider foundations of our democracy and the global challenges that lie ahead in the twenty-first century.

PART IV

PUTTING IT RIGHT

7

The Next Chapter of
British Liberty

*'The character of our country will be defined by how
we write the next chapter of British liberty.'*

GORDON BROWN, 2007

In 1995 Will Hutton lamented the lack of limits on centralized state control in Britain: 'The executive branch is held only nominally accountable to Parliament. There is no formal independence of the judiciary. There is no codified bill of rights. There is no presumption that the activity of the state should be open and transparent.'

Yet despite these warnings from the left, a constellation of factors swelled to create a perfect storm which swept the country from 1997, inflicting widespread damage on the idea and exercise of liberty that Britain has nurtured for centuries. A latent Marxist disdain for liberty, New Labour's electoral strategy of triangulation, a fixation on the twenty-four-hour news cycle, a policy of enthusiastic European integration and a large parliamentary majority combined to create the conditions for an unprecedented assault on British liberty.

A decade on, Hutton's concerns have been exacerbated rather than remedied, resulting in a tectonic shift in the fault lines that demarcate the relationship between the citizen and the state. At a time when it is often said that ideological divisions between the major political parties have narrowed, there is a marked divergence in approach. An editorial in the *Daily Telegraph* argues: 'There is now a clear divide between the two main political parties on the future direction of Britain: one believes that a powerful, controlling state is the best way to achieve a socially just society; the other that power should be devolved to local communities and to individual citizens.'

The *Sunday Times* characterizes the debate in similar terms: 'The choice is not right or left, but how you define the relationship between citizen and state.'

On the left, there is raw shock and profound bafflement. The *Observer* warns: 'After a decade, the account shows a devastating loss of the freedoms that we once regarded as our birthright, the self-evident and self-perpetuating virtue of the British people and their constitution.'

While all the main political parties approach the next UK general election with a commitment to constitutional reform, including a Bill of Rights, the ensuing debate reveals very different approaches to human rights.

Twenty-first-century Britain, competing in a globalized world, needs, more than ever, to recast the relationship between the individual and the state in a way that preserves its legacy of liberty and protects its democratic prerogatives. The debate on a Bill of Rights offers a precious opportunity to restore and entrench our fundamental liberties, establish an autonomous regime of British human rights law consistent with the overarching minimum standards set out under the Convention and reinforce – rather than undermine – the other supporting pillars of our liberal democracy. Calls to expand human rights even further risk devaluing the currency of rights, undermining their popular credibility and shredding the political consensus that might otherwise be achieved.

To address the current problem it needs to be put in perspective. Whether it is the assault on liberty, or the risks of rights inflation, we are not standing at the cliff edge of impending totalitarian disaster. The assault on liberty today pales in comparison with the tyrannical threats posed by fascism or communism in the twentieth century. The spread of CCTV has proved intrusive and ineffective, but its use in public areas is hardly 'Orwellian', as one deputy Chief Constable has suggested – there are no CCTV cameras in our homes yet. The characterization of database checks on those working with children as 'Stalinist' by another critic also misses the mark – Stalin was evil and ruthlessly efficient, whereas this government's approach to databases is naïve and inept. So, too, plans for giant screens to broadcast the Olympics in towns and cities in 2012 may offend against good taste, but they hardly herald the arrival of *1984*, as another commentator suggests. Overstating the danger to British liberty risks misunderstanding it. The threat comes from the steady accretion of security powers, the incremental extension in the reach of the state and the cold indifference of faceless bureaucracies – not secret police and torture chambers. Likewise, the proliferation of rights may be eroding the rule of law and democratic accountability by stealth, but foreign judges are not planning an imminent coup at Westminster.

Yet, because the threat is subtle, steady and surreptitious – rather than presenting any clear-cut, short-term danger – it is elusive, more difficult to guard against and easily displaced by more newsworthy controversies of the day. The risks are more akin to those in the parable of the boiling frog. It is said that if you place a frog in a boiling pan, it will jump straight out. But if you place a frog in a pan of water at room temperature, and then slowly increase the heat, the frog's internal constitution does not pick up the slow change in temperature, so it gradually becomes groggy and disoriented and eventually dies. Bandied around boardrooms and consultancies, the parable has entered the folklore of commercial strategy as a warning against failing to discern and address subtle, long-term but fundamental and strategic threats to companies fixated on short-term profit margins.

The assault on liberty and the risks of proliferating rights present a similar kind of threat. While many ordinary, innocent people endure a diverse range of disproportionate infringements of their basic rights, daily intrusions into their privacy and increasing meddling in their lives, each new measure or abuse has been explained away by ministers or officials – as either isolated abuse or necessary tactics in the fight against crime and terrorism. The threat may not be Orwellian or Stalinist, but it is all the more acute because we have gradually become inured to the constant ebbing away of our freedoms. We may not be facing dictatorship or despotism, but we are being continually short-changed by the state. Whether or not we notice it on a day-to-day basis, the remorseless salami-slicing of our liberties risks leaving a permanent scar on Britain.

Likewise, the creeping jurisdiction of the courts by stealth is not easily identified with any single defining moment. It has had a more sluggish, comatosing effect – draining public services, undermining public protection, increasing dependency on the state, diluting personal responsibility and side-stepping democratic accountability. Britain signed up to a ban on torture in 1950 that aimed to prevent the repetition of Nazi medical experiments on vulnerable minorities in the death camps. Yet fifty years on the same rules now dictate to parents how they can discipline their children. We started out with a right to private life, to prevent disproportionate intrusions into the home, which now effectively allows dangerous criminals to negotiate the terms of their release from prison.

While attempts to project these trends forward into the future are inherently imprecise, we need to assess the risk of long-term damage of continuing to ignore the current direction Britain is taking. If the voracious appetite of the state is not checked, what will Britain look like in 2020? How long will police be able to detain suspects without charge – forty-two, fifty-six, ninety days or even indefinitely? What will happen to the tradition of peaceful protest – and what subjects will be out of bounds, as the pernicious combination of security and political correctness provides rationales for closing down more and more subjects of legitimate debate? Will jury trials be gradually confined to ever declining categories of cases, eventually to be extinguished as an ancient relic of a bygone era? How much of our personal data will be stored on ID cards and vulnerable government databases – and shared across not just Whitehall and local authorities but also an expanding EU and other international partners? Will a universal DNA database turn us into a nation of suspects? What is left to stop councils from using surveillance powers to investigate every aspect of local residents' lives? If Britain continues on this course over the next few years we will eventually cross the Rubicon in the relationship between the citizen and the state, shedding all the old presumptions in favour of the former and against the latter, leaving behind a few remnants of our fundamental freedoms as lonely exceptions to the commonplace exercise of intrusive power by the state. What once seemed unthinkable now looks possible and, if it goes unchecked, will soon start to look increasingly probable.

As our fundamental liberties quietly recede, will they continue to be replaced by new brands of rights, conjured up by human rights lawyers and campaigners seeking to expand their horizons? To what extent will healthcare, education, housing and other social services be reformulated into human rights, placing additional burdens on the state and the taxpayer without the proper means of democratic legislative oversight? Perhaps it will become more relevant to ask which areas of public policy will not be cast as rights. What will be the consequence of the concurrent abdication of personal and social responsibility, increasingly eclipsed by the one-way traffic of proliferating rights, the associated compensation culture and an obsession with health and safety? What will fill the vacuum of authority, surrendered by nervous teachers in the classroom, risk-averse police officers on the street and wary citizens whose sense of civic duty has worn thin, in the absence of support from law enforcement authorities? On current projections, armed with a burgeoning arsenal of new rights, the foxes will continue their siege of the chicken coop. The public will be increasingly forced to understand rather than withstand the threats from violent criminals, whose privacy and sensibilities are upgraded to the status of inviolable rights. Truculent children will be immunized in their disruptive classroom tussles with demoralized teachers. The ongoing metamorphosis of the right to life will attract the desperate and destitute from all over the world to Britain, not just as a historic safe haven from persecution, but increasingly as an international oasis of healthcare and social support. The taxpayer will be weighed down by the increasing burdens on the public purse, magnified by the financial impact of proliferating rights. The fabric of society will suffer a debilitating sclerosis as the state strives hopelessly to deploy human rights to engineer social outcomes, warping all sense of balance in the relationship between rights, risks and responsibilities.

Looking forward, the twenty-first century offers the mixed blessings of globalization – the opportunities of the global village, coupled with new risks and threats. Times of change generate uncertainty for the individual and put new strains on society.

There is little point in pretending that these challenges can be solved through a process of labelling interests as human rights, of whichever particular brand. There are no simplistic prescriptions, no quick fixes. However, our ancient tradition of liberty remains as relevant today as ever and can continue to guide us in the future. By preserving it, Britain will be better placed to withstand the challenges that globalization throws up. Liberal – rather than social, let alone socialist – democracy will better prepare our economy, society and democracy to endure the rigours, and prosper, during the uncertain times ahead.

Historically, Britain's tradition of liberty has been a source of great economic strength. During the Renaissance, ground-breaking thinkers in Europe like Copernicus, Galileo and Bacon ran a real risk of persecution with scientific innovations and assertions that challenged religious dogma. Britain was one of the first to decouple scientific and theological study, breaking religious control over scientific endeavour and releasing the individual creativity that fuelled the industrial revolution. Jeffrey Sachs, the development economist, points out that international living standards increased by a mere 50 per cent over the eight-hundred-year period leading up to the nineteenth century. In contrast, triggered by the industrial revolution in Britain, the world's average per capita income grew ninefold between 1800 and 2000. Sachs argues that Britain was the crucible for the industrial revolution, at least in part, because of its comparatively strong protection of liberty at that time: 'Britain had strengthening institutions of political liberty. Britain's parliament and its traditions of free speech and open debate were powerful contributors to the uptake of new ideas. They were also increasingly powerful protectors of private property rights, which in turn underpinned individual initiative.'

As globalization and the information revolution throw up a new, but not entirely dissimilar, range of challenges for the twenty-first century, the ability to thrive in an increasingly competitive global economy is, again, likely to reward the creativity, ingenuity and initiative promoted in a pluralistic society – which prizes and protects individual liberty and encourages the free flow of information and ideas.

There remains a strong correlation between those countries that guarantee political freedoms and civil liberties and promote economic freedoms, and their levels of economic prosperity. There is a compelling case for Britain to seek to retain its comparative advantage in this area, in the face of rising economic competition from other emerging economies, such as China and Russia. Their authoritarian political systems will struggle to accommodate the political pressures that derive from the burgeoning middle classes that will inevitably follow, if they succeed in sustaining high levels of economic growth. In the absence of reform, poor governance, political instability, social unrest and corruption will affect the economic performance of a range of up-and-coming economies. Equally, Britain's best chance of effectively competing with emerging democracies like India, and older democracies in Europe and North America, is as a free and open economy, bolstered by robust democratic institutions and a liberal culture of freedom, individual creativity, risk-taking and personal responsibility.

That opportunity is now being jeopardized by the inflated size and role of the state. The UK economy cannot grow and compete internationally while sustaining such a bloated bureaucracy. Both the growth of the Big Brother state and the proliferation of rights have contributed to this. It has been estimated that the current government has squandered £20 billion on ineffective and authoritarian measures, including ID cards, the DNA database and CCTV camera deployments – costing around £800 per British household. The abuse of power is invariably accompanied by the abuse of taxpayers' money, which means we are paying a high price – in terms of both our freedom and our finances – for the ballooning presence of the state in our everyday lives. Nor has the government's massive investment of resources in law enforcement – allied to its assault on the British justice system – yielded a significant return, either in terms of its impact on crime or any consequential economic dividend. In fact, the government's failure to get a grip on crime has saddled the economy with costs of £60 billion per year – with an estimated £13 billion per year in direct costs to business.

Meanwhile, the taxpayer has also had to pick up the bill to cover the costs of rights inflation and the accompanying compensation culture. There are no specific government figures setting out the costs to government in legal liabilities and the provision of extra public services since the Human Rights Act. But they form part of a clear national trend. Over the last ten years, the size of the British state has grown dramatically. The share of the country's wealth spent by government has risen by 7.2 per cent between 1999 and 2006, to 45 per cent of GDP. While governments in most other comparable common law countries – for example, the US, Australia, New Zealand and Canada – spend below 40 per cent of their national wealth, profligate government spending in Britain has even surpassed continental countries like Germany, where the government spends 44 per cent of GDP. This marks a dramatic shift in the centre of British gravity, away from those countries with which the UK shares a liberal tradition, and towards European variants of socialism. It reflects the government's sustained commitment to the redistribution of wealth, including through the active promotion of new rights and a drive to put the UK at the heart of Europe. However, it ignores the counsel of economists like Irwin Stelzer, who warned in 2008:

> [T]hat there is a 'tipping point' at which the government's share
> of the economy becomes so large that the private sector cannot

function efficiently. My guess was that if the government claimed more than 40 per cent of national income, then bad things would begin to happen. And so they have, just shortly after Chancellor Brown raised the Government's share of GDP past that tipping point.

The size of the state is now harming Britain's economic performance. One tangible consequence of the claims culture has been an increase in the proportion of households in the UK claiming benefits, rising from 24 per cent in 1997 to 39 per cent in 2008. Over the same period, the number of people claiming benefits has risen by four million and, in addition, the state now employs almost one million more people. Over a third of the working-age population is now totally dependent on the state for their income.

While the economy is paying a high price for the exponential increase in the size of – and dependency on – the state, the returns on this immense investment in the public sector, promised by New Labour, have proved illusory. British global competitiveness and economic productivity have fallen and there has been no improvement in social mobility. According to *The Economist*, Britain now ranks a mere twentieth in its international league table of global competitiveness, the UK business environment having dropped from fifth to tenth place and its innovation rating also slipping further behind the international competition. British economic resilience has also suffered, with economist Anatole Kaletsky accurately predicting that 'in contrast to every previous slowdown since the early 1990s, Britain could well do worse than America and continental Europe in 2008' – and the International Monetary Fund warning that the UK will be worse hit by the credit crunch than any other big economy. While ministers talk up the need for the smack of firm government to guide Britain through recession, the UK's vulnerability has been exacerbated by the dual state failures of massive public debt, caused by irresponsible government spending, and ineffective – rather than insufficient – regulation of the banking sector.

Nor has the inflation of the state improved British economic productivity, which has steadily deteriorated since 1997 and languishes behind our major international competitors. The government-funded Economic and Social Research Council has highlighted the 'large impact' of the 'poor relative productivity performance in the public sector', given the dramatic increase in the size of the state.

Perhaps most disappointing, the government has failed to improve social mobility. New Labour set store by its ability to use the mechanics of state to correct social inequality and expand opportunity. In 1994, Will Hutton lambasted 'The thirty, thirty, forty society', which he claimed had stratified the country according to 'new social fissures in the working population' – 30 per cent disadvantaged, 30 per cent marginalized and 40 per cent privileged. Both Tony Blair and Gordon Brown took their cue from this social diagnosis. Approaching his final term in office, Blair staked his legacy on the vision of 'an opportunity society where all have an equal chance to succeed; that could and should be 21st century Britain under a Labour Government'. Gordon Brown has followed, calling social mobility 'a national crusade'. Yet, after over a decade in office, social mobility in Britain remains low by international standards and stubbornly stagnant. The massive expansion of rights over the last eleven years – along with other forms of public sector investment – has not given those from poor backgrounds a leg up, singularly failing to improve their prospects of climbing Britain's socio-economic ladder. New Labour's pledge to use the state to level the social playing field has proved a mirage.

In economic terms, the growth of the state – both its increasing authoritarianism and its inflation to service new claims on public services – has failed to repay the enormous investment since 1997.

As *The Economist* concluded in 2008: 'Given that government in Britain chews up 45% of GDP, one percentage point more than in Germany and five more than the OECD average, the accent should be on shrinking the state.'

At a social level, the protection of individual liberty can help brace Britain for the challenges of the twenty-first century. Liberty promotes a healthy and resilient society, capable of absorbing and assimilating diverse influences – particularly relevant during times of change. Personal freedom allows what Mill called 'experiments in living'. He argued: 'It is important to give the freest scope possible to uncustomary things, in order that it may in time appear which of these are fit to be converted into customs.'

Freedom under law should be reasserted over the government's corrosive policy of multiculturalism, which has divided communities rather than bringing them together. Pervasive political correctness, and counter-productive attempts to protect the sensitivities of minority or vulnerable groups, should give way to more rigorous debate. The British tradition of liberty provides the individual citizen, religious communities and other minority groups with the freedom to follow their faith and convictions, consistent with a singular, secular law that protects both freedom of conscience and the wider public interest in a clear and consistent demarcation of public – including criminal – law. An approach that entrenches freedom under law will allow for broad debate, competing views and provide an outlet for the frustrations and grievances felt by both local communities and the wider public.

All sides in controversial debates – on gay adoption, homosexuality in the clergy, the role of sharia law or the direction of foreign policy – need to be heard and tested through robust and critical argument. The parameters of tolerant debate ought to be able to accommodate views that some individuals and groups may find offensive or insulting, but categorically exclude those who incite violence. We should be able, in Voltaire's words, to 'disapprove of what you say, but ... defend to the death your right to say it'. It is legitimate to question the doctrine of any religion, however insulting some may find it. The Danish cartoons were insensitive, but should not be censured by any freedom-loving democracy. Nor should Austria have prosecuted the British historian David Irving for Holocaust denial, despite the repugnance of his views. In the absence of any direct attempt to incite violence against Jews, his revisionist version of history – and credibility – should be left to other historians to shoot down. Irving's trial gave him undue publicity and made him a martyr amongst his racist supporters.

As the twenty-first century advances, scientific innovation will fuel further ethical controversies and political debate, whether on the time limit for abortion, genetically modified crops, stem cell research or measures to address global warming and environmental damage. Maximizing public debate, giving voice to the full range of diverse views – scientific and religious – will be critical to striking a durable social consensus. We should heed Mill's advice that '[h]e who knows only his side of the case, knows little of that'.

If liberty can strengthen British society, the further proliferation of new rights threatens to aggravate its weaknesses, eroding notions of personal, parental and civic responsibility at a time of rising family breakdown and anti-social behaviour. Attitudinal changes have shorn parents, police, teachers and other community figures in authority of their traditional respect. In return, the compensation culture has saddled public servants with stultifying bureaucracy and paralysing legal liabilities.

In addition to the economic and social benefits of restoring a focus on British liberty, it offers a means of reviving confidence in our democracy and reconnecting politics with an apathetic public. Freedom of speech, coupled with a rambunctious media, has traditionally kept British politics far cleaner than most other countries. For example, the restraints on the media in France would be unthinkable in Britain. They helped shield Jacques Chirac and Alain Juppé during their respective terms as President and Prime Minister, despite serious allegations of corruption. They allowed Jacques Barrot to be appointed to the European Commission in 2004, without disclosing a suspended prison term for a criminal conviction for embezzling political party funds – later revealed by a British Member of the European Parliament. Allegations of loans for peerages and illegal party funding in Britain, as culpable as they may be, pale into insignificance compared to the serious claims that French law shields from scrutiny. Transparency International, an NGO that measures corruption worldwide, ranks Britain joint twelfth in the world – France ranked nineteenth. Other common-law countries that take a similar approach to protecting free speech – Australia, Canada and New Zealand – are also amongst the highest-ranking countries. British politics may not be perfect, but free speech helps keep its politics relatively clean by international standards.

During periods of political controversy, most recently over the war in Iraq, the right to peaceful protest provides an important outlet for opposing views on highly contentious national issues. The curtailment of the freedom to demonstrate against unpopular policies undermines public trust and sharpens the sense of disconnection between the public and its political decision-makers. At a time of increasing apathy and scepticism about politics, free speech and peaceful protest afford a measure of popular engagement in the democratic process. The restriction and prosecution of protests against the war in Iraq near Parliament – the heart of our democracy – cut off avenues for the peaceful expression of public discontent at a time when they were needed most.

Looking to the future, Britain is well placed to take advantage of the IT revolution that is changing the way popular debate takes place. As newspaper circulation figures decline, websites, blogs and social networks are opening up moral, political and social discourse to new audiences. In Britain today there are sixty computers for every one hundred people and nearly seven million internet hosts, giving more and more people an interest in and a voice on matters of national debate, well beyond the conventional confines of the Westminster village, rendering freedom of speech more relevant to the average citizen than ever before.

Ultimately what we need is a Bill of Rights, to galvanize a national debate on the constitutional direction Britain is taking and reach out across and beyond party political divides. A Bill of Rights will not automatically solve any of the challenges we face, nor guarantee any of the UK's wider national interests. Many of the policy or legislative failures cited in earlier chapters require specific remedies – ID cards should be scrapped, RIPA reviewed and the health and safety regime revised. However, constitutional reform does contribute to what the political historian Peter Hennessy has described as making the weather – defining the political terms of trade that shape our country.

A wider public debate on a Bill of Rights would allow a national stocktaking of recent developments and future direction. It would strengthen the democratic credentials of any reform – one possibility would be to consult the public directly on the outcome by referendum. A Bill of Rights would, by definition, root our conception of rights in British law and restore a sense of national ownership, rather than unnecessarily importing wholesale the Strasbourg model – a model that includes not only the original Convention rights, influenced by British drafters, but also the swathes of new rights invented by the Strasbourg Court. It would help reverse the popular disconnect with, and rising scepticism about, human rights. A British Bill of Rights would, therefore, have two fundamental advantages over the Human Rights Act or any other alternative constitutional arrangements. First, it would allow the UK to anchor and reorientate a conception of human rights in the British liberal tradition. Second, a home-grown Bill of Rights would help bridge the democratic deficit generated by the seemingly endless judicial legislation emanating from Strasbourg.

The *Observer* commentator Henry Porter has characterized the case for such a Bill of Rights as a resuscitation of the British idea of liberty:

> There is a profound but unacknowledged crisis in this country. Our liberties have been attacked, but we have also suffered a collapse in what I would call the liberty reflex, both in and outside parliament. Twenty years ago … the media would have been inflamed; former members of the National Council for Civil Liberties (now Liberty) such as Harriet Harman and Patricia Hewitt would have been talking about a police state; and there would almost certainly have been marches and protests. But today we just let it go.
>
> This is why I believe a new Bill of Rights is imperative. But it must be a Bill of Rights that is clearly British in origin and that draws its potency from our traditions and culture, and from the settlements of 1689 and Magna Carta, insisting for example on the right to trial by jury, which is not found in European charters and conventions. There is no question that such a bill would overlap with some of the alleged guarantees in the [Human Rights Act], but, crucially, the drafting would be part of a process of general political renewal, in which there was a rebalancing of powers at the very top of our democracy. To my mind it should be restricted to what I have referred to as headline rights and should not include economic rights, which seem to me to be aspirations that can dilute the potency of a Bill of Rights.

It goes without saying that it should be entrenched: that is placed beyond the reach of the authoritarian tendencies that are obviously alive in the civil service and the current administration and permitted by an easily manipulated parliamentary majority.

A Bill of Rights offers Britain the opportunity to celebrate its liberal tradition – the inspiration of Locke, Mill and Berlin, and the legacy of Magna Carta. It would protect the ancient rights that this country has fought to defend through the centuries, at enormous human cost. It would preserve the freedom, respect – but also the responsibilities – of the individual. It would humble an increasingly arrogant and abusive state, obliging greater humility from government ministers and officials in justifying the assumption of power, authority and the control they exercise in our daily lives. It would re-establish some balance in the relationship between the citizen and the state, and restore a presumption in favour of preserving individual liberty – a presumption that might still be rebutted with compelling cause, but not on spurious grounds or trivial whims.

Since becoming Prime Minister, Gordon Brown has regularly steeped his policy ideas – including on human rights – in the language of 'Britishness'. In a speech in 2007, he boldly claimed: 'The character of our country will be defined by how we write the next chapter of British liberty – by whether we do so responsibly and in a way that respects and builds on our traditions, and progressively adds to and enlarges rather than reduces the sphere of freedom.'

Yet with the introduction of ID cards, his fixation on forty-two days' pre-charge detention, the extension of the database state and the expansion of a surveillance society, Gordon Brown lays a reasonable claim to being the most authoritarian Prime Minister in post-war history. He has attacked without compulsion the bedrock values, the very Britishness, he claims to stand for.

This disdain for British liberty flies in the face of a growing consensus. There is political concern across all three major political parties about the government's cavalier approach to habeas corpus, free speech, creeping surveillance and trial by jury. Attempts to extend pre-charge detention to forty-two days have attracted almost universal condemnation in the press, puncturing the myth that the right-wing British media only ever rubbishes human rights.

Outside the Westminster village it is often suggested that the public support forty-two days' pre-charge detention, but it all depends on what you ask – and how. If you ask whether the police should be able to hold 'suspected terrorists' in 'exceptional circumstances' for forty-two days, it loads the question in favour of an affirmative response. People hear 'terrorist' – and a suspicious one at that – and 69 per cent accept that forty-two days might be necessary in an emergency. However, if you ask how long police should be able to hold in pre-charge detention 'people who may be innocent or guilty of a terrorist offence' – a more impartial question, bearing in mind that half of those held for twenty-eight days to date have turned out to be innocent – then 61 per cent answer that the limit should be twenty-eight days or less. Probe further, and give people the option of either forty-two or twenty-eight days coupled with a relaxation of the ban on post-charge questioning, and 70 per cent opt for the latter. More broadly, 71 per cent of the public believe that the government has attacked civil liberties and 59 per cent believe Britain has become a nation of snoopers.

When David Davis, then the Shadow Home Secretary, resigned from Parliament following the House of Commons vote on forty-two days – in protest at the relentless assault on British liberty – his by-election campaign on this single issue attracted support from well beyond his natural political base. Conservative, Labour and Liberal Democrat MPs backed him. He garnered support from a host of unexpected figures outside the conventional world of politics – Bob Geldof, Nigel Kennedy, Terry Waite, General Mike Rose, Colonel Tim Collins, Shami Chakrabati and Martin Bell were just a few of those who came out publicly in his support. Even more telling still, his decision was greeted with an unprecedented wave of public approval. Sixty-nine per cent of the public approved of Davis's principled stand. His campaign received thousands of emails and letters of support from ordinary people sick and tired of bearing the brunt of incessant interference by the state. They matched moral support with financial support. From pensioners posting cheques for £100 to previously unrelated businessmen who sent in much larger sums, Davis struck a chord with the wider public – defying the pollsters and commentators who claimed that no one cares about British liberty.

While there is a growing consensus in favour of protecting British liberty, attitudes shift if the debate is broadened to include additional human rights – and the Human Rights Act. Politicians diverge, the tabloid media complains of a human rights 'bonanza', 'shams' and 'bogus claims', and public opinion becomes more critical if not hostile. The government's own research backs this up. A Ministry of Justice survey in 2008 found that the government's approach to human rights had led to public confusion and concern. The findings show public support for the protection of fundamental rights, but negative attitudes towards the Human Rights Act. It found support for an approach that protects fundamental liberties – associated most closely in the public mind with liberty of the person, freedom of speech, freedom of conscience, freedom of worship, the right to a fair trial, personal privacy and freedom of movement. But it revealed popular concern about the current direction 'whereby individuals can selfishly exercise too much power against the system and find justification for antisocial behaviour in terms of their "rights"'. It also highlighted a common complaint that human rights 'burden [public service] providers and encourage unscrupulous individuals to seek unjustified compensation'. Many associate human rights with political correctness, lack of discipline amongst the younger generation and the compensation culture. While 84 per cent support a law to protect fundamental rights, 57 per cent believe that 'Too many people take advantage of the Human Rights Act.'

The inflation of rights beyond fundamental liberties has devalued their currency, tarnishing the credibility of human rights in general, at a time when British liberty has never been more important. A Bill of Rights provides an opportunity to refocus on liberty and stem the flow of novel rights, confining them to the realm of policy and the level of normal legal protection afforded to every other economic, social and political interest or claim. It offers the best chance of forging a strong national consensus on fundamental rights.

In contrast, some campaigners are lobbying for a Bill of Rights that further expands human rights well beyond even their current broad scope. Parliament's Joint Committee on Human Rights (JCHR) published a report in 2008 calling on the government to enact a Bill of Rights including a range of new economic and social rights – among them human rights to healthcare services, education, accommodation and even benchmark standards of living for everyone in Britain. Supporters of economic and social rights on the left, such as JCHR Chairman Andrew Dismore, often cite South Africa's Constitution, the negotiation of which was heavily influenced by the socialist African National Congress Party in alliance with the South African Communist Party.

This approach is muddled and bound to lead to confusion. In proposing '[a] duty of progressive realisation of economic and social rights by reasonable legislative and other measures, within available resources', it confuses the basic notion of constitutionally guaranteed rights and the policy goals of political parties and – once in office – governments. Fundamental liberties reflect the most basic, minimum, freedoms that everyone in Britain should have as of right. There is greater – although by no means unanimous – political consensus on such threshold rights. In contrast, the differing views on economic and social policy aspirations for the country – which divide opinion across and amongst political parties – should be debated in Parliament and public, and decided at general elections. They depend on moral and political considerations and available resources, all of which are too fluid to be rigidly cast in stone as constitutional rights enforced by judges.

The draft model proposed by the JCHR seeks to bury these basic democratic choices in legal language, stipulating rights to '*appropriate* health care services', 'free full-time education *suitable* to [individual] needs', '*adequate* accommodation *appropriate* to [individual] needs' and an '*adequate* standard of living' (my italics). Words like 'appropriate', 'suitable' and 'adequate' are subjective and value-driven, deliberately designed to allow a degree of flexibility. But ultimately, even under the JCHR's 'light touch' approach to judicial review, it will be left to judges to decide in court what levels of healthcare, education or accommodation are 'appropriate' – i.e. what is fair – for everyone. This approach to human rights represents an astonishing abdication of democratic choice, in deciding economic and social policy, to unaccountable judges. Worryingly, the government shows signs of gradually moving towards an acceptance of the case for incorporating these extensive new economic and social rights into its plans for constitutional reform. This is a mistake. The fluid and competing priorities of economic and social policy in the twenty-first century should be debated and determined by accountable ministers and democratically elected law-makers – not by lawyers in court.

As Lord Bingham has argued, if proposals for further constitutional reform are carried forward, they 'should lay down enforceable rights and duties and not resort to the expression of hopes and aspirations'. More broadly, he adds, such reform:

> ... should, so far as achievable, be neutral, not only (of course) as between political parties but also as between systems of social and economic organisation. If the history of the last 50 years shows nothing else, it surely shows that the beliefs of one generation become the heresies of the next. Constitutional provisions should never be allowed to hamper growth, prevent diversity or restrict the scope for new ideas.

In one sense, a more restrictive constitutional approach to human rights is the reflection of a particular view of liberal democracy. Nevertheless, it remains neutral in that it seeks to maximise freedom and diversity, and preserve the scope for elected law-makers – rather than courts – to decide the socio-economic direction of the country.

A Bill of Rights should, therefore, be limited to the core of rights in the European Convention, as originally inspired and formulated, adding only those quintessentially British rights left out. The original Convention reflected the British idea that rights protect the citizen from the state and uphold our fundamental freedoms. The right to life, prohibition of torture, liberty of the person, right to a fair trial, right to respect for privacy and the various freedoms of conscience – thought, religion, speech and association – give expression to the traditional British commitment to liberty. Those core Convention rights have also been a model for wider international human rights treaties, including the principal UN human rights treaty, the International Covenant on Civil and Political Rights. However, a British Bill of Rights would also have the major advantage of allowing us to tailor the text to our own national traditions, priorities and customs. For example, trial by jury can be properly protected, and freedom of speech given greater emphasis than would be the case in other European countries.

A Bill of Rights should also make full use of the doctrine of the margin of appreciation under the Convention, to spell out in greater detail the scope of rights and their corresponding qualifications, correcting one of the failures of the Human Rights Act. It should focus our judiciary on its primary task, which is to give effect to British rights instead of trying to divine and decipher the murky case law emanating from Strasbourg. Refocusing the domestic courts on the strict judicial task of applying those enshrined, fundamental liberties would put a brake on the invention of novel categories of rights.

History demonstrates the temptation that governments – of all political persuasions – will be tempted to take action that undermines our fundamental liberties. While all governments in office have a natural reflex to try to curtail our freedoms to some degree, the last decade has brought that risk into sharper focus. The Labour Party entered office on an election manifesto genuinely committed to safeguarding civil liberties, but has taken unprecedented steps to undermine them. In reality, fundamental liberties cannot depend for their protection on either the government of the day or the will of Parliament. The vote in favour of forty-two days in the House of Commons in June 2008 demonstrates the weakness of relying on Parliament as the sole check. The deployment of the resources of state to push through the vote on a deeply unpopular and draconian measure, amidst widespread reports by Labour rebels of bullying, intimidation and financial inducements, illustrates how easy it is for a government – through Parliament – to ride roughshod over our fundamental freedoms.

Nor has the Human Rights Act prevented this sustained assault on British liberty. While the courts may declare primary legislation incompatible with Convention rights, the government can delay, obstruct and ultimately corral Parliament to ignore or fudge judicial findings of human rights violations. Despite countless infringements of British liberties, the law was altered just ten times, between 2000 and 2007, in response to violations under the Human Rights Act. The Human Rights Act was designed as a compromise between the need for greater protection of rights and concerns about parliamentary sovereignty, but it falls between both stools. If a court declares legislation incompatible with the Human Rights Act, it cannot uphold the right or strike down the offending law, so the individual is not properly protected. In the meantime, ministers can rush through changes to the law by order, using a fast-track procedure. So, in such politically contentious cases there is barely any real parliamentary scrutiny either.

Experience over the last decade supports the case for entrenching greater constitutional protection for our fundamental freedoms. Options include strengthening judicial power, including the power of the courts to strike down those provisions of a law that violate the fundamental liberties set out in a Bill of Rights. This can be done by amending the Parliament Act, which lays down the procedure under which new law is passed. It could require, for any law that conflicts with our Bill of Rights, that it will only be upheld in court if it has been passed either by both the House of Commons and the House of Lords, or by some form of special majority (rather than just 51 per cent of the votes cast). Parliament, as the central source of democratic legitimacy, would thereby retain the ultimate right to revise, amend or overrule the protections set out in a Bill of Rights. This would allow a measure of flexibility to adapt to changes in circumstances and realities over the long term. However, by entrenching a limited number of core rights, it would be much more difficult for governments to pass knee-jerk, reactive or populist measures that do not withstand serious scrutiny. This would strike the right balance between protecting liberty and preserving democratic accountability.

It would also give judges considerable new power. Citizens would be able to wield – and judges enforce – a core of strictly defined rights, effectively trumping attempts by government, or Parliament, to ignore or interfere with fundamental liberties. The main objection to giving our judges 'strike-down' power to protect the individual from abuse by the state is that it would infringe parliamentary sovereignty. However, the exponential increase in EU law-making power and other delegations of legislative power have altered the traditional Diceyan conception of parliamentary sovereignty – the idea of a single level of law made exclusively by Parliament. While there are already wide areas where Parliament no longer reigns supreme, entrenching a core set of rights would still allow parliamentary amendment or repeal, thereby preserving parliamentary sovereignty. But it would make it much less easy for Parliament to override our fundamental freedoms on a political whim.

While the current role of the courts under the Human Rights Act cannot protect our fundamental freedoms, it also exposes the UK to judicial legislation at home and from Strasbourg. So the reality is that judges are already exercising significant political and, more worryingly, a degree of legislative power. A Bill of Rights would strengthen the exercise of judicial power in return for refocusing and limiting it to the application of fewer – core – rights. Crucially, the legislative role would be removed, and returned to our elected representatives in Parliament, who would draw up the Bill of Rights. That would leave British judges with the limited, but critically important, job of weighing up competing rights, or balancing individual rights with the wider public interest. Judges would not be creating new rights, just applying those already set by our democratically elected Parliament. This refocused remit would be more consistent with the judicial role than the current blurring of the judicial and law-making functions under the Human Rights Act.

Even then, UK judges would inevitably risk being drawn into political controversy when interpreting the application of rights, for example, in areas such as counter-terrorism or criminal justice. Under a Bill of Rights, the courts could determine that forty-two days' pre-charge detention is a disproportionate response to the terrorist threat level, uphold the right of peaceful protest in the face of excessive security legislation and review the use of intrusive surveillance to monitor compliance with trivial laws. In such cases, there would inevitably be concern that unelected judges are standing in the way of security laws passed by Parliament. That is why it would be important for Parliament to spell out in greater detail and itself endorse – through a Bill of Rights – the limitations on its own power. Equally, there is a difference between judges making decisions in controversial areas, which they have always done, and judicial creation of new law. Judges have often been engaged in politically sensitive areas. Where it involves the interpretation of legal questions, it is not inherently at odds with the execution of their judicial responsibilities. Sentencing serious criminals often attracts political reaction, but remains a fundamentally judicial business. Challenges to government powers – on grounds other than human rights – can also properly be reviewed by the courts, for example the recent challenge to the government's decision to halt the corruption investigation into a Saudi arms deal involving BAE systems. Even in politically controversial areas, it remains the judge's role to dispassionately apply – but not rewrite – the law.

In this way, a Bill of Rights would protect freedom under law, while reinforcing the other pillars of our liberal democracy – the rule of law, separation of powers and democratic accountability. To bridge the current democratic deficit, the international relationship between British and Strasbourg courts also needs to be refined – recalibrated to reflect their proper roles. While UK courts should be responsible for enforcing UK rights, the Strasbourg Court can currently impact on the UK in two ways. First, where a claim against the British government is taken through the UK courts and fails, but the claimant petitions the Strasbourg Court. Second, where UK courts apply rulings from Strasbourg in other cases brought against other countries. While we cannot avoid the first without pulling out of the Convention altogether, many of the problems in practice have resulted from the second – the impact of the wider, expansive and unpredictable Strasbourg case law through the Human Rights Act. Yet there is nothing in the Convention which requires a country to adhere to the rulings of the Strasbourg Court in cases to which it is not a party.

Under a Bill of Rights, the UK courts would not need to follow or even be guided by the unwieldy and inconsistent Strasbourg case law. The normal rules of judicial interpretation already allow reference to European – and other important international human rights – jurisprudence if it is relevant, and when it may be useful. The House of Lords should be treated as the final court of appeal in the UK, and our judges should focus exclusively on giving effect to a Bill of Rights, rather than fretting about the political implications of any subsequent application to Strasbourg – which are for governments to worry about. The French and German constitutional courts already adopt this approach, in different ways, leaving them greater latitude in determining the interpretation of Convention rights. French officials have consistently, and with relative ease, ignored the full extent of the restrictions on deportation of terrorists and extremists laid down by the Strasbourg Court in the *Chahal* case, while their opposite numbers in Whitehall struggle and strive to apply the ruling to the letter. The German courts apply their Basic Law, which is in many places wider than the Strasbourg case law, but in some areas more restrictive. Even the British government has now explicitly recognized the unnecessary strictures placed on the UK by the Human Rights Act, and acknowledged the scope for making greater use of the margin of appreciation to reprioritize the pecking order of rights in this country.

A Bill of Rights would offer an opportunity to ground human rights in British history and traditions. The redefinition of the judicial relationship would confine the UK courts to the application of our basic rights and curb the importation of new rights through the back door, by mitigating the impact of the relentless flow of judicial legislation from Strasbourg. That way we can protect our fundamental liberties, meet our treaty obligations and return democratic control over the human rights process to British law and UK courts.

Nevertheless, a Bill of Rights cannot immunize the UK from adverse rulings from the Strasbourg Court, and there are limits on how far the UK can refine its interpretation of Convention rights. For example, the Strasbourg Court is unlikely to accept any dilution of the absolute ban on torture, to allow deportation of those that pose a risk to our security but would face torture if returned home. However, a Bill of Rights would allow the government to specify a clearer burden of proof of the risk of persecution, before it is claimed as grounds for blocking deportation proceedings. It could also limit the ban on deportation to clear-cut cases of torture – excluding other comparatively minor categories of mistreatment. That would give Britain greater scope to expel those threatening public safety and reduce the scope for abuse of the rules, while preserving our commitment to the absolute prohibition on torture. It would be a defensible position, based on principle, that would meet the standards set out in the UN Convention Against Torture and minimize the countervailing risks of adverse judgments from Strasbourg. In practice, both the risks and consequences of being overruled by Strasbourg – if we replace the Human Rights Act with a Bill of Rights – have been overstated. In one recent Italian case, the Strasbourg Court refused to dilute its earlier broad rulings on deportation of those at risk if returned home, but pointedly observed that in practice it had 'only rarely' blocked deportation on grounds of torture. The UK government's own research has pointed out that domestic French courts already get away with applying less strict standards than their British counterparts:

> ... claims based on appeals to Article 3 [the prohibition of torture and inhuman or degrading treatment] have met with far less sympathy in the French courts ... of the eleven cases in France in which issues surrounding torture were raised [between 2000 and 2007], the courts rejected all claims based on Article 3 ... claims based on this article are rarely if ever successful. In part, this is a result of the fact that the courts are generally unwilling to question the evidence on which initial administrative decisions to deport or extradite individuals are made ...

So the French courts have not applied the same strict standards as their British counterparts, but have rarely been hauled up by the Strasbourg Court. As the UK Ministry of Justice concedes, the practical reality is that before the Human Rights Act, 'the time taken and the expense involved meant that only the most serious allegations could be dealt with at Strasbourg'. Given that a Bill of Rights would ensure protection – in Britain – in those, most serious, cases, the worst case scenario is that the Strasbourg Court might take a different view in other less serious cases – including, for example, attempts to block deportation that are really claims for medical treatment rather than violations of the ban against torture. In those relatively limited circumstances, the consequences of adverse rulings from Strasbourg have been exaggerated.

The review mechanism for monitoring compliance with Strasbourg rulings involves diplomatic peer review amongst the member states of the Council of Europe. The ultimate sanction for ignoring the Strasbourg Court is suspension or expulsion, which requires a two-thirds majority of the forty-seven European countries – and no country has ever been thrown out of the Council of Europe. The bottom line is that the kinds of issue, that create a serious problem during the diplomatic review process that follows an adverse ruling from the Strasbourg Court, are military coups and widespread or flagrant violations of fundamental rights. Amidst the much worse human rights records of other European countries reviewed in the Council of Europe, the practical repercussions for Britain of resisting Strasbourg's more expansive rulings in comparatively less serious cases would be slight.

This is not just about Britain having the courage to make full use of the diplomatic review process to cock a snook at the Strasbourg Court in those less serious cases where we think – on principle, not expediency – that it has got its case law wrong. It is also a question of positively influencing the direction of the Strasbourg Court. There is widespread misunderstanding about the role of international courts. Under international law, the relationship between national and international courts is two-way. International courts are not courts of appeal – they expect to engage in a dialogue with national courts. For example, the rules of the International Court of Justice (ICJ) – the principal judicial organ of the UN – make express provision to enable the ICJ judges to draw on the approach of national courts in determining international law. Similarly, the Strasbourg Court already draws heavily from the practice of national courts. The enactment of a Bill of Rights would provide an opportunity to strengthen the British contribution to that process, including by resisting the direction of judicial legislation from Strasbourg. As the former President of the Strasbourg Court, Luzius Wildhaber, characterized the relationship, it involves 'a two-way process whereby developments in the domestic legal system influence Strasbourg to change its case-law'. Furthermore, the Strasbourg Court is much more likely to be receptive to national approaches that stray from the strict letter of its own approach, where they are based on the judicial application of domestic constitutional guarantees that reflect and respect the core rights set out in the Convention – rather than conflicts arising from knee-jerk legislation or headline-grabbing security measures.

Nonetheless, this approach does not come without any risk at all. The adoption of this model might increase the risk of some divergence between the Strasbourg Court and UK courts in relatively marginal cases. But there are no risk-free alternatives. Those risks must be balanced against the much greater risks involved in the direction in which Britain is currently heading – the risks of inflating rights, fuelled by judicial legislation from Strasbourg. This model offers the best alternative – a principled and transparent approach which protects our fundamental freedoms while strengthening democratic accountability.

Some have suggested that replacing the Human Rights Act with a Bill of Rights would require UK withdrawal from the Convention, the Council of Europe and even the EU. That kind of scaremongering ignores fifty years of British practice prior to the Human Rights Act and the experience of other constitutional courts throughout Europe. David Pannick QC argues that: 'Abolishing the Human Rights Act would be pointless if people retain the right to take their grievances to Strasbourg. Alternatively, we pull out of the Convention altogether, which means we have to pull out of the European Community. You can't have it both ways.'

Ben Emmerson QC agrees: '[I]f a Bill of Rights offered protection that was less than that offered by the Strasbourg jurisprudence, it would fail to prevent cases going there.'

Pannick and Emmerson oversimplify the position in two ways. First, they gloss over the distinction between cases brought against the UK and the wider Strasbourg case law involving cases against all other countries. We can avoid directly importing the Strasbourg case law into UK law – it is not required by the Convention and other countries have chosen not to. While it is correct to say that, if Britain does not comply with all the Strasbourg case law, it will still be possible for claims to be lodged with the Strasbourg Court, this legalistic view ignores the practical realities. As the House of Lords has complained, the Strasbourg Court's case law is haphazard, so the fact that it decided one way in a particular case brought against one country, does not guarantee the same result in other cases brought against Britain – which is all the more reason for Britain to steer its own course, according to its own high standards.

Equally, if the UK replaces the Human Rights Act with a Bill of Rights, far fewer claimants will – in practice – take advantage of Strasbourg's more expansive human rights rulings, because they would not be able to rely on them in the UK courts, but only before the Strasbourg Court. While there are human rights cases ongoing in Britain every day, the Strasbourg Court can only hear a selection of high-priority cases, including much more serious allegations of human rights violations. In 2006, 60 per cent of pending claims lodged with the Strasbourg Court comprised complaints against five countries – Turkey, Russia, Romania, Ukraine and Poland. So, repealing the Human Rights Act would significantly reduce the direct impact of the Strasbourg case law to the most serious cases brought against the UK, which reach the Strasbourg Court. Yet under a Bill of Rights, the most serious violations of fundamental liberties would already be dealt with by UK courts. Far from being pointless, a Bill of Rights would have a decisive, practical effect. On the other hand, the Human Rights Act has not immunized the UK from adverse rulings by the Strasbourg Court – claimants can and still do take their grievances against the UK to Strasbourg.

Pannick's second criticism also fails a basic reality check. The suggestion that there is an umbilical link tying the Strasbourg case law, the Convention and membership of the EU may make for an elaborate legal opinion, but it is politically naïve. It would be possible to disapply the Strasbourg case law, through a Bill of Rights, and stay within the Convention and the Council of Europe. Even if Britain pulled out of the Convention – which is neither necessary nor desirable – while it would certainly generate real anxiety among other European countries, it would not automatically lead to our ejection from the EU. In the absence of serious and sustained human rights abuses by the UK, there would be no appetite amongst other European countries to question British membership. The diplomatic realities are that, while British withdrawal from the Convention would be a unilateral action, British ejection from the EU would require multilateral agreement – requiring an implausible consensus amongst the remaining members. On the contrary, the prospect of British departure would generate serious concern and opposition amongst many of our European friends. Anyone with any experience of EU diplomacy will know the difficulty it has in reaching a consensus on anything, let alone the prospect of kicking out one of its key members. Ultimately, British membership of the EU would be a political – not legal – question, decided by statesmen not lawyers.

Wider developments in the EU are, however, creating additional complications. An increasing number of Directives and Regulations touch on human rights law and the government's enthusiasm for the Lisbon Treaty has created serious legal uncertainty. It remains unclear what effect the EU's Charter of Fundamental Rights would have in UK law, if the Lisbon Treaty ever entered into force. At best, it would create unhelpful duplication. At worst, it would impose on Britain an additional tier of expanding EU human rights law – the limits of which would be decided by the European Court of Justice in Luxembourg rather than courts in the UK.

If replacing the Human Rights Act with a Bill of Rights would not require Britain to withdraw from the Convention, nor has the case for withdrawal yet been convincingly made. While some Eurosceptics, such as Lord Tebbit, advocate withdrawal to return law-making authority to the UK, others like the UK Independence Party support the repeal of the Human Rights Act without withdrawal from the Convention. Some campaign groups, like MigrationWatch, promote withdrawal to deal with the specific problem of deporting terrorist suspects who face torture at home. However, as already considered, there are less drastic ways to stem the flow of judicial legislation from Strasbourg, and a Bill of Rights could give the UK greater clarity and flexibility over deportation decisions (albeit not to the extent sought by MigrationWatch).

The reality is that the Convention – and the Strasbourg Court – are both important and imperfect. Equally, the Strasbourg case law is not static, which means the UK can positively influence its development. In addition to enacting a Bill of Rights – which will address many of the problems – there remains a range of ways for the British government to constructively engage with and improve the Strasbourg Court, including challenging its rulings, derogating from the Convention under certain conditions, seeking a coalition of states to amend the Convention or even trying to negotiate UN Security Council resolutions to guide its approach to security issues. As a matter of priority, the UK could – and should – take the initiative in the Council of Europe to address the root of the problem, namely the number of non-judicial appointments at the Strasbourg Court. There are too many academics, diplomats and lawyers – rather than real judges – in Strasbourg. In fact, there is increasing recognition of the importance of 'quality control' in the election of judges to international courts – reflected in the procedures developed at other international courts, such as the International Criminal Court and European Union Civil Service Tribunal.

For those genuinely committed to strengthening the long-term health of the international rule of law, the mixed calibre of international judges is a real cause for concern. This range of alternative means of engaging with and influencing the Strasbourg Court ought to defer the need to consider the nuclear option of withdrawal from the Convention.

Notwithstanding criticisms of the Strasbourg Court, we should also acknowledge that membership of the Convention and the Council of Europe has proved a valuable element in UK foreign policy. There are good reasons for Britain to remain a party. Membership strengthens our credibility in pressing human rights issues against dictators and other authoritarian regimes across the world. It is easier for Britain to put diplomatic pressure on other countries to respect their international human rights obligations, while avoiding spurious claims of double standards, if it remains a party to what is widely regarded internationally as the leading human rights treaty. The UK and its European partners also use Convention standards as a key benchmark for assessing the human rights credentials of countries applying to join or engage in partnerships with the EU – a foreign policy objective common to all the main political parties. Withdrawal from the Convention would send a negative signal to the wider world about Britain's commitment to human rights, whether dealing with our international partners, reforming governments in the Balkans or dictators beyond.

CONCLUSION

Human rights in Britain are adrift from their moorings. Liberal democracy in this country has been attacked from opposite sides, both passively absorbed with a degree of fatalism. More than two hundred years ago, the British statesman and philosopher Edmund Burke warned that 'the people never give up their liberties but under some delusion'. Throughout the last decade, the assault on British liberty in the name of security has been fraudulently misrepresented as the inevitable price to pay in an era in which 'the rules of the game are changing'. So, too, the proliferation of rights has been inaccurately portrayed as an inescapable, non-negotiable condition of EU membership. Liberty lost, and democracy denied, we are submissively acquiescing in a seismic shift in the fault lines of the relationship between the state and the citizen – without either willing it or objecting to it.

Yet neither complacency nor apathy can hide the fact that the problems are of our own making, the decisions are voluntary not pre-determined and there are alternative courses Britain is free to chart. There is cross-party recognition that government has grown abusive, arbitrary and arrogant in the exercise of its powers. There is wider public support for restoring some balance in the relationship between the citizen and the state – as well as concern that rights are being used to take unfair advantage of 'the system'. We need a broad national debate on these issues, because they go to the heart of our democracy – who we are, what we stand for and what kind of country we will bequeath our children and grandchildren. There is only so much individual freedom we can forfeit before it irreversibly changes the character of our country and our citizenship of it. Amidst comparatively trivial proposals to promote 'Britishness' through greater flag-waving, changing the national anthem or an extra bank holiday, nothing more captures this elusive definition than the fundamental freedoms nurtured in, and defended by, this country over eight hundred years since Magna Carta. This is the real debate about what it means to be British.

As this book went to press, the government was embroiled in an unprecedented controversy, as counter-terrorism police arrested opposition MP, Damian Green, searching his home and office at the House of Commons and seizing computers, phones and privileged documents. The heavy-handed raid was triggered by Mr Green acting as a conduit into the public domain of leaked documents, disclosing serial incompetence at the Home Office – airing issues of manifest public interest, and no less political embarrassment. The arrest of an elected representative for telling the truth should sound a warning siren. This dual attack on liberty and democracy shows just how far we have come since 1997, and should dispel the myth – once and for all – that only those with something to hide have anything to fear.

In the lead-up to the next general election, all three main political parties will present proposals for constitutional reform. The upcoming debate on a Bill of Rights offers a precious opportunity to reconsider our approach, reverse the assault on liberty and restore rights to their proper place within the wider architecture of our liberal democracy.

NOTES

xv **'The liberties stripped from the weak'** *Guardian*, 10 December 2007.

xv **'Human rights is merely a sweetener'** *Daily Mail*, 6 November 2007.

xv **Wave upon wave** Stella Rimington, quoted in the *Daily Mail*, 13 July 2007.

3 **'the foundation of principles'** Winston Churchill, *A History of the English-Speaking Peoples*, chapter VII, volume 2, p. 79, 1956. For recent accounts of the history of Magna Carta, see also Ralph Turner, *King John: England's Evil King?*, 2005; Frank McLynn, *Lionheart and Lackland: King Richard, King John and the Wars of Conquest*, 2006; and Geoffrey Hindley, *The Magna Carta: The Story of the Origins of Liberty*, 2008.

5 **'indefinite imprisonment'** Paragraph 74, *A(FC) and Others v Secretary of State for the Home Department*, judgment of the House of Lords dated 16 December 2004, [2004] UKHL 56, also known as the Belmarsh judgment.

7 **'groped in the dim light'** Churchill, *A History of the English-Speaking Peoples*, chapter VII, volume 2.

8 **'a man's house is his castle'** Edward Coke, *The Third Part of the Institutes of the Laws of England*, chapter 73, 1628.

11 **It is based on a unique** See *Entick v Carrington* (1765), 19 St Tr 1030.

13 **He represents an early** See Thomas Hobbes, *Leviathan*, first published in 1651.

13 **'[A]ll men may be restrained'** John Locke, *Second Treaties of Government*, chapter 2, first published in 1689.

13 **'take away, or impair'** Ibid., paragraph 6.

14 **'freedom of men'** Ibid., paragraph 22, chapter 4.

14 **'because it may be'** Ibid., paragraph 143, chapter 12.

14 **'[it] is a feature'** Lord Mustill, *R v Home Secretary, ex p Fire Brigades' Union* [1995] 2 AC at 567.

15 **'tyranny of the majority'** See in particular, John Stuart Mill, *On Liberty*, 1859, published by Everyman, 1994.

15 '[T]hat's the only purpose' Ibid., chapter 1, p. 81.

15 'diversity of character and culture' Ibid., chapter 3, p. 138.

15 '[I]t is important' Ibid., chapter 3, p. 135

15 '[h]e who knows only his side' Ibid., chapter 2, p. 104.

16 'Democracy is two wolves' Unsourced, but widely attributed.

16 'the slaughter of individuals' 'Two Concepts of Liberty', 1958, Isaiah Berlin, published in *Liberty*, OUP, 2002, p. 212.

16 'from the crooked timber' Ibid., p. 216.

16 'the area within which' Ibid., p. 169.

16 'matter of argument' Ibid., p. 171.

17 'Liberty is not the only goal' Ibid., p. 172

17 'Everything is what it is' Ibid.

18 'cost blood' A. C. Grayling, *Towards the Light*, chapter 1, p. 6, published by Bloomsbury, 2007.

18 'a war, viewed' House of Commons, 3 September 1939.

19 'Liberty, therefore, is' Karl Marx, *On the Jewish Question*, 1843.

19 'Freedom is capitalist' Vladimir Ilyich Lenin, *The State and Revolution*, chapter 5, section 2, 1917.

19 'Freedom is the recognition' Quoted in Alan Mackay, *The Harvest of a Quiet Eye*, 1977.

20 'Liberty is precious' Quoted in Sidney and Beatrice Webb, *Soviet Communism*, 1935.

20 It is estimated Jonathan Glover, *Humanity: A Moral History of the Twentieth Century*, p. 237, published by Jonathan Cape, 1999.

20 Communist China's Great Leap Ibid., p. 284.

20 The Khmer Rouge Ibid., p. 309.

20 'mass repressions' President Khrushchev's speech to Twentieth Party Congress of the Communist Party of the Soviet Union, 25 February 1956.

21 'Since the State' A. Robertson and J. Merrills, *Human Rights in the World*, chapter 1, p. 10, published by Manchester University Press, 1996.

22 Looking around the table See Peter Oborne, *The Triumph of the Political Class*, chapter 7, published by Simon and Schuster, 2007. See also A. Roth and B. Criddle, *Parliamentary Profiles*, 1997–2002.

27 'We must plan for' Karl Popper, *The Open Society and its Enemies*, 1945.

28 While the government In November 2006 the Director General briefed publicly that it was monitoring 1600 individuals involved in

terrorism. The updated figure in November 2007 was 2000.

29 **Yet, at the same time, violent** See Chapter 4.

29 **'A pattern is emerging'** Jenny McCartney, *Sunday Telegraph*, 11 May 2008.

31 **'[T]he great privilege'** Winston Churchill, 21 November 1943, in a telegram to the Home Secretary explaining his decision to release Oswald Mosley.

32 **The book was** For an account of human rights cases during the 1970s and 1980s, see the sixth edition of Geoffrey Robertson's *Freedom, the Individual and the Law*, published by Penguin, 1989.

33 **'Let no one'** Prime Minister's Press Conference, 5 August 2005.

35 **In 2006, the Director General** Reported on BBC Online, 10 November 2006.

35 **By 2007, her successor** Speech by Jonathan Evans, Head of MI5, to the Society of Editors, 5 November 2007.

35 **Despite some indications** See, for example, Gordon Brown's speech on liberty at the University of Westminster, 25 October 2007.

36 **Yet at the time** Widely reported. See *The Times*, 12 June 2008.

36 Statement by the Home Secretary to Parliament, 13 October 2008.

37 **complex terrorism investigations** Report by Justice, *From Arrest to Charge in 48 Hours: Complex terrorism cases in the US since 9/11*, November 2007.

39 **Far from being** See the comments of Ken Jones, President of ACPO, to *Observer*, 15 July 2007.

39 **While the Commissioner** Sir Ian Blair's evidence to the Home Affairs Select Committee, 9 October 2007.

41 **The Civil Contingencies** See section 19(1) (c) of the Civil Contingencies Act 1994, which defines the kinds of emergency covered by the legislation.

42 **'epidemic'** Ibid.

44 **wholly innocent individual** The case is summarized in *The Week*, 23 February 2008. See also the judgment of the Court of Appeal in *Raissi v Secretary of State for the Home Department*, 14 February 2008 [2008] EWCA Civ 72.

44 **The FBI quickly** See the report in *Washington Post*, 18 December 2001.

45 **'It behoves us all'** Interview, *Daily Mail*, 13 July 2007.

45 **'on a practical basis'** Maiden speech of Baroness Manningham-Buller, House of Lords, 7 July 2008.

46 **Chief Constables and other** Widely reported, including by *The Times*,
    6 June 2008. See also Andy Hayman, *The Times*, 6 October 2008.

46 **'If we now go back'** House of Lords debate, 13 December 2005,
    col. 1175.

46 **'Make no mistake'** Lord Dear, *Guardian*, 31 March 2008.

47 **'I want to have absolute'** *Today* programme, BBC Radio 4,
    14 November 2007.

47 **In 2007, the head of** DAC Peter Clarke, 'Learning From Experience –
    Counter Terrorism in the UK since 9/11', 24 April 2007, *Policy
    Exchange*.

48 **'Muslim groups said'** Equality Impact Assessment to the 2008
    Counter-Terrorism Bill, published by the Home Office in July 2007.

49 **'The series of terrorist'** Peter Clarke, former head of counter-terrorism
    at the Metropolitan Police, *The Times*, 9 September 2008.

51 **'to look tough on terror'** YouGov/Liberty poll, March 2008.

51 **Stop and search** *Arrest for Recorded Crime (Notifiable Offences) and the
    Operation of Certain Police Powers under PACE England and Wales
    2006/07*, Ministry of Justice, July 2008.

51 **The rate of convictions** The figures are available on the Home Office
    website.

51 **It was disclosed that** Reported at BBC Online, 12 December 2007.

52 **a thirty-four-year-old** Reported variously, including in *The Times*,
    17 October 2005.

52 **The family was surrounded** Reported variously, including BBC
    Online, 23 July 2008.

53 **Only thirty individuals** As of November 2007.

53 **There were eighteen** See the quarterly ministerial updates to
    Parliament on the control order regime, issued by written ministerial
    statement.

53 **'small number of cases'** Paragraph 27, Third Report by the
    Independent Reviewer, Lord Carlile, pursuant to Section 14(3) of the
    Prevention of Terrorism Act 2005, 18 February 2008.

53 **Lord Carlile** Ibid., at paragraph 26.

54 **Privacy campaign groups** See Liberty's Response to the Home Office
    Document 'National Identity Scheme Delivery Plan 2008', June 2008.

55 **'… beginning to represent'** Oral evidence to the Home Affairs Select
    Committee, House of Commons, 8 June 2004.

55 **However, the overwhelming** For a rebuttal of each argument in favour

of ID cards, see *Identity Crisis – the Case against ID cards*, Peter Lilley MP, published by the Bow Group, February 2005.

55 **'massive identity fraud'** Jerry Fishenden, writing in *Scotsman*, 18 October 2005.

55 **Even if that loophole** Reported in *The Times*, 6 August 2008.

56 **'Perhaps in the past'** Tony McNulty, speech to IPPR, reported widely, including in *The Times*, 4 August 2005.

56 **Unsurprisingly, as the ongoing** YouGov poll, published December 2007.

56 **Given these flaws** Identity Project Report, London School of Economics, June 2005.

57 **'the liberty of speaking'** Thomas Jefferson, Reply to Philadelphia Democratic Republicans, 1808.

58 **In response to** *The Governance of Britain – Constitutional Renewal*, published by the Ministry of Justice, March 2008.

58 **The use of ASBO** Widely reported, including on BBC Online, 3 May 2006.

59 **'cult'** See the *Guardian*, 20 May 2008. The prosecution was subsequently dropped.

59 **'Undercover Mosque'** Widely reported.

60 **In another case, a whistle-blower** See Martin Bright, 'Talking to Terrorists', *New Statesman*, 20 February 2006; and Martin Bright, 'When Progressives Treat with Reactionaries', *Policy Exchange*, July 2006.

61 **'If you shout out'** Cited in *Daily Telegraph*, 6 January 2007.

61 **The Metropolitan Police** A Metropolitan Police spokesperson was quoted in *Daily Telegraph*, 7 February 2006.

61 **In another notorious case** The case of Abu Hamza has been widely reported across the media.

62 **In 2004, a year before** Ken Livingstone's evidence to the Home Affairs Select Committee, 13 September 2005.

65 **'Trial by jury is'** Lord Devlin, *Trial by Jury*, published by Stevens, 1956.

66 **Following an enormous** Based on figures on government expenditure on 'public order and safety', OECD statistical database 2008.

66 **Yet few are willing** *Crime in England and Wales 2007/08*, published by the Home Office, July 2008.

66 **Since 1997, police-recorded** Ibid.

66 **We now have over** Home Office papers deposited in the House of Commons, 2 June 2008.

67 **'An epidemic of violence'** See 'The Burden of Crime in the EU', EU
ICS 2005; 'Anti-social behaviour across Europe', ADT Europe, May
2006; and *Time* magazine (front cover), 7 April 2008.

67 **Human rights lawyers** For example, see Geoffrey Robertson, *Freedom,
the Individual and the Law*, published by Penguin,1989.

68 **Traditional socialists** See Hugh Collins, *Marxism and Law*, published
by OUP, 1982.

68 **'... the judiciary'** Will Hutton, *The State We're In*, chapter 2, p. 36,
published by Vintage, 1995.

69 **'My thesis is that'** J. A. G. Griffiths, *The Politics of the Judiciary*,
conclusion, p. 319, published by Fontana, 1991.

69 **'In both democratic'** Ibid., p. 328–9.

69 **'tough on crime'** The phrase was coined by Tony Blair during his
period as Shadow Home Secretary.

71 **One fifteen-year-old boy** See the collation of cases online by
Statewatch's 'ASBOwatch'.

71 **Research by the British Institute** Reported by BBC Online, who
commissioned the research, 23 February 2007. See also the reports
regarding use of ASBOs for children with Tourette's syndrome, BBC
Online, 15 August 2005.

71 **An ASBO was** See the case of Philip Howard, in chapter 2.

72 **'I cannot emphasise'** Widely reported. See *Daily Mail*, 24 January
2007, and *Metro*, 11 August 2008.

72 **In another bizarre** Variously reported in January and February 2008,
including by BBC Online; and *Metro*, 7 February 2008.

72 **But he accepted** *The Forester*, 6 March 2008.

72 **ASBOs are so** See 'Tackling Anti-Social Behaviour', National Audit
Office, published December 2006.

73 **'Baby-ASBOS'** Reported widely, including *Daily Telegraph*, 18 March
2008.

74 **'Police should always'** Sir Robert Peel's 'Nine Principles of Policing'.

74 **Ms Watmough** Reported variously, including *Manchester Evening
News*, 21 May 2008.

74 **Kate Badger** Variously reported. See *Daily Telegraph*, 31 January 2008.

75 **His wife paid** Reported in *The Times*, 25 July 2008.

75 **The risk of abuse** Reported in *Daily Telegraph*, 3 May 2008.

75 **Barbara Jubb** Reported widely, including in *Metro*, 16 May 2007 and
by BBC Online, 17 May 2007.

76 **For example, in Peterborough** Widely reported, including in *The Times*, 30 May 2008.

76 **'the power to fine'** Letter from Stephen Wooler, Her Majesty's Chief Inspector of the Crown Prosecution Service, to the Attorney General, published with Her Majesty's Chief Inspector of the Crown Prosecution Service Annual Report 2006/7, 17 July 2007.

76 **'offenders brought to justice'** See the *Criminal Statistics 2006*, Ministry of Justice. Cited in *Daily Telegraph*, 30 November 2007, noting that only 49 per cent of total offences 'brought to justice' resulted from a conviction in court.

77 **Disorder being paid** Of the 201,200 PNDs issued in 2006, 52 per cent (104,500) were paid in full without any court action. Almost half were not paid (*Criminal Statistics 2006*, Ministry of Justice, November 2007).

77 **'How far do you'** Cindy Barnett, Chair of the Magistrates' Association, interviewed in *Daily Telegraph*, 10 May 2007.

78 **When William Cobbett** A. C. Grayling, *Towards the Light*, chapter 5, p. 176, published by Bloomsbury, 2007.

79 **'a microcosm'** See Lord Simon's speech during the House of Lords debate on the Criminal Justice (Mode of Trial) Bill, 2 December 1999.

81 **'I am much happier'** Reported at BBC Online, 28 January 2008.

81 **'We have knifings'** *Wall Street Journal*, 22 January 2008.

82 **And that means** Harriet Harman, 'Justice Deserted – The Subversion of the Jury', p. 29, published by the National Council for Civil Liberties, 1979.

83 **'The size and nature'** 'Review of the Investigation and Criminal Proceedings Relating to the Jubilee Line Case', HM Crown Prosecution Service Inspectorate, June 2006.

83 **The Serious Fraud** The Serious Fraud Office's Annual Report 2006/7 is available at www.sfo.gov.uk

83 **'The problem of'** Press release by Peter Thornton QC on behalf of the Bar Council, 13 March 2007.

84 **When the legislation** Lord Goldsmith, Attorney General, *Hansard*, 20 March 2007.

84 **In February 2008** Reported in *The Times*, 11 February 2008.

85 **In the meantime** Reported variously, including *News of the World*, 6 April 2008, and *Daily Telegraph*, 22 March 2008.

85 **Concerns about transparency** Reported variously, including in *The Times*, on 18 March and 11 April 2008.

89 **Knowledge without** Samuel Johnson, *Rasselas*, chapter 41, 1759.

89 **Lawyers and commentators** See Geoffrey Robertson, *Freedom, the Individual and the Law*, published by Penguin, 1989.

90 **'Surveillance society'** Richard Thomas, Information Commissioner, interviewed in *The Times*, 16 August 2004.

90 **'Today I fear'** Press release, Information Commissioner, 2 November 2006.

91 **'transformational government'** Sir David Varney, *Service Transformation: A better service for citizens and businesses, a better deal for the taxpayer*, published by HM Treasury, December 2006.

91 **'The public do not'** Ibid., p. 20.

91 **The report characterized** Ibid., chapter 5.

92 **As for Sir David** Widely reported.

92 **In the wake of** Poll by Populus for *The Times*, 21 November 2007.

92 **Nor was it an** Response to Written Parliamentary Questions, *Hansard*, 29 October 2007.

93 **'A man's house'** Edward Coke, *The Third Part of the Institutes of the Laws of England*, chapter 73, 1628.

93 **Following a surge** See Harry Snook, *Crossing the Threshold*, published by the Centre for Policy Studies, April 2007; and 'Powers of Entry', published by the Home Office, 15 July 2008.

94 **By 2008, there were** See the Reports of the Interception of Communications Commissioner for 2006 and 2007, published on 28 January 2008 and 22 July 2008 respectively.

94 **In addition to bugging** Annual Reports of the Chief Surveillance Commissioner 2006/7 and 2007/8, published 16 July 2007 and 22 July 2008 respectively.

94 **fifty-nine categories** See *Daily Telegraph*, 12 April 2008. Compare Schedule 1, Parts I and II, of the Regulation of Investigatory Powers 2000 as enacted, with the Schedule as amended in 2008.

95 **In one case** Widely reported between 10 and 11 April 2008, including in *Bournemouth Echo*, *Metro* and *Daily Telegraph*.

95 **I was quite** Interviews with *Bournemouth Echo*, 10 and 11 April 2008.

95 **'for the purpose'** See section 28(3) (b) of RIPA.

95 **The powers are** Reported in *Daily Telegraph*, 14 May 2008.

95 **Elsewhere, a similar** Investigation by the Press Association news agency, reported by BBC Online, 27 April 2008.

96 **'inexperience'** Annual Report of the Chief Surveillance Commissioner 2007/8.

96 **It is a skewed** Council responses to Freedom of Information requests to 152 councils were widely reported, including in *Daily Mail* and *Daily Telegraph*, 5 June 2008.

97 **Applicants for jobs** Reported widely on 21 and 22 May 2006, including on BBC Online and in *The Times*.

97 **The following year** Widely reported. The story followed an investigation by *News of the World*, reported on 28 January 2007.

98 **In 2002, school caretaker** The investigation and trial were extensively reported in the media.

98 **The Bichard Report** Home Office, *Bichard Inquiry Recommendations – Fourth Progress Report*, May 2007.

98 **Police computer records** Widely reported. See, in particular, *Daily Telegraph*, 26 February 2008.

99 **Recent database fiascos** See Chapter 2, above.

99 **ID cards rely** A BBC Online investigation in 2007 found that forged identity documents were being sold over the internet to under-age drinkers for £10.

100 **It recommended establishing** Sir James Crosby, *Challenges and Opportunities in Identity Assurance*, published by HM Treasury, 2008.

100 **In May 2008 the government** Reported in *Sunday Times*, 5 October 2008.

101 **'citizens enquiry'** Report published by the Human Genetics Commission, 30 July 2008.

101 **As a result of** See the response to Written Parliamentary Questions, *Hansard*, 29 September 2008; and Gareth Crossman, *Overlooked: Surveillance and Privacy in Modern Britain*, chapter 6, published by Liberty, October 2007.

102 **the government is not** See *Modernising Police Powers: Review of the Police and Criminal Evidence Act 1984 Consultation Paper*, Home Office, 16 March 2007; and police comments reported on BBC Online, 23 February 2008.

102 **The DNA database** See *National DNA Database Annual Report 2005–6*, Home Office, March 2007; response to Written Parliamentary Questions, *Hansard*, 10 July 2007; and the report in *Daily Telegraph*, 27 August 2007.

102 **DNA samples** Response to Written Parliamentary Questions, *Hansard*, 13 December 2007.

102 **convicted of serious** A prisoner sampling exercise was conducted in

2003; see response to Written Parliamentary Questions, *Hansard*, 16 April 2007; and proposals to close the loophole exempting terrorist suspects on control orders were set out in the Counter-Terrorism Bill published in 2008.

102 **infringe personal privacy** *Ten Myths about the Police National DNA Database*, GeneWatch, February 2008.

103 **'I don't trust the police'** Reported in *Independent*, 7 May 2006.

104 **'standard procedure'** Reported in *Daily Telegraph*, 7 March 2008.

104 **'Stop and search'** Widely reported, including in *Daily Telegraph*, 5 November 2006.

105 **The figures were trashed** GeneWatch UK Briefing, June 2008, available on their website.

105 **'guilty who haven't'** *The Times*, 17 June 2008.

106 **The proportion of recorded** See Gareth Crossman, *Overlooked: Surveillance and Privacy in Modern Britain*, p. 2 and chapter 6, published by Liberty, 2007; and *Ten Myths about the Police National DNA Database*, GeneWatch, February 2008.

106 **Equally, Scotland's** Ibid.

106 **While graphic or tragic** *The Times*, 26 February 2008.

106 **Again, Dixie** The cases of Mark Dixie and Steve Wright were widely reported in the media.

107 **In February 2007** Reported in *Independent*, 22 February 2007.

108 **'CCTV was originally'** Detective Chief Inspector Mick Neville, head of CCTV at the Metropolitan Police, interviewed in *Guardian*, 6 May 2008.

109 **From 1997, the government** On the expansion and effectiveness of CCTV, see 'Assessing the Impact of CCTV', Home Office Research Study 292, February 2005; 'National CCTV Strategy', published as a joint Home Office/ACPO report, October 2007; and 'A Report on the Surveillance Society', p. 19, Surveillance Studies Network, September 2006.

109 **Additional funds followed** 'A Report on the Surveillance Society', p. 19, Surveillance Studies Network, September 2006.

110 **generating complaints** *Guardian*, 20 October 2007.

110 **Further plans** *Daily Telegraph*, 12 April 2008.

110 **'chilling effect'** Crossman, *Overlooked: Surveillance and Privacy in Modern Britain*, chapter 4, published by Liberty, 2007.

110 **In one case, CCTV** Reported by BBC Online, 13 January 2006.

110 **claimed there was no** Ibid., 3 July 2007.

111 **'… a powerful'** PLP Brief, 'Challenge to Tories on CCTV', from Jacqui Smith and Tony McNulty, 17 June 2008.

112 **'public support for CCTV'** 'Assessing the Impact of CCTV', Home Office Research Study 292, February 2005, in particular chapter 3.

112 **These figures were** See the evidence of Deputy Chief Constable Graeme Gerrard, Head of CCTV at ACPO, to the House of Lords Constitution Committee, 16 January 2008.

112 **The reasons became** 'National CCTV Strategy', published as a joint Home Office/ACPO report, October 2007.

112 **Even when camera** Ibid., p. 12.

113 **In contrast, while** Ibid., chapter 5.

113 **'presentation of CCTV'** Ibid., p. 37, and more generally chapter 8.

113 **Basic failures** Ibid., p. 15.

114 **These talking cameras** Reported in *Time* magazine, 11 February 2008.

114 **'the available studies'** 'Dilemmas of Privacy and Surveillance, Challenges of Technological Change', Royal Academy of Engineering, March 2007.

115 **'somebody's been taking'** David Aaronovitch, 'Liberty in Peril?', *Observer* Debate, 4 July 2008.

115 **As a result, the British** See, for example, the Prüm Treaty now incorporated into EU law.

116 **'Stork is not'** See reports in *Computer Weekly*, 1 October 2007, and on Kablenet.com on 29 November 2007.

116 **'endemic surveillance society'** '2007 International Privacy Ranking', Privacy International, 28 December 2007.

117 **Seventy-seven per cent** ICM poll commissioned by the Information Commissioner. The survey was conducted between 27 and 28 February 2008, with the results published in March 2008.

117 **A report in 2006** 'A Report on the Surveillance Society', p. 63, Surveillance Studies Network, September 2006.

119 **'We need to take'** 20 October 2008.

123 **'Government big enough'** Variously attributed, first to Thomas Jefferson and later to Gerald Ford and Barry Goldwater.

126 **Equally, some of** See Francesca Klug, 'Why Human Rights?', *Catalyst*, May/June 2007 issue.

127 **'[T]he treaty'** Mr S. Hoare, UK delegate, Council of Europe, June

1950, reported at p. 52 of the *travaux préparatoires* to Article 1 of the Convention, available at www.echr.coe.int

127 **'contains a definition'** Kenneth Younger, 1950, cited by Geoffrey Marston, in 'The United Kingdom's Part in the Preparation of the European Convention on Human Rights', *The International and Comparative Law Quarterly*, Vol. 42, No. 4, October 1993, p. 796.

128 **'small paradise'** Ibid., at p. 804.

128 **'To allow Governments'** Ibid., at p. 806.

128 **'The real vice'** Ibid., at p. 818.

129 **In Golder v UK** *Golder v UK*, judgment of 21 February 1975 (1979–80) 1 EHRR 524.

130 **'their work for them'** Ibid., at paragraph 37. Separate Opinion, Judge Fitzmaurice.

130 **In Tyrer v UK** *Tyrer v UK*, judgment of 25 April 1978 (1979–80) 2 EHRR 1.

130 **'The Court must'** Ibid., paragraph 31.

131 **'present-day conditions'** *Cossey v UK* (1981) 13 EHRR 622, at paragraph 3.6.3 of the Court's judgment.

132 **The Strasbourg Court** See, for example, the judgment in *Selmouni v France*, 28 July 1999 (2000) 29 EHRR 403.

132 **On the contrary** See 'Reflections on the Early Years of the New Strasbourg Court', Cripps Lecture to the Howard League for Penal Reform 2006, given by Sir Nicholas Bratza QC, UK Judge at the Strasbourg Court.

132 **'I also concede'** Judge Franz Matscher, 'Methods of Interpretation of the Convention', in R. MacDonald, F. Matscher and H. Petzold, *The European System for the Protection of Human Rights*, 1993.

133 **In 2007, only** The CVs of the judges are publicly available, including from the Strasbourg Court website.

133 **'I was a don'** Cited in Peter Hennessy, *The Prime Minister: The Office and its Holders since 1945*, published by Penguin, 2000.

134 **'the politicised process'** 'Judicial Independence: Law and Practice of Appointments to the European Court of Human Rights', *INTERIGHTS*, May 2003, p. 4.

134 **Amongst the problems** Ibid., p. 9.

134 **Strasbourg judgements** See Article 46 of the Convention.

135 **This was motivated** See paragraph 63, Report of the Evaluation Group to the Committee of Ministers on the European Court of

Human Rights, 27 September 2001; and Alistair Mowbray, *The Development of Positive Obligations under the European Convention on Human Rights by the European Court on Human Rights*, chapter 9, published by Hart Publishing, 2004.

135 **In one case** *A v UK*, judgment of 23 September 1998 (1999) 27 EHRR 611.

136 **In the case in hand** See the report of the European Commission of Human Rights, in *A v UK*, adopted on 18 September 1997.

137 **'revolutionise our legal world'** *The Economist*, 24 August 2000.

137 **'As British courts'** Ibid.

138 **'in the United Kingdom'** Lord Hoffman, 'Human Rights and the House of Lords', *62 Modern Law Review*, March 1999, p. 161.

138 **'... the passing'** Ibid.

138 **The act also expressly** There is an increasing range of academic commentary on the effect of the Human Rights Act. A good overview is 'The Human Rights Act Six Years On: Where are We Now?', Richard Clayton QC [2007] EHRLR, Issue 1, 11. For further critical opinion, see the submissions by legal practitioners to the Society of Conservative Lawyers in 2006 and 2007, available at: www.conservativelawyers.com/research.htm

139 **'The problem which'** Lord Rodger, at paragraph 67, *Al-Skeini v Secretary of State*, 13 June 2007 [2007] UKHL 26. For a further example of the difficulties in following the Strasbourg case law, see *N (FC) v Secretary of State for the Home Department*, 5 May 2005 [2005] UKHL 31.

140 **account when ruling** Section 2.

140 **'it is ordinarily'** Lord Bingham at paragraph 28, *Kay v Lambeth LBC*, 8 March 2006 [2006] UKHL 10.

140 **In 1999, Lord Hoffman** Lord Hoffman, 'Human Rights and the House of Lords', *62 Modern Law Review*, March 1999, p. 166.

141 **'From this, in my judgment'** Paragraph 62, judgment of Arden LJ, *Jain v Trent Strategic Health Authority*, 22 November 2007 [2007] EWCA Civ 1186.

141 **'The duty of national'** Paragraph 20, *R (Ullah) v Special Adjudicator*, 17 June 2004 [2004] 2 AC 323, at 350.

141 **'The role of'** Keir Starmer QC, *European Human Rights Law*, published by Legal Action Group, 1999, p. 187.

141 **So the Strasbourg Court** On the application of the principle of

subsidiarity under the Convention, see also D. J. Harris, M. O'Boyle and C. Warbrick, *Law of the European Convention on Human Rights*, published by Butterworths, 1995, p. 14; and C. Ovey and R. White, *Jacobs and White: The European Convention on Human Rights*, published by Oxford University Press, 2006, p. 18.

142 **'is prepared to extend'** Ibid.

142 **As a result** The margin of appreciation derives from Articles 1 and 13 of the Convention, both omitted from the Human Rights Act. For an explanation of this omission, see Keir Starmer QC, *European Human Rights Law*, published by Legal Action Group 1999, p. 190.

142 **'[s]o far as it'** Section 3 (1) of the Human Rights Act 1998.

142 **'instructs the courts'** Francis Bennion, 'Human Rights: A Threat to Law?', 2003, 26(2) UNSWLJ 418, p. 433.

143 **Where this happens** For a range of views on the impact of the Human Rights Act, see Richard Clayton QC, 'The Human Rights Act Six Years On: Where are We Now?' [2007] EHRLR, Issue 1; E. Faulks and A. Warnock, 'The Impact of the Human Rights Act in the Courts', submission to the Society of Conservative Lawyers, May 2007; Lord Steyn, '2000–2005: Laying the Foundations of Human Rights Law in the United Kingdom', [2005] EHRLR, Issue 4, p. 349; F. Klug and K. Starmer, 'Standing Back from the Human Rights Act: how effective is it five years on?' [2005] PL Winter; and Francesca Klug, 'The Human Rights Act 1998: Winners & Losers', paper submitted to *Justice*, 9 August 2002.

143 **Whereas the constitutional** See the comments of Lord Phillips MR, at paragraphs 21–22, in *Ullah v Special Adjudicator* [2003] 1 WLR 770. For an overview of the approach of German and French courts, see 'Judicial Comparisons in Human rights Cases', UK Comparative Law Series, Vol. 22, 2003.

143 **France, Italy and Germany** See paragraphs 264–269 of the Home Affairs Select Committee's Second Report 2003/04, 'Asylum Applications', published 26 January 2004. In relation to German practice, see also *Council of Europe Yearbook of the European Convention on Human Rights*, 1997, pp. 760–65. In relation to Italian practice, see 'Italy: A Briefing to the UN Committee against Torture', Amnesty International, April 2007.

143 **The French courts** Ibid., pp. 3–7. See also the criticisms of French deportation procedure in 'In the Name of Prevention', *Human Rights*

Watch, June 2007; *Gebremedhin v France*, judgment of 26 April 2007; and the Hautefeux Act, subsequently adopted in France in November 2007. See also concerns voiced in the UN Torture Committee, recorded in UN document CAT/C/SR.681, dated 22 November 2005.

144 **But it is clear** See the *travaux préparatoires* to Article 1 of the ECHR, particularly at p. 49, available at www.echr.coe.int. The expanded definition of jurisdiction was explained by the Strasbourg Court in *Issa v Turkey* (2004) 41 EHRR 567.

144 **'[T]he Convention'** Paragraph 71, judgment of the Strasbourg Court in *Issa v Turkey* (2004) 41 EHRR 567.

144 **In Britain, it was** See *Al-Skeini v Secretary of State for Defence* (13 June 2007) [2007] UKHL 26.

145 **'that can be reasonably'** Paragraph 116, *Osman v UK* (1998) 29 EHRR 245.

145 **It ruled that** See also *Z v UK* (2001) EHRR 97, in which the Strasbourg Court adapted its approach in *Osman*.

145 **Since the Human Rights Act** *Van Colle v Chief Constable of Hertfordshire Police*, 2006, 3 AER 963.

145 **While the decision** Compare, for example, the judgments of Lord Bingham and Lord Phillips in the joined cases of *Chief Constable of Hertfordshire Police v Van Colle; Smith v Chief Constable of Sussex*, 30 July 2008 [2008] UKHL 50.

146 Reported in *Daily Telegraph*, 14 January 2008.

148 **'liability may lead'** Lord Keith, delivering the judgment in *Hill v Chief Constable of West Yorkshire*, House of Lords [1989] AC 53.

148 **'challenging the autonomy** Lord Hoffman, 'Human Rights and the House of Lords', 62 *Modern Law Review*, March 1999, pp. 163–6.

149 **Relying on the Osman** See G. Monti, 'Osman v UK – Transforming English Negligence Law into French Administrative Law?', October 1999, 48 ICLQ 757.

150 **died from hyperthermia** Reported in *Guardian* and *Independent* on 12 April 2008. See *Smith v Secretary of State for Defence*, judgment delivered by Mr Justice Collins in the High Court on 11 April 2008.

151 **The Strasbourg Court** See Ovey and White, *Jacobs and White: The European Convention on Human Rights*, chapter 4, published by Oxford University Press, 2006. See also paragraph 219 of the judgment of the Strasbourg Court in *Cyprus v Turkey*, 10 May 2001.

152 **The ban on torture** See the *travaux préparatoires* to Article 3 of the ECHR, available at ww.echr.coe.int

152 **The original intention** It is clear that Article 3 Convention was not originally intended to have this effect from negotiating history recorded in the *travaux préparatoires* to the Convention and a comparison with Article 33 of the United Nations Refugee Convention 1951.

153 **'grossly defamatory'** Keir Starmer QC, *European Human Rights Law*, p. 403, published by Legal Action Group, 1999. See, in particular, *East African Asian*, Case (1981) 3 EHHR 76; and *D'Haeses, Le Compte v Belgium* (1984) 6 EHRR 114.

153 **exponentially expanded** For example, see the House of Lords' reasoning in *R (Adam, Limbuela and Tesema) v Home Secretary*, 3 November 2005 [2005] UKHL 66.

153 **'a late applicant'** Paragraph 7, judgment of Lord Bingham.

153 **Similar logic** *R (ex parte Husain) v Asylum Support Adjudicator* [2001] EWHC Admin 852.

153 **A drug trafficker** *D v UK* (1997) 24 EHRR 423. See *N v UK*, judgment of 27 May 2008, particularly at paragraph 45, regarding the general principles to be applied to the deportation of those with serious illness.

154 **The UK courts** See the judgment of the House of Lords in *N (FC) v Secretary of State for the Home Department*, 5 May 2005 [2005] UKHL 31, especially the arguments of Lord Nicholls.

154 **estimated to cost** Widely reported. See BBC Online, 13 November 2006.

154 **claims citing the prohibition** See *A v UK*, judgment of 23 September 1998 (1999) 27 EHRR 611.

154 **The ban on torture** *Z v UK*, judgment of 10 May 2001 (2002) 34 EHRR 97.

154 **This legal minefield** See, for example, *W v UK*, judgment of 8 July 1987, Series A, No. 121; and *Eriksson v Sweden*, judgment of 22 June 1989, A.156 (1989).

155 **sued on human rights grounds** *Ignaccolo-Zenida v Romania*, judgment of 25 January 2000 (2001) 31 EHRR 97.

155 **suspicion of involvement** *Chahal v UK*, judgment of 15 November 1996 (1997) 23 EHRR 413.

156 **a convicted armed robber** *Ahmed v Austria,* judgment of 17 December 1996 (1997) 24 EHRR 278.

156 **'indiscriminate violence'** Paragraph 3.5, Humanitarian Protection, *Asylum Protection Instructions*, October 2006.

156 **life of prostitution** *AA (Uganda) v Secretary of State for the Home Department*, 22 May [2008] WLR(D) 170.

156 **As already considered** See European Convention on Human Rights, *Asylum Protection Instructions*, October 2006, p. 15.

156 **'... the expulsion'** Paragraph 45, *N v UK*, judgment of 27 May 2008.

157 **'I express the obligation'** Lord Nicholls at paragraph 16, judgment of the House of Lords in *N (FC) v Secretary of State for the Home Department*, 5 May 2005 [2005] UKHL 31.

157 **'It may be said'** Lord Hope, ibid.

158 **That rule is stricter** See the United Nations Refugee Convention 1951 and the United Nations Convention against Torture 1985.

158 **Finally, these developments** See paragraphs 264–269 of the Home Affairs Select Committee's Second Report 200304, 'Asylum Applications', published 26 January 2004.

158 **Many countries outside** See *Suresh v Canada*, 2002, SCC 1, File No. 27790, 11 January 2002.

159 **It receives** According to figures released by the UN High Commissioner for Refugees, cited in the 'Pocket World in Figures', *The Economist*, 2008 edn.

159 **Beyond the ban** For a good overview, see Alistair Mowbray, *The Development of Positive Obligations under the European Convention on Human Rights by the European Court on Human Rights*, 2004, pp. 89–96, published by Hart Publishing, 2004.

159 **In April 2008** *R (Black) v Secretary of State for Justice*, 15 April 2008 [2008] EWCA Civ 359.

159 **Unlike libertarians** See *Hirst v UK*, judgment of the Strasbourg Court, 6 October 2005; *Dickson v UK*, Strasbourg Court, 4 December 2007; and Maria Eagle's answer to a written Parliamentary Question by Andrew Turner, 1 May 2008.

159 **Outside the prison gates** See *Simms v Simms; A v A* [2002] EWHC 2734 (Fam); *A v A* [2003] Fam 83.

160 **the judges interpreted** *Bensaid v UK* [2001] INLR 325, at paragraph 47; and *Nasri v France*, judgment of 13 July 1995 (1996) 21 EHRR 458.

160 **Somewhat counter-intuitively** *Airey v Ireland*, judgment of 9 October 1979 (1979–80), 2EHRR 305.

160 **This new right** See *Van Kück v Germany*, judgment of 12 June 2003 (2003) 37 EHRR 973; and *Goodwin v UK*, judgment of 11 July 2002 (2002) 35 EHHR 447.

160 **Compare the paratrooper** Widely reported. See *Sunday Times*, 25 May 2008.

162 **highly critical** *Otto-Preminger-Institut v Austria*, judgment of 20 September 1994 (1995) 19 EHRR 34.

162 **'a positive obligation'** Paragraph 95, *Chapman v UK* (2001) 33 EHRR 399.

162 **accepted the possibility** See *Marcic v Thames Water Utilities Limited*, 4 December 2003 [2003] UKHL 66. The claim succeeded as far as the Court of Appeal, but was overturned on the facts of the case in the House of Lords.

162 **protection from pollution** *Lopez Ostra v Spain* (1995) 20 EHRR 277.

162 **right to compel** Ibid. See also *Powell and Rayner v UK* (1990), judgment of 21 February 1990, 12 EHRR 355; and *Hatton and others v UK*, 8 July 2003 (2003) 37 EHRR 611.

162 **Some of the new** See, for example, Article 15(c) of Directive 2004/83/EC and Directive 2004/58/EC, both adopted on 29 April 2004.

163 **Many of the claims** The data was disclosed under the Freedom of Information Act and reported in *The Times*, 3 December 2007.

164 **departments have refused** See the series of responses recorded in *Hansard*, during October 2007.

164 **Police have withheld** These cases have been widely reported in the media.

164 **'What about OUR rights?'** Headline, *Sun*, 6 January 2007.

164 **government review** 'Review of the Implementation of the Human Rights Act', Department of Constitutional Affairs, July 2006.

165 **'have to look after him'** Widely reported, and quoted by the Lord Chancellor in a speech at Manchester University, 9 February 2007.

165 **'Why have our police'** Headline, *Daily Mail*, 8 June 2006.

165 **pledged to redouble** Speech by the Lord Chancellor, Manchester University, 9 February 2007.

166 **'respect the spirit'** See 'Human Rights Insight Project', Ministry of Justice, January 2008, pp. iv, 5.

166 **In a futile** See Home Secretary's statement to the House of Commons, 17 July 2008; and the Policing Green Paper published

on the same day, especially the 'policing pledge', p. 29.

166 **government is adopting** 'A consultation on the NHS Constitution', 30 June 2008.

166 '**[t]he courts may**' Ibid., paragraphs 2.5–2.6.

167 '**A technological revolution**' *The Times*, 2 July 2008.

167 **refused NHS funding** Published in *Sunday Times*, 24 August 2008.

167 '**There is a finite pot**' Comments by Andrew Dillon, NICE's chief executive, and Sir Michael Rawlins, NICE's chairman, reported on BBC Online, 24 August 2008.

169 '**Nor is there**' *Spirit of the Laws*, Part 2, Book 11, Chapter 6, 1748, published by Cambridge University Press, 2002.

171 '**extends far beyond**' Francesca Klug, 'Why Human Rights?', *Catalyst*, May/June 2007.

174 '**real injustices**' Polly Toynbee, 'The left should beware the right-wing wolf in civil liberties sheep's clothing', *Guardian*, 14 December 2007.

175 '**… it is a confusion**' Isaiah Berlin, *Two Concepts of Liberty*, chapter I, p. 172, 1958, published in *Liberty* by Oxford University Press, 2002.

177 '**… although proper**' Key Recommendation 4, *HMIP Independent Review into the Case of Anthony Rice*, May 2006.

177 '**We find it regrettable**' Ibid., at paragraph 8.3.12.

178 '**appear to have let**' Ibid., at paragraph 9.1.25

178 '**This whole process**' Ibid., at paragraph 10.2.17.

179 **their release** See pp. 16 and 17, National Probation Service Performance Report 20 and Weighted Scorecard 2005/06, Director of Probation, June 2006.

179 '**misunderstanding of human rights**' Review of the Implementation of the Human Rights Act, Department of Constitutional Affairs, p. 27, July 2006.

179 **A review by the NHS trust** Widely reported. The Report by South London and Maudsley NHS Trust was released onto its website and then withdrawn. It is cited variously, including *Daily Telegraph*, 14 April 2008.

179 '**concentration on rights**' Judge Trigger, Liverpool Crown Court, sentencing Adam Swellings for his role in the murder of Garry Newlove. The case was reported variously, Judge Trigger's remarks cited in *Daily Telegraph*, 18 January 2008.

179 **Official complaints** IPCC Annual Report 2007/8, p. 3.

180 '**"work the paper"**' Chatterton and Bingham, 24/7 Response Policing

in the Modern Police Organisation, December 2006, available at
www.polfed.org.

180 **A report by HMIC** *Leading from the Frontline*, HMIC, July 2008.

180 **'erosion of a basic level'** Ibid., at p. 84.

181 **'This prosecution'** Cited in *Daily Telegraph*, 27 June 2003.

182 **'to eliminate risk'** 'Review of Practices and Procedures adopted by
Thames Valley Police in connection with fatal shootings at Highmoor
Cross on Sunday 6 June 2004', by Detective Superintendent Michael
Tighe, submitted as evidence to the Home Affairs Select Committee
inquiry into Police Reform, 22 February 2005.

183 **'Physical contact'** See paragraphs 1.3 to 1.7, 'Health & Safety –
Water Related Incidents', Devon & Cornwall Constabulary, 5 August
2005.

184 **hundreds of homes** Widely reported, including *Daily Telegraph*,
9 May 2008.

184 **'not looking for'** Reported widely, including *The Times*, 12 January
2007.

184 **increasing signs that** There have been numerous examples of union
concern. Unfounded or unfair claims against teachers have been
reported widely in the media, including those against Bob
MacKenzie, Graham Davies, Claire Cooper and Judi Sunderland.

185 **official advice** See BBC Online reports on 14 August 1998 and 4 June
2004 respectively.

185 **'It's just being sensible'** Widely reported, including BBC Online, 4
October 2004.

185 **'The myth'** 6 September 2007, 'Great health and safety myths', issued
by the Health and Safety Executive.

185 **'... danger of using'** Speech by Jonathan Hughes-D'Aeth to the
Independent Schools Council, cited widely including *The Times* and
Daily Telegraph, 5 June 2008.

186 **The decision undermined** Widely reported, 18 July 2008.

186 **bouncy castle** Widely reported. See the judgment in *Harris v Perry,
Perry and Harris*, 8 May 2008 [2008] EWHC 990 (QB).

186 **Pancake Race** These incidents have been widely reported in the
media, including: *Argus Lite*, 18 May 2008; *Daily Telegraph*, 7 June
2008; and *The Times*, 5 February and 14 July 2008.

186 **The Federation of Small Businesses** Reported widely, including in
The Times, 13 October 2007.

187 **'It's not as if'** Widely reported, including in *Daily Telegraph*, 5 August 2008.

187 **'The grass on the embankment'** Reported in *Daily Telegraph* and *Daily Mail*, 8 September 2008.

188 **According to the Forestry Commission** Reported in *The Economist*, 21 June 2008.

188 **'How did it get'** *Guardian*, 11 August 2008.

189 **Mr Tyers was forced** Widely reported. The trial judge and Mr Tyers are quoted at length in *Daily Mail*, 31 January 2007.

190 **'I certainly will think'** Widely reported, including BBC Online and *Daily Mail*, 25 March 2008.

190 **'Research shows that'** Cited at 'Robocop Britain: The most expensive justice system in the world', Reform, 2 September 2008.

191 **The Justice Secretary** *Hansard*, 9 January 2008.

192 **'The Convention is drafted'** *R v Chief Immigration Officer, Heathrow Airport ex parte Bibi* (1976) 1 WLR 979 at 985B.

192 **'… confusion to our laws'** Francis Bennion, 'Human Rights: A Threat to Law?', 2003, 26 (2) UNSWLJ 418 at 432.

195 **proper democratic accountability** See Chapter 3.

195 **'[i]t would be'** 'The Bill of Rights', Lectures at Harvard Law School, 1958.

201 **'The character'** Speech given to the University of Westminster, 25 October 2007.

201 **'The executive branch'** Will Hutton, *The State We're In*, chapter 1, published by Vintage, 1995.

202 **'There is now a clear'** 7 October 2007.

202 **'The choice is not right or left'** Martin Ivens, *Sunday Times*, 13 April 2008.

202 **'After a decade'** Henry Porter, *Observer*, 9 March 2008.

203 **'Orwellian'** Deputy Chief Constable of Hampshire, Ian Redhead, reported in *Daily Telegraph*, 22 May 2007.

203 **'Stalinist'** Brendan O'Neill, *Guardian*, 12 December 2007.

203 **plans for giant screens** Ross Clark, *The Times*, 25 June 2008.

207 **During the Renaissance** See A. C. Grayling, *Towards the Light*, chapter 3, published by Bloomsbury, 2007.

207 **'Britain has strengthened'** Jeffrey Sachs, *The End of Poverty*, p. 33, published by Penguin, 2005.

208 **There remains a strong correlation** By way of illustration compare

the Freedom Ratings (compiled by Freedom House) with the Index
of Economic Freedom (produced by the Heritage Foundation and
Wall Street Journal) and respective countries' GDP and GDP per
capita (collated in 'Pocket World in Figures', 2008 edn, by *The
Economist*).

208 **It has been estimated** 'The Cost of Big Brother Government',
Taxpayers Alliance, July 2008.

209 **the government's failure** See the response to Parliamentary
Questions by the Rt Hon. David Hanson MP, Minister for Justice,
11 March 2008; and 'The Invisible Crime: A Business Crime Survey',
British Chambers of Commerce, April 2008.

209 **The share of the country's wealth** See *OECD in Figures*, 2001 and
2007.

210 **'My guess was that'** *Daily Telegraph*, 11 September 2008. See also
Irwin Stelzer, 'Taxes in a Global Economy: Efficiency, Fairness and
Incentives', *Politeia*, 2008.

210 **Over the same period** Treasury and Department of Work and
Pension figures, cited in Maurice Saatchi, 'Enemy of the People',
pp. 19–28, for the Centre for Policy Studies, published 9 July 2008.

210 **Over a third** Various ONS statistics.

210 **British global competitiveness** See ONS figures and the World
Economic Forum Global Competitiveness Index.

210 **According to the economist** See 'Pocket World in Figures', *The
Economist*, 2006, 2007 and 2008 edns.

210 **accurately predicting** See 'The storm to come', Anatole Kaletsky
writing in 'The World in 2008', published by *The Economist*; 'World
Economic Outlook', International Monetary Fund, published
October 2008; and the polls of economic forecasters published in
The Economist during October 2008.

211 **'large impact'** 'The UK's Productivity Gap', Economic and Social
Research Council, p. 27, 2004.

211 **'an opportunity society'** Tony Blair, Speech to Labour Party
Conference, 28 September 2004.

211 **'a national crusade'** Gordon Brown, House of Commons, 23 June
2008.

211 **after over a decade** Dr J. Blanden and Professor S. Machin, *Recent
Changes in Intergenerational Mobility in Britain*, Centre for Economic
Performance, LSE, published in December 2007.

212 **'Given that government'** 'Now what?', *The Economist*, 12 July 2008.

212 **'It is important'** John Stuart Mill, *On Liberty*, chapter 3, p. 135, 1859, published by Everyman, 1994.

213 **'[h]e who knows'** Ibid., chapter 2, p. 102.

214 **They allowed Jacques Barrot** Reported at BBC Online, 22 November 2004.

214 **Other common-law countries** See www.transparency.org

215 **In Britain today** See 'Pocket World in Figures', *The Economist*, 2008.

215 **However, constitutional reform** Peter Hennessy, *The Prime Minister: The Office and its Holders since 1945*, p. 530, published by Penguin, 2000.

217 **'It goes without saying'** Henry Porter, Submission to the Joint Committee on Human Rights, 3 March 2008.

217 **'The character of our country'** Speech given to the University of Westminster, 25 October 2007.

218 **Attempts to extend** See the review of press opposition to forty-two days on Liberty's website, www.liberty-human-rights.org.uk.

218 **People hear 'terrorist'** YouGov poll for *Daily Telegraph*, June 2008.

218 **if you ask** ICM poll for Joseph Rowntree Reform Trust, 9 July 2008.

218 **Probe further** YouGov/Liberty poll, March 2008.

218 **More broadly, 71 per cent** See the poll for politics.co.uk, 9 July 2008, and the ICM survey for *Mail on Sunday*, 14 June 2008.

219 **Sixty-nine per cent** ICM poll for *Mail on Sunday*, 14 June 2008.

219 **'bonanza'** See Chapter 5.

219 **A Ministry of Justice survey** 'Human Rights Insight Project', Ministry of Justice, pp. 7–8 and 17–19, January 2008.

219 **The findings show** Ibid., pp. 17–18 and 26–9.

219 **It found support** Ibid., pp. 8 and 28. These were the specific rights that garnered 10 per cent or more positive associations from respondents.

219 **'whereby individuals can'** Ibid., p. 19.

220 **'and encourage unscrupulous'** Ibid.

220 **many associate human rights** Ibid, pp. 21–2.

220 **'Too many people'** Ibid., p. 29.

220 **Parliament's Joint Committee** 'A Bill of Rights for the UK?', JCHR, pp. 53–5, 10 August 2008.

220 **Supporters of economic** See Andrew Dismore's comment piece for *Guardian*, 10 August 2008.

221 **in office – governments** 'A Bill of Rights for the UK?', JCHR, p. 48, 10 August 2008.

221 **JCHR's 'light touch'** Ibid., p. 55.

221 **Worryingly, the government** Ibid., pp. 45–7.

222 **'hopes and aspirations'** 'A Written Constitution?', Lord Bingham, Annual Lecture to the Judicial Studies Board, 2004.

224 **Despite countless infringements** Sixteenth Report of the Joint Committee on Human Rights, p. 40, 18 June 2007.

224 **It could require** The range of options for entrenching rights are considered in greater detail in 'A British Bill of Rights, Justice', 2007.

227 **French officials have consistently** See the criticisms of French deportation procedure in 'In the Name of Prevention', Human Rights Watch, June 2007; and also the concerns voiced in the UN Torture Committee, recorded in UN document CAT/C/SR.681, dated 22 November 2005.

228 **acknowledged the scope** 'Review of the Implementation of the Human Rights Act', Department of Constitutional Affairs, p. 39, July 2006. See also, for example, Richard Clayton QC, 'The Human Rights Act Six Years On: Where Are We Now?', 2007 EHRLR, Issue 1, p. 11. On the approach of German and French courts, see 'Judicial Comparisons in Human rights Cases', UK Comparative Law Series, volume 22, 2003.

228 **It would be a defensible position** See the rules applicable to deportation in Article 3 of the UN Convention Against Torture 1985.

229 **'only rarely'** See paragraph 142, *Saadi v Italy*, judgment of the Strasbourg Court, 28 February 2008.

229 **'… claims based on appeal'** B. Goold, L. Lazarus and G. Swiney, 'Public Protection, Proportionality, and the Search for Balance', pp. 24–5, Ministry of Justice, September 2007.

229 **'the time taken'** 'Review of the Implementation of the Human Rights Act', p. 8, Department of Constitutional Affairs, July 2006.

230 **the rule of the International Court** Article 38(1) (d) of the ICJ Statute.

231 **'system influence Strasbourg'** Speech by President Wildhaber, opening the judicial year in Strasbourg, 23 January 2003 (available at www.echr.coe.int).

231 **'Abolishing the Human Rights Act'** Reported, *The Times*, 27 June 2006.

231 **'[I]f a Bill of Rights'** Ibid.
232 **60% of pending claims** See 'Reflections on the Early Years of the New Strasbourg Court', Cripps Lecture to the Howard League for Penal Reform 2006, given by Sir Nicholas Bratza QC, UK Judge at the Strasbourg Court.
233 **It remains unclear** See Protocol 7 to the Lisbon Treaty, which sets out the application of the Charter of Fundamental Rights to the UK. See also paragraphs 54–62 of the Thirty-fifth Report of the House of Commons European Scrutiny Committee, 2 October 2007.
234 **While some Eurosceptics** Point 10, UKIP Election Manifesto, 2005.
234 **in addition to enacting** Interestingly, despite concerns expressed, the government has never sought to address the Strasbourg rules on deportation in this way, so it remains an untested alternative. See the response by Jim Murphy for the government to Parliamentary Questions on 17 November 2007, *Hansard*. Operative paragraph 3(f) of UN Security Council resolution 1373 (2001) provides an example of the UN Security Council addressing the balance between the security interest in deporting terrorist suspects and the rights of asylum seekers.
237 **'the system'** See 'Human Rights Insight Project', Ministry of Justice, January 2008.

INDEX